Studies in Economic Reform and Social Justice

Social Costs of Markets and Economic Theory

Edited by

Frederic S. Lee

WILEY

Studies in Economic Reform and Social Justice

Social Costs of Markets and Economic Theory

Edited by
Frederic S. Lee

WILEY

This edition first published 2013

Registered Office
John Wiley & Sons Ltd, The Atrium, Southern Gate, Chichester, West Sussex, PO19 8SQ, United Kingdom

Editorial Offices
350 Main Street, Malden, MA 02148-5020, USA
9600 Garsington Road, Oxford, OX4 2DQ, UK
The Atrium, Southern Gate, Chichester, West Sussex, PO19 8SQ, UK

For details of our global editorial offices, for customer services, and for information about how to apply for permission to reuse the copyright material in this book, please see our website at www.wiley.com/wiley-blackwell.

Library of Congress Cataloging-in-Publication Data

Social costs of markets and economic theory / edited by Frederic S. Lee.
pages cm.—(Studies in economic reform and social justice)
Includes index.
ISBN 978-1-118-86940-6 (hardcover)—ISBN 978-1-118-86938-3 (pbk.) 1. Income distribution–United States. 2. Work environment–United States. 3. United States–Economic conditions. I. Lee, Frederic S., 1949–
HC110.I5S65 2013
330.01—dc23

2013041012

A catalogue record for this book is available from the Library of Congress.

Set in 10 on 13pt Garamond Light by Toppan Best-set Premedia Limited
Printed in Singapore by Markono Print Media Pte Ltd.

01—2013

Contents

Editor's Introduction

This issue of the *American Journal of Economics and Sociology* is on the social costs of markets. It continues the broad theme on the social nature of markets and the social provisioning process that began with the April 2011 issue on the social economy and the methods to investigate the social economy, followed by the November 2011 issue that dealt with modeling the economy and the social provisioning process as a historical-social, disaggregated system of economic activity, and the April 2013 issue on markets, competition, and the economy as a social system. To start, the "social costs of markets" is an interesting concept. If they exist or even thought to exist, then capitalism as a system of markets may be critically interrogated, which is a possibility that mainstream economists work hard at avoiding if not outright suppressing. On the other hand, the social costs of markets raise the specter that is haunting mainstream economics and the 1 percent—the specter of meaningful work, economic equality, distributive justice, and critical economic thinking. In short, the issue is not really about the social costs of individual markets, but about the social costs of the system of markets under capitalism.

It is hard enough to get mainstream economists to admit that there are significant costs of a capitalist market system without going further and saying that the mainstream theory used to examine social costs is wrong and that a democratic-socialist planned economy of some sort would reduce significantly the social costs of markets. However, it is quite easy to develop historical and analytical narratives of the social costs of the capitalist market system. Jon Wisman and Matt Davis provide a riveting story of the degrading of work, decline of community, and rising inequality in the United States from 1870 to 1930. This resulted, they argue, in the undermining of "hard work" as a way to socially distinguished oneself. To correct for this, social respect and social standing became identified with consumption. In this manner consumption became a palliative as a way to deal with the harsh social costs of a capitalist market system. Reinforcing this point, Bradford Van Arnum and Michele Naples make clear how the financialization

American Journal of Economics and Sociology, Vol. 72, No. 5 (November, 2013).
DOI: 10.1111/ajes.12046

of the U.S. economy since the 1960s has exacerbated the decline in producing useful things for households and facilitated the march to greater income inequality, both which increase the social costs of markets. Finally, John Pullen examines the ideologically laced arguments concerning the unequal ownership of natural resources in relation to distributive justice. What is evident is that those who accept capitalism and more specifically the neoliberal version of it are the most vociferous in condemning any redistribution of income, wealth, and ownership rights that would lessen economic and social inequality and lead to a more just society. But as noted above, inequality of income, wealth, and the ownership of natural resources is generating increasing social costs. Hence, the time has come to challenge the mainstream position that a capitalist market system does not in principle generate social costs and is the best of all possible economic systems.

If there is an attempt to connect the existence of social costs with a critique of mainstream theory, then the push-back by mainstream economists becomes significant, as Sebastian Berger shows in his discussion of the correspondence between K. W. Kapp and J. M. Clark over the former's manuscript on social costs eventually published as the *Social Costs of Private Enterprise*. In particular, Clark, who promoted the social control of business in the interwar period, felt that Kapp was going a step too far in his analysis of social costs because the core of his analysis involved a rejection of neoclassical-mainstream theory while the policy implications involved a rejection of capitalism. Clark was of the opinion that through some form of social control capitalism, markets, and business could be made to work better and nicer, hence his opposition. Further opposition to Kapp came from the neoliberals, especially those at Chicago, who hijacked the concept of social costs and effectively neutralized it. This point is further examined by Altug Yalcintas who convincingly shows that Coase's theorem on social costs was deliberately transformed into its neoliberal opposite by George Stigler. It was then insinuated into mainstream theory, never to be extracted.

What is important here is that critiques of and even novel variations in mainstream theory that do not ideological support capitalism or especially the neoliberal vision of capitalism are attacked by mainstream economists. Thus, by inference, it is near impossible to find a way to have an honest theoretical engagement between mainstream economics qua economists and those who are interested in developing an alternative to mainstream economics; what takes place is the efforts by the former to suppress and eliminate the latter. There are many ways in which this happens. One way to do this is through using a leading economics dictionary to redefine the alternative heterodox theory as mainstream. This Orwellian approach was, as Oscar Carpintero details in his article, carried out by the editors of *The New Palgrave Dictionary of Economics* (second edition) with regard to ecological economics.

Assuming that an alternative to mainstream theory exists or at least can be constructed, the ontological methodological question that needs addressing and answering is the degree to which the alternative theory is a social explanation of economic activity and social provisioning. That is, the fundamental question is whether heterodox economics should be a natural qua physics or biological science or a social science. Georgis Liagouras interrogates the attempt by Geoffrey Hodgson and Thorbjorn Knudsen to ground economics in a Darwinian evolutionary framework. He finds the attempt unsuccessful and hence suggests that economics must be a social science and hence grounded in the social and not in the natural world. Perhaps the next question that needs answering is whether there are any real, substantive differences between heterodox and mainstream economists and their theories. Michele Di Majo examines this issue and shows that, at least among Italian economists, there are differences between mainstream and heterodox economists: (1) in terms of individual and academic characteristics and political views; (2) that heterodox economists maybe less fractious as a group than mainstream economists; and (3) that heterodox economists not only disagree with mainstream policy prescriptions, they also have a shared body of alternative theory from which they derive a common set of policy prescriptions. It is because their policy prescriptions are different, that is, being critical of the pro-market, neoliberal policies supported by mainstream economists, that their theory is attacked and heterodox Italian economists are driven out of Italian universities.

To develop an alternative, heterodox economic theory requires engagement with various heterodox approaches. Nuno Martins does this in terms of heterodox economics and the classical political economy. In particular, he identifies various components associated with classical political economy that actually belong to the emerging neoclassical economics. Therefore, the moral of Martins's article is that it is important to determine which components of the various alternative heterodox approaches are theoretically compatible with each other, or at least identify those components that are mainstream in nature and avoid them. An example of this careful engagement is Theofanis Papageorgiou, Ioannis Katselidis, and Panayotis Michaelides's comparative analysis of Veblen's, Commons's, and Schumpeter's views on institutions. They found that all three saw that institutions are social and help regulate and coordinate economics activities leading to social provisioning; that is to say, from their perspective a market economy is not a self-regulating economy, but a socially regulated economy—the question is who does the social regulation for whose benefit.

Another aspect of developing an alternative heterodox theory is the need to rework existing heterodox theory. In her article, Zdravka Todorova argues that household consumption patterns in the context of the social provisioning process routinely engage in what Veblen called conspicuous consumption. And because such consumption is socially constructed, the clear implication is that the consumption patterns of households are socially determined by business enterprises, the ruling classes, and the nature of the capitalist system itself. In this case, markets are institutional mechanism through which nonmarket forces—capitalist system and the ruling class and business enterprises—drive household consumption and manipulate household consumption decisions. Is this a social cost of markets—perhaps so.

Whether capitalist markets have social costs depends on who controls them. For the 1 percent the answer is no since markets work in their favor; however, for the rest of the 99 percent or at least the 90 percent the answer is yes. But to make this argument "stick" it is necessary to develop (1) an alternative heterodox economic theory of how the capitalist market system works and (2) an insightful, comprehensive critique of mainstream theory that questions both its internal theoretical coherence and its capabilities of explaining how the market system actually works. This issue of the *AJES* is a contribution to the constructive agenda, but much more remains to be done.

FL

An Essay on Distributive Justice and the Equal Ownership of Natural Resources

By JOHN PULLEN*†

ABSTRACT. The article argues that, in seeking to establish criteria for distributive justice, consideration should be given to the manner in which Earth's natural resources are owned. The views of seven notable authorities on this issue are presented, ranging from an unrestricted right of private ownership to some form of public or collective ownership. The possibility of a system of ownership that is private but equal is discussed.

Many reformers have argued, for economic and/or ethical reasons, that ownership of the natural resources of Earth should be wider and fairer, but relatively few have had the temerity to propose that it should be equal, and that unless it is equal it will not be equitable. Many have insisted on the right of every human being to a share of natural resources sufficient for a survival subsistence, but few have declared that a mere survival share is not good enough, and that the demands of distributive justice will not be met until everyone has an equal share of natural resources.

History has shown, and continues to show every day, how enormous wealth can accrue to individuals or companies that obtain control of a significant portion of Earth's valuable natural resources, such as land, coal, iron ore, and gold. The unequal distribution of the value of natural resources is also regarded (by those who obtain less than an equal share) as a grave social injustice and as a denial of democratic rights. They also argue that the poverty suffered by masses of people is mainly due to an unjust distribution of the value of natural resources.

In this article the arguments for and against an equal sharing of the value of natural resources are presented by comparison and contrast with the views expressed on this issue by the following seven

*I gratefully acknowledge the advice of Donald Winch, Fred Lee and four referees.
†University of New England, Australia, jpullen2@une.edu.au.

American Journal of Economics and Sociology, Vol. 72, No. 5 (November, 2013).
DOI: 10.1111/ajes.12035

writers—John Locke, Thomas Paine, John Stuart Mill, Henry George, Friedrich Hayek, John Rawls, and Robert Nozick—selected because their views provide an adequate spread between individualist and collectivist extremes, and thus open up for discussion the possibility of a middle position in which equality of ownership of the value of natural resources can co-exist within the framework of a democratic system based on private property.

Those who assert equal rights to natural resources usually interpret "equal" to mean "common," and proceed to advocate land nationalization or some form of community or cooperative ownership, and to reject private ownership of land. Some who have recognized the justice of an *equal* sharing of natural resources have drawn back from an explicit avowal of that principle because they perceive it as a utopian ideal, incapable of realization in practice.

This article has three aims: (1) to investigate the argument that distributive justice requires an equal sharing of the value of natural resources; (2) to ask whether such a policy could be effected within a nonsocialist political framework, and without rejection of the principle of private ownership of land and other natural resources; and (3) to consider whether it is a practical possibility.

Definition of "Nature" and "Natural Resources"

In this article the terms "nature" and "natural resources" are used synonymously and refer to those things that exist independently of human beings and are external to human beings; for example, land in its unimproved condition, excluding any improvements made by humans; sunlight; air; the sea; rain water, excluding the value due to storage and purification; resources such as oil, coal, gas, gold, diamonds, silver, iron ore, excluding their value due to exploration, extraction, and transport; all forms of plant and animal life, excluding the value due to cultivation, husbanding; in short, everything provided independently of human agency. The terms "Earth," "Earth's resources," and "world's resources" are also used in this sense.

In defining "nature" and "natural resources" in this way, those elements that make up the genetic endowment and the internal, received constitution of human beings are excluded. The term "natural resources" thus refers to natural resources that are external to human beings, as distinct from the natural resources internal to human beings. It is recognized, however, that received human talents are part of "nature" and part of Earth's "natural resources" if those terms were to be used in a wider sense. The question of the ownership of internal natural resources and human talents has been explored by, for example, John Rawls (1971), who argued that talents should be regarded as a common pool, and that anyone who has more than an average share should compensate those who have less. Such a principle provides a theoretical basis in moral philosophy for a social welfare system that assists the genetically less-privileged members of society. The issue is too large, and perhaps already too well canvassed, to be considered here. This article therefore distinguishes between nature's gifts that are external to human beings and nature's gifts that are internal, and applies the principle of equal rights only to the former.[1]

Natural Rights: Equal Rights and Equal Shares

The case for an equal ownership, or even a wider and fairer ownership, of Earth's resources, is often presented in terms of natural rights. Advocates see the right of each individual to an equal portion of Earth's resources as a right inherent in the nature of each and every human being. They see it as fundamental, self-evident, and inalienable, like the right to life, liberty, and the pursuit of happiness. They argue that every person born into the world has a right to life, and a right to own and use the resources of the world; and that the right of one person to natural resources is equal to the right of every other person to natural resources. It is a powerful argument that appeals especially to the elemental hopes, aspirations, and instincts of all who currently enjoy less than an equal portion of Earth's resources. It is frequently supported by the theological argument that the Creator would not have intended that the ownership of the material resources of the universe should be restricted to a relatively small number of human creatures.

The fact that a right to an equal and private share of the value of Earth's resources has rarely been discussed, let alone accepted, throughout history does not negate or diminish its validity in the minds of advocates. They distinguish between the existence of a natural right on the one hand, and its popular acceptance and implementation on the other. They point to other rights that are now widely accepted as natural rights even though in earlier times they were not accepted, such as the right not to be a slave, the right to vote, the right of free speech, and the right of married women to own property. The general acceptance of human rights in these areas has been a slow evolutionary movement in human consciousness. Will the evolution of consciousness one day lead to the recognition and realization of the right of all to an equal share of the value of natural resources?

The natural rights argument for an equal sharing of the value of natural resources has many detractors. Some say there is no such thing as a natural right; that the only justifiable basis for laws and rights is the power of the state; and that the only valid laws are positive laws, not natural laws. They reject the principle that we have equal natural rights to Earth because they deny the existence of natural rights of any kind. Others accept that there are certain principles or rules that can be deemed to be natural laws and natural rights, but deny that an equal sharing of Earth's resources is one of them. Much of the controversy would be avoided if the question of equal access to Earth's resources were discussed in terms of equal "shares" rather than equal "rights." The arguments might then become less moralistic, less metaphysical, and less adversarial, and could be focused on pragmatic and utilitarian considerations.

Equal or Common: Private or Public

The principle of equal rights to natural resources is open to more than one interpretation. In the first place, the expression "equal rights" could be interpreted to refer to a situation where each member of society (however "member" and "society" are defined) has the right of individual private ownership of an equal share of the value of the natural resources of the society, with ownership implying the right to use or dispose of the share. In this sense, the equal right could be described as a distributive and private right rather than a common or collective right. An alternative interpretation of "equal rights" is one that refers to a situation where natural resources are owned collectively or communally by the state or government. It could be described as "public property" or "state ownership"[2] or "common rights." Under a system of equal private rights, natural resources would be shared equally, with each share being the private property of its owner; whereas under a system of common rights, the natural resource would be the property of the society as a whole, and used for purposes determined by the government. The latter system would mean a negation of the right of private ownership of land and other natural resources; the former system would be consistent with the right of private ownership of land and other natural resources. The argument under discussion in this article refers to equal rights in the former, distributive, private sense.

Equal Physical Shares or Equal Shares of Value

The calculation of each person's equal share of land would have to take into consideration not merely the quantity of land, but also factors affecting its quality and its economic potential—such as soil fertility, climate, water supply, proximity to towns, transport facilities, aesthetic aspect, and its prospects for increased value in the future. Also, each person's share would need to be periodically adjusted in response to changes in population, thus reducing security of tenure and weakening the motives for efficient cultivation and long-term improvements of the soil. Equal physical apportionment would be even more difficult in the case of natural resources other than agricultural land—for example, oil, coal, minerals, air waves, and the ocean. To introduce equality in the ownership of the actual natural resources themselves would therefore be hopelessly impractical, however desirable in theory.

But some writers have argued that distributive justice does not require an impossible physical equalization of natural resources. In their view, the demands of distributive justice can be adequately satisfied by an equal sharing of the *value* of the resources, a process that would obviate the need to divide the physical resources into equal portions, and would not abolish or diminish security of tenure.

Those who lack the desire, or the opportunity, or the ability to own an identifiable portion of the physical resources need not be deprived of an equal share of their value.[3]

Taxation and Self-Ownership

An equal distribution of the value of natural resources presupposes that their value is capable of being assessed and amalgamated. The method of amalgamation usually proposed is taxation. But amalgamation by means of taxation cannot be justified if taxation itself is ethically unjustifiable.

An ethical argument against the taxation of private income and wealth is that it involves a violation of the right of self-ownership. The principle of self-ownership has been used by some commentators as a decisive obstacle to redistributive taxation in general; and could therefore be used as an argument against an equal redistribution of the value of Earth's resources in particular.

However, this anti-taxation and anti-transfer argument seems to depend on a restricted vision of the nature of the self, and of the nature of the production process. There seems to be an assumption that when an individual engages in the production of a commodity or service, the product is produced by the individual alone, and that therefore, using a labor theory of property, it belongs absolutely and entirely to that individual, with the consequence that the state cannot legitimately claim by taxation any part of the product. This argument overlooks the role played in the production process by society and by external natural processes, acting in combination with the individual. It involves an overindividualistic interpretation of the nature of the production process.

Thomas Paine on the Taxation and Redistribution of the Value of Natural Resources, and on the Ethical Justification of Taxation

An early recognition of the role of society in the production process can be found in Thomas Paine's *The Rights of Man* (1791–1792) written in response to the ultra-conservative and anti-interventionist views of Edmund Burke's *Reflections on the Revolution in France*

(1790). Paine argued that society contributes to the productive efforts of the individual laborer or capitalist, and that an individual's income is not produced by the individual alone. Personal property, he said, is "the effect of society." For the individual who is separated from society the amount of personal property that can be acquired is limited, even if you "give him an island or a continent to possess . . . All accumulation, therefore, of personal property, beyond what a man's hands can produce, is derived to him by living in society." And society's participation in production provides an ethical justification for taxation: "on every principle of justice, of gratitude, and of civilisation." The individual who accumulates personal property owes part of it "back again to society from whence the whole came" (Paine [1791–1792] 1948: I. 620).[4]

A neglect of the essential role of society in the production process, and an overemphasis on the productivity of the individual seems to stem from a narrow and disputable concept of self. But if we admit, with Paine, that a causative role in production is performed by social forces and institutions beyond the individual, then the individual's ethical claim to the product can only be partial or limited, not absolute. Ownership of self may or may not be an absolute right,[5] but even if it is absolute, it cannot logically be a basis for claiming an individual's absolute right to the products of production, simply because the individual is only part of the production process. The product is always a joint product, not a sole product. It may be difficult or impossible to distinguish the respective contributions of the individual and society, but the joint nature of the production is undeniable.

In speaking of self—as in yourself, myself, himself, herself, oneself—we tend to think of a body-mind entity, distinct and separate from other entities. Our customary notion of self is that of a self-centered self. We tend egocentrically to forget that, although we use resources internal to ourselves in the furtherance of our development—physically, mentally, economically—and are to some extent therefore self-made, we are also aided and influenced by forces and inputs received from outside ourselves—by genetic endowments, by external natural resources (such as air, sunlight, water, and the fertility of the soil), and by the society in which we live (its customs, culture, institutions, and infrastructures). Without these inputs from outside the self we would be either incapable of existing or far less developed and far less productive. The "self" being a multi-causal amalgam of the influences emanating from within and from outside the individual person, the concept of "self-made man" is, strictly speaking, a self-contradiction and an absurdity.

The problem of distinguishing the relative contributions of the individual and society is similar to the problem underlying the controversy in economics over the validity of the marginal productivity theory of distribution, namely, the problem of separating and rewarding the contributions of the marginal products of the factors of production. It is arguable that the traditional four-fold classification of the factors of products—land, labor, capital, and enterprise—should be expanded to include a fifth factor—society.

The argument for absolute individual ownership of products and against taxation is often treated as an automatic logical inference from the argument for self-ownership. Conflation of the two arguments creates an emotional bias in favor of private ownership and against state taxation and ownership. To deny ownership of self is regarded as support for slavery or servitude, and as an affront to personal freedom and dignity. By treating ownership of self and ownership of products as two aspects of the same problem, a denial of absolute ownership of the products to which one has made a productive contribution is therefore emotively seen as akin to denial of the right to ownership of self and of the right to life, liberty, and the pursuit of happiness.

If we accept as a principle of private property rights that things belong to those who have produced them, or that their ownership should be in proportion to the various productive contributions in the case of joint or multi-causal products, and if we accept that society has played a role in the production of the things that the *self-centered self* normally and erroneously thinks are produced entirely by itself, then society and its agent, the state, must have a legitimate right to at least some portion of that production. For the *self-centered self* to claim an *absolute* right to the products and income in the production of which it has contributed is therefore logically unfounded. An individual's right of ownership of a joint product can only be partial or limited, and the political and ideological arguments over the property rights of the individual and the state become a question of proportion or degree rather than confrontational denial. There is an indisputable logic in favor of the right of society (or its agent, the state) to take by taxation some portion of the products in whose production individual members of society have participated. This right is even stronger if the external natural resources are regarded as assets to be shared equally by all members of the society.

If the role of society as a causal contributor to the productivity and income of the individual were to be described as that of a sleeping partner, that would be an example of how words can govern thought, or of how the choice of a word to describe an event can generate a misapprehension of the nature of the event. The use of the expression "sleeping partner" would demean and downgrade the physical, social, and cultural functions of society in human affairs; and tend to interpret society's role as merely inert, passive, or minor.

Paine also justified a tax-and-transfer policy on the grounds that the landless poor had been wrongfully deprived of their natural right to property in land when common lands became exclusive private property. He recognized that the land then became more productive, but argued that those who no longer had access to land had been forced into poverty, and that there should be compensation for "all those who have been thrown out of their natural inheritance." He proposed that this compensation be paid "by subtracting from property a portion equal in value to the natural inheritance it has absorbed" (Paine [1791–1792] 1948: I. 612–613). The mechanics of this compensation proposal were left rather vague, but as Philp (1989:88) suggests, it seems to imply that proprietors of land should pay a ground-rent to the state. We are not told how the ground-rent is to be calculated—whether on the quantity of land, or its fertility, or its market value—but it has similarities to the policy of land-value taxation later proposed by John Stuart Mill, Henry George, and others.

Paine's ground-rent proposal has some similarities with the argument for equal ownership of natural resources, but differs in several respects. It was applied by Paine only to agricultural land, not to urban land, and not to other natural resources such as coal, water, and precious metals. Paine's redistributionist policies were conceived as welfare payments or social assistance for the underprivileged and the deserving poor—such as child benefits, education benefits, income supplements and pensions for the aged, maternity benefits, and funeral benefits—not as payments that all citizens were to receive as their rightful share of the value of the nation's natural resources. Moreover, as they were conceived as remedies for temporary distress, they would cease if individual circumstances improved; and the implication is that they would be pitched merely at a subsistence or basic-necessities level.[6] Paine's revolutionary tendencies did not extend to advocating *equal* rights to external natural resources.

It is true that the principle of equal rights to Earth's resources is implicit in the writings of those who argue that *all* the means of production, both those provided by nature and those made by humans, should belong to the state. But the converse is not true. All communists are believers in equal rights to Earth's resources, but not all believers in equal rights to Earth's resources are communists. Paine, although not explicitly enunciating the principle of *equal* rights to nature's gifts, sought a fairer distribution of nature's gifts while maintaining a nonsocialistic belief in free enterprise and laissez-faire as a general economic principle. He did not see any contradiction between laissez-faire and a fairer distribution of natural resources.

Locke's Proviso: Equal Shares or Subsistence Shares?

In the property theory enunciated by or associated with John Locke, the right to private ownership of anything is established by the labor of the claimant, whether it be the labor of collecting food, the labor of growing food, or the labor of constructing a dwelling. Locke recognized that labor does not act alone, but requires access to external natural resources, such as air, water, soil, or produced materials. Private property in the products of labor therefore cannot be justified unless the laborer has a legitimate claim to private property in the required resources and materials. Locke based the right to own and use external natural resources on the fact of human existence. By the very fact of their existence on the earth, humans have the right to use the resources provided by nature. However, he modified this latter right by adding a condition—often called Locke's "proviso." We have a right to use external natural resources provided there is "enough and as good left in common for others" (Locke [1764] 1952: 17).

This limiting condition could be interpreted in different ways. An egalitarian interpretation is that all should have an equal share of natural resources. An alternative interpretation is that Locke merely intended that the demands of distributive justice will be met as long as the natural resources available to everyone are at least sufficient for subsistence, even though some might have a greater share than others.

This nonegalitarian interpretation dilutes the more radical implications of the actual words. In its support, one could argue that Locke was a paid advocate for the upper or landed class of English society in their defense against monarchical absolutism, and that he would never have conceived or intended that *all* the members of a nation should have an equal share of its natural resources.

However, several difficulties confront a nonegalitarian interpretation of Locke's intentions. A nonegalitarian interpretation involves a falsification of the actual words of the text. The words "enough and as good" taken literally, at their face value, are an unequivocal statement of equality of distribution. Irrespective of Locke's motivations or intentions, the fact remains that his words enunciate a portentously radical principle of property rights, and carry an inescapable egalitarian message.

The use of the term "proviso" to describe Locke's words serves to weaken or even negate their egalitarianism. It suggests that Locke was enunciating a mere limiting condition of minor or secondary significance, and one that does not seriously impair the validity of a labor-only theory of property that would justify the partitioning of Earth's resources on the basis of the labor expended by the first claimants, even if that labor involved force, conquest, imperialistic aggression, hereditary succession, or chance discovery. Describing those words as a "proviso" relegates them to the inferior status of an exception to a principle rather than acknowledging it as a second principle of equal status with the labor principle, even though the two principles are in conflict. If "as long as there is enough and as good left in common for others" is regarded as a separate principle, rather than a mere limitation or exception to another principle, it cannot be blithely dismissed as a minor quibble, and ceases to be overshadowed by the labor-only principle. Neither principle then enjoys a dominant role, and the egalitarian implications of the so-called proviso remain unmistakable.

The question of what Locke really meant or intended by his "proviso" is of course important from an historical perspective, but the "proviso" remains important if removed from its historical context, and considered independently of Locke, as a proposition in social ethics or political philosophy. The principle that ownership and use of natural resources should be organized in such a way that there will be "enough and as good left in common for others," that is, in a way that gives everyone an equal share, is a principle that demands reasoned consideration, and either reasoned justification or reasoned refutation. It cannot be dismissed simply by arguing that Locke did not intend it to have egalitarian consequences. Its validity (or invalidity) as a principle applicable to society today is not dependent on what Locke meant, or indeed on whether Locke said it.

Locke's "spoilage" limitation, which permits private use of natural resources only on the condition that they are not spoiled or wasted by nonuse or misuse, provides an *upper limit* to private rights but does not ensure *equal rights*. As commentators have observed, the spoilage limitation is easily avoided by employing others to extend one's own labor power, and by financial control of a more-than-equal share of the physical resources.

The linguistic distinction between a principle and a proviso can be compared with the artificiality of the distinction between "yes . . . if" statements and "no . . . unless" statements. The anti-egalitarian attitude to natural resources states: individual ownership of natural resources *is* permissible, *if* there is enough and as good left in common for others. The egalitarian attitude states: individual ownership of natural resources *is not* permissible, *unless* there is enough and as good left in common for others. Anti-egalitarian interpreters prefer the former statement because it reduces the restriction to the status of an exception. Egalitarian interpreters prefer the latter statement because it elevates the restriction to the status of a principle.

Locke's argument that those in extreme want have the right to take the underutilized property rights of others provides another limitation to the uninhibited private ownership of natural resources, but while endorsing a fundamental right to subsistence, it is not an argument for equal rights. It also leaves unanswered the question of what constitutes subsistence. Does it mean a basic level of food, health, and housing, sufficient for the survival of the individual worker and for the procreation of the next generation of workers? Or is "subsistence" to be understood in a culture-specific sense that would vary according to the living standards acceptable in different times and places, and that therefore might demand for all a considerable level of conveniences and comforts, and even luxuries?

John Stuart Mill and the Unearned Increment

The principle of equal rights to the value of natural resources was not explicitly formulated by John Stuart Mill, but his concept of the unearned increment of land has been interpreted as a powerful argument for a *wider* distribution or socialization of the increments in land value, and might plausibly be interpreted as an argument for their *equal* distribution.

In Mill's view, landowners receive an income without being producers and without deserving it.

> Landed proprietors are the only class, of any number or importance, who have a claim to a share in the distribution of the produce, through their ownership of something which neither they nor any one else have produced. (Mill [1848] 1909: 422)

The following passages clearly and forcefully indicate that in Mill's view the acquisition by a relatively small number of landowners of the value of a nation's land is undeserved, unwarranted, unfair, and a grave social injustice.

> The ordinary progress of a society which increases in wealth, is at all times tending to augment the incomes of landlords, to give them both a greater amount and a greater proportion of the wealth of the community, independently of any trouble or outlay incurred by themselves. They grow richer, as it were in their sleep, without working risk or economising. What right have they, on the general principle of social justice, to this accession of riches? (Mill [1848] 1909: 818)

He continued this indictment of current land ownership, arguing that "a few families, from the mere accident of their possessing certain tracts of land" acquire enormous riches "without their having themselves aided in the acquisition by the smallest exertion, outlay, or risk." This increase in the value of land, or at least part of it, should be appropriated by the state, and applied to "the benefit of society, instead of allowing it to become an unearned appendage to the riches of a particular class" (Mill [1848] 1909: 834).

The concept of the unearned increment of land, as developed by John Stuart Mill and others, can be seen as one step towards an equalization of the value of external natural resources—for two reasons: (1) by taxing increases in the value of land it gave fiscal recognition to the principle that increases in land value that occur independently of the individual landowner should be shared by all members of society; and (2) it showed that an equal sharing of land can be brought about by equal sharing of the *value* of the land, without attempting the impossible task of dividing the land into equal physical portions.

However, Mill's use of the concept of unearned increment, and its subsequent promotion by land reformers such as Henry George, has had some unforeseen counterproductive effects. His use of the term "unearned" had a powerful emotional and ethical appeal, but has given rise to the persuasive counterargument that increments in land value are not the only increments that can be called unearned. If the increments in land value are to be taken by taxation and used for the equal benefit of all, simply because they are unearned, then the argument should lead to the taxation of *all* unearned increments, whether of land or labor or capital. Life itself is an "unearned" benefit for the child, as are the child's genetic endowments. To impose a special tax on land increments simply because they are unearned would logically justify similar taxes on the products of all genetically-endowed talents. The term "unearned increment" thus opens up a ready avenue of criticism of land-value taxation and distracts attention from the fundamental principle of an equal sharing of the value of nature's gifts.

Henry George: Private and Equal Rights to Land

Perhaps the most ardent nonsocialist advocate of equal rights to nature's gifts has been Henry George. The principle of equal rights to land appeared frequently in his writings and lectures; for example:

> The equal right to life, liberty and the pursuit of happiness, does it not necessarily involve the equal right to land, without which neither life, liberty, nor the freedom to pursue happiness is possible? (Field and George [1885] 1936: 14)
>
> The equal right of all men to the use of land is as clear as their equal right to breathe the air—it is a right proclaimed by the fact of their existence . . . If we are all here by the equal permission of the Creator, we are all here . . . with an equal right to the use of all that nature so impartially offers. (George [1879] 1956: 338)

George's position amounted to an assertion that the Lockean proviso cannot be satisfied unless there is *equal* access to natural resources, and that distributive justice requires that those who own natural resources should compensate those who do not. He maintained that the economic system would then be more productive and more equitable.[7]

Henry George is sometimes accused of being a socialist or communist because of his often-quoted statement "we must make land common property" (George [1879] 1956: 328), but as argued elsewhere (Pullen 2001) his policy on private property in land was not as clear as that quoted statement suggests. He concocted an unnecessary, idiosyncratic, and confusing distinction between private property in land and private possession of land. He seems to have believed that the *essence* of private ownership consists of ownership of the increments in the value of the land, so that when these increments are taxed and become the property of the state, he believed *private* property is transformed into *common* property. A title holder would retain security of possession and the right to sell, lease, or bequeath, but George chose to describe the title holder's resulting situation as private possession rather than private property. However, there would seem to be no legal or ethical reason for the title not to be called "private property," or at least "conditional private property," even though the increments in land value are reserved to the state. This interpretation of George's concept of private property is vindicated by the fact that on more than one occasion he was reported as saying that, under his scheme of land-value taxation, the title holder would retain a fee simple title to the land.

Karl Marx welcomed George's land tax proposal as a movement towards a communist ideal, though criticizing it for not going far enough in that direction, and for distracting Georgists from the communist ideal.[8] George categorically denied that he was a socialist or that his principle of land-value taxation embodied socialist tendencies. Whereas Marx wanted to abolish private property rights in the means of production, George wanted to abolish inequality of private property rights in the value of natural resources. Marx disliked capitalism and wanted to replace it with socialism; George wanted to reform and improve capitalism. In a most non-Marxist manner, he asserted that he saw no conflict between the interests of capital and labor.

Critics who interpret George as a socialist point to his support for state ownership of railroads and the telegraph, and it is conceivable that, were he alive today, he might be advocating state ownership of other means of transport, such as airlines and motorways, and of other forms of communication, such as telephone and internet. But against this evidence of pro-government tendencies, he was critical of individuals who rely too heavily on government, and do not do enough for themselves. If government involvement is necessary, he indicated a preference for local rather than state or national government. However, he recognized a legitimate role for government, and he recognized the legitimacy of taxation. But the only tax he was prepared to condone was a tax on land values. He believed that the individual producer has exclusive property rights to his product, and that income tax and all other taxes are an unjust infringement by the state of the private property right of individuals. Although George commendably emphasized the role played by society in the formation of land values, he recognized but gave far less emphasis to the role played by society in assisting the productivity and the income of the individual.

A significant contribution by George to the debate on the ownership of natural resources was his distinction between physical ownership and fiscal ownership. Equality of ownership in the physical resources themselves would be a practical impossibility, but equality of ownership of the value of the resources, he argued, would be feasible.

A similar idea, using different terminology, has been presented more recently by distinguishing between "control rights" and "income rights" in property. The right to own, use, and transfer assets can be retained even though the right to income from the assets is subject to redistributive taxation: "the essence of self-ownership can be preserved while instituting mechanisms designed to maintain equality of condition" (Christman 1991: 28).

Friedrich Hayek on Distributive Justice

Friedrich Hayek regarded the concept of social justice (and its synonym, distributive justice) as "intellectually disreputable," "as nothing more than an empty formula," and as having "no meaning whatever." He argued that justice is meaningful "only as a rule of human conduct," and that "there can be no distributive justice where no one distributes" (Hayek 1979: 3–4). His view of distributive justice reflects his view that society is no more than a collection of individuals, not an entity distinct from its members, and certainly not a person capable of performing, or being morally responsible for, just or unjust distributive actions. He regarded concepts of justice and injustice as meaningful only when they are judgments about the behavior of individual persons; they are therefore not relevant to society as a whole, which is not a human person.

According to Hayek, if governments do not intervene to redistribute income and wealth, the distribution will be determined by the market process, which is "a game of skill as well as a game of chance" and in which some players will prove to be more successful than others. The less successful might resent the outcome, and might wish it to be corrected "by some authoritarian act of re-distribution" but there would be no reason for saying that it is either just or unjust. On the contrary, according to Hayek, the game of the market unimpeded by governmental redistributionist measures brings great benefits. It has been responsible for the relatively high incomes now enjoyed by many people; and the introduction of redistributive measures based on a mistaken concept of social justice would result in reduced saving, investment, and productivity (Hayek 1979: 7, 11, 12, 14).

Hayek believed that the free market system has come about, not because it was conceived and introduced by individuals or by governments, but because of "an evolving process of cultural selection," by "cultural evolution through learning," and by "the competitive selection of cultural institutions." The free market system has prevailed not because humans thought it would be the most successful system but simply because it "turned out to be so." It is an institution that has been shaped by "a process of trial and error," and that has also shaped our intelligence in understanding its merits, although there remains in our midst some "non-domesticated barbarians" who refuse to accept it "although they still claim all its benefits" (Hayek 1979: 15).

Needless to say, having denied the very concept of distributive justice, Hayek did not put forward a normative case for reform in the existing distribution of the value of external natural resources.

There are some possible counterarguments to Hayek's position. His concept of cultural institutions, developed by trial and error, not by individual human thought, comes close to an admission of the existence of an entity other than a collection of individual persons. In other words, his concept of cultural institutions seems to be an alternative for the concept of society. He rejected the concept of society but seems to reinstate it under the name "cultural institutions," and thereby reinstates the possibility of social justice and social injustice.

His assertion that there is no such thing as society, and no such thing as social justice, verges on a denial of the possibility of collective action and collective responsibility. If one person commits rape and murder, Hayek would say there has been an act of injustice. If two persons commit rape and murder, he would say there have been two acts of injustice. If 100,000 people acting together commit rape and murder, he would say there have been 100,000 acts of injustice, but would refuse to describe it as a collective act of injustice or a social injustice. When expressed in those terms, the issue seems to become merely semantic, and would cease to be an issue if the word "society" were expunged from the dictionary, and replaced by one such as "collection," "crowd," or "mob." If people as individuals are capable of acting unjustly and can be held responsible for their actions, surely they can also do so collectively, whether they are called a "collection" or a "society."

Hayek's view that the free market system is the culmination of the competitive selection of cultural institutions seems to imply that the evolution of cultural institutions has reached eschatological fulfillment in the free market; that any attempt to guide its future development by consciously planned redistributive reforms—such as an equal sharing of the value of external natural resources—would be both anti-social and anti-evolutionary. It precludes any further improvement of our social institutions, or any changes in the existing pattern of wealth distribution, other than those affected by the skill and luck of the players in the game of the market. Hayek seems to have taken over Marx's role as a discoverer of the law of motion of the history of cultural institutions. It is a millenarian belief that, with respect to the distribution of ownership of nature's gifts, whatever is now, is best.

John Rawls on Equal Basic Rights

The publication of *A Theory of Justice* ([1971] 1972) by John Rawls stimulated debate about the meaning of justice in general and of distributive justice in particular. Rawls repeatedly referred to equal rights, enunciating as "a first principle" that all persons should have "equal basic rights and liberties" (Rawls 1999: 62), but did not refer, even as a topic for discussion or rebuttal, to equal rights to nature's gifts as one of the basic rights. He neither asserted nor denied that distributive justice requires an equal partition of the value of natural resources; he simply did not address the question.

Rawls's silence on the question of proprietary rights to natural resources was a consequence of the unusual and unsubstantiated assumptions on which he chose to develop his theory of justice. He began by asserting that the initial distribution of property rights in the means of production is irrelevant to both distributive justice and the economy's production potential because whatever the initial distribution, impersonal market forces will lead to a comparability of outcomes. The specification of basic property rights can therefore, according to Rawls, be ignored.

Rawls's faith in the power of the market to produce comparable outcomes irrespective of the initial pattern of property rights leads him to some surprising positions with regard to natural resources. He maintained ([1971] 1972: 61) that the distribution of wealth must be consistent with both equality of citizenship and equality of opportunity; but in discussing equality of citizenship, he seems to have been oblivious to the argument that, without equal rights to the value of natural resources, there will always be two classes of citizens—first-class citizens who have more than an equal share of the value of Earth's resources and second-class citizens who have less than an equal share.

In discussing equality of opportunity he omitted any reference to an equal sharing of the value of natural resources, but advocated equal sharing of the products of human talents. He claimed that human talents should be regarded as a common pool, and proposed that anyone who has more than an equal share should compensate those who have less (Rawls [1971] 1972: 338). There seems to be an anomaly or contradiction in this position. Human talents, inasmuch as they are genetic endowments, are internal natural resources. Rawls declared that the initial distribution of property rights in external natural resources—such as land, oil, and coal.—is not relevant to distributive justice because the market will ensure a comparable result even though the initial distribution is unequal; but he was not prepared to rely on the market to ensure comparability when the natural resources internal to the human person are initially distributed unequally.

It is surprising that Rawls, in his search for the bases of equality of opportunity, did not recognize that equality of opportunity would be greatly enhanced by equal access to the value of the nation's natural resources. One might even argue that an equal sharing of the value of natural resources is an absolutely essential precondition for equality of opportunity. Though by no means a sufficient condition, it must surely be a necessary condition.

Rawls claimed that "the great evils of human history . . . follow from political injustice" and that "the gravest forms of political injustice are eliminated by following just (or at least decent) social policies and establishing just (or at least decent) basic institutions" (Rawls 1999: 6–7). It would be difficult to deny the large element of truth in these statements, but it would also be difficult to accept that Rawls had provided a convincing or satisfactory analysis of the social policies and institutions necessary for the establishment of political justice. The argument being canvassed here is that there can be no lasting peace and prosperity within a nation or between nations without at least a substantial degree of equality in the distribution of the value of nature's gifts.

Rawls enunciated, as one of the "important requirements" for political stability, that there should be a "decent distribution of income and wealth" (Rawls 1999: 50):

> all citizens must be assured the all-purpose means necessary for them to take intelligent and effective advantage of their basic freedoms . . . and to lead reasonable and worthwhile lives. (Rawls 1999: 50, 114)

He also stressed the political consequences if this decent distribution did not prevail:

> In the absence of this condition, those with wealth and income tend to dominate those with less and increasingly to control political power in their own favor. (Rawls 1999: 50)

There will obviously be a wide variety of views on what constitutes "intelligent and effective advantage," on what is understood by "reasonable and worthwhile lives," and on the criteria for determining a decent distribution. Some will interpret a decent distribution as a basic standard of working-class comfort—enough food to maintain health, adequate housing, a modicum of conveniences and comforts, a reasonable time for rest and recuperation, and sufficient education and training to perform productive work—in short, a standard of living that will enable workers to maintain their health and strength, and to procreate the next generation of workers. Others, however, might interpret a decent distribution of income and wealth in a more liberal manner that would make available a significantly higher standard for all. A key element in this debate must surely be the question of whether *all* persons are to have an *equal* share of the value of nature's resources, or whether nature's resources, and the financial benefits derived from them, are to be restricted to relatively few.

In discussing the degree of inequality that would be morally acceptable, Rawls held that when the least advantaged have sufficient means to make intelligent and effective use of their freedoms and to lead reasonable and worthwhile lives, "there is no further need to narrow the gap" (Rawls 1999: 114). Some critics could interpret this in a way that lends moral justification to a degree of inequality that is quite indecent, and that even if there is equality in all other determinants of prosperity—talents, work effort, financial prudence, etc.—significant inequalities in the sharing of the value of natural resources will inevitably lead to a situation where the landed few enjoy far more worthwhile lives than the landless many.

The following was one of a number of principles of justice formulated by Rawls: "All social values—liberty and opportunity, income and wealth, and the bases of self-respect—are to be distributed equally unless an unequal distribution of any, or all, of these values is to everyone's advantage" (Rawls [1971] 1972: 62). It has never been empirically proved, as far as I am aware, and it is difficult to imagine how it ever could be empirically proved, that an *unequal* distribution of the value of a nation's natural resources could be to everyone's advantage. Those who attempt to justify unequal distribution of the value of natural resources appeal, for example, to the economies of scale that can be achieved on larger agricultural holdings, or to the massive capital expenditure in machinery and transport required for the efficient extraction and processing of large mineral holdings. The argument has some validity in the context of equal physical shares, but loses validity in the context of equal shares of the *value* of natural resources.

Robert Nozick on Distributive Justice

The redistributionist tendencies of John Rawls did not find favor with Robert Nozick. In his *Anarchy, State and Utopia* (1974), he argued for laissez-faire, against the welfare state, and against any attempts by government to achieve a more equal sharing of income and wealth. For Nozick, the state's role should be restricted to providing its citizens with protection against theft and violence (internal and external), and to enforcing contracts. For the state to do more, he argued, would be to violate individual rights. A more than minimal state is immoral: "The minimal state is the most extensive state that can be justified. Any state more extensive violates people's rights" (Nozick 1974: 149).

Nozick's principle of distributive justice is based on his "entitlement theory," as summed up in the statement:

> The complete principle of distributive justice would say simply that a distribution is just if everyone is entitled to the holdings they possess under the distribution. (Nozick 1974: 151)

This of course leads to the question: How is entitlement to a person's holdings determined? Nozick's answer invokes two principles: the principle of justice in acquisition, and the principle of justice in transfer.

The principle of justice in transfer is defined (negatively) by excluding the commonly accepted elements of unjust transfer—such as fraud, misrepresentation, and undue coercion. The definition is largely uncontroversial, but leaves open the question of whether or to what extent inequality of bargaining power in the transfer process constitutes unjust exploitation. Nozick's definition of justice in acquisition is more controversial. He appears to believe that there are no rules of distributive justice that apply to unheld things: "You may find an unheld thing now and appropriate it" (Nozick 1974: 151n). He believes that the first arrival or the first comer has the right to claim private ownership of the natural resources of a newly discovered and uninhabited area, but that this right is unlimited only if the object is available in unlimited quantities—"It will be implausible to view improving an object as giving full ownership of it, if the stock of unowned objects that might be improved is limited" (Nozick 1974: 175). His use of the term "implausible" is significant. Why is the situation said to be merely implausible, rather than unjust? If he had used the term "unjust," he would have had to acknowledge that there is an ethical principle of acquisition that differs from and is additional to the "first arrival" principle, or the "labor embodied" principle, or the "first improver" principle. He acknowledges that the "crucial point is whether appropriation of an unowned object worsens the situation of others" (Nozick 1974: 175). This leads him to a discussion of Locke's proviso, which he interprets as the right to a share of natural resources that is sufficient for subsistence, but not the right to an equal share. He does not give serious consideration to either the justice or the expediency of a policy of equal sharing of the value of natural resources, and gives only a brief and dismissive mention of writers such as Henry George who have advocated an equal sharing of nature's gifts.

> No workable or coherent value-added property scheme has yet been devised, and any such scheme presumably would fall to objections (similar to those) that fell the theory of Henry George. (Nozick 1974: 175)

In dismissing George so summarily, Nozick seems to have been unaware of the central role in George's thought of the principle of an equal distribution of the value of natural resources. In omitting any consideration of this fundamental aspect of George's thought, Nozick was following the pattern of commentaries on George prevalent in most of the secondary literature, where the emphasis is on other aspects of George's systems, such as the Single Tax, anti-protectionism, decentralization of government, and racial restrictions on immigration. From a philosophical perspective, these aspects are far less significant than the principle of the equal distribution of the value of natural resources. Without this principle, George's system could still be judged on merely pragmatic and economic grounds, but would lose a major philosophical or moral rationale.

Thus, Nozick's principle of acquisition does not give adequate consideration to the claim that distributive justice requires *equal* sharing of the value of natural resources; does not refute the principle of *equal* sharing either on philosophical grounds or on the utilitarian grounds of the greatest good of the greatest number; and does not recognize that the principle of equal rights to nature's gifts needs to be given due weight, along with the principle of first arrival and the principle of justice in transfer, in a comprehensive theory of distributive justice.

Objections to the Principle of an Equal Sharing of the Value of Natural Resources, as a Prerequisite of Distributive Justice

Having outlined the principle of an equal sharing of the value of natural resources, and having seen how some well-known theorists have or have not treated this principle, consideration is now given to some possible objections either to the principle itself or to its practical application.

The A Priori Objection

If the principle of equal shares of the value of natural resources is presented exclusively or mainly as an *a priori* statement, then an obvious objection would be that it is no more valid than its contrary; it cannot be proved or disproved by reasoning, and is a moral judgment that will appeal to some but not to others, depending on each individual's moral sense or moral instincts or moral predisposition. Irrespective of whether or not there is such a thing as the equal right of all to natural resources, and despite the prevalence of *a priori* judgments amongst advocates, the case for an equal sharing of nature's gifts is not entirely dependent on or restricted to *a priori* judgments, but is arguable on empirical or consequentialist grounds, which may not be conclusive, but are at least probable and persuasive. It could be argued that equal sharing of the value of land and other natural resources will create a wider distribution of wealth and income, and that this will mean, following a Keynesian logic, more effective demand in the hands of those with a higher propensity to consume, with a consequence of increased production, employment, and general well-being. A supplementary economic and amoral argument is that an equal sharing of the value of natural resources will reduce the monopoly power of those individuals and companies that have a controlling ownership of the world's resources, and thus lead to higher production and lower prices. These are therefore not unreasonable empirical reasons for thinking that the opportunity for all citizens to lead worthwhile lives will be greater in a society where the value of nature's resources is shared equally and from which all benefit equally, than in one where there is gross inequality in the ownership of the value of nature's resources.

A totally convincing utilitarian or consequentialist argument in favor of the principle of equal shares of land would require an impossible social experiment under strict laboratory controls, comparing the progress of (at least) two societies similar in all respects except that one adopted equal shares and the other did not. But it would be illogical to reject the principle of equal shares to the value of land simply because it lacks strict empirical justification. Many other *a priori* principles have come to be accepted not only as natural rights (as noted above), but also as *equal* natural rights, even though they have never been empirically or consequentially tested by controlled experiments, and even though their consequentialist basis is only probable. It should be remembered that the case for the existing *unequal* ownership of nature's resources has also never been subjected to strict empirical testing.

The Political Objection: Socialist or Capitalist?

The principle of an equal distribution of the value of natural resources is seen by some as a dictate of natural law and as a prerequisite of distributive justice; but others see and fear it as distributive injustice and as a step towards a socialist, Marxist, or communist regime. The question therefore is, can the principle of an equal division of the value of natural resources be reconciled with free enterprise capitalism? Is it a rejection of capitalism, or a nonsocialist modification of capitalism—a modification that, according to its advocates, would improve the capitalist system by removing the restrictive, or anti-competitive effects of monopolization or oligopolization of natural resources?

The implementation of a policy of equal sharing of the value of natural resources would involve a radical change from the typical current situation of unequal sharing. The legislative processes required to effect the change might be seen as a major intervention by government in the free market. But it should not be forgotten that the existence of the institution of *unequal* sharing of the value of natural resources, despite being long accepted as the norm, is itself the result of government legislation and intervention. The change from unequal sharing to equal sharing is a substitution of one form of government intervention for another.

A system of equal sharing of the value of natural resources could be achieved by the nationalization of natural resources and the abolition of their private ownership. But it could also be achieved, without abolishing private ownership, by requiring private owners to pay to the state a rent, or fee, or tax, based on the value of the resource, and by the state using the revenue for the equal benefit of all. Such a reallocation of funds from private to public purposes would alter the public/private balance, and would not appeal to those who have an ideological preference for private enterprise, or who suffer from a morbid fear of government. They would judge it as an attempt to convert capitalism to socialism. Some socialistic element is undoubtedly involved; at the moment of being transferred by rent, fee, or tax, the funds are obviously being socialized or nationalized. But the ultimate impact will depend on the manner in which the funds are subsequently dispersed. If they are spent on public works or public services that over time provide approximately equal benefits for all private individuals in the society, then the socialistic stage will be only a temporary means to an end in which benefits will be effectively privatized. This privatization will be even more directly and more obviously achieved if the funds accruing in the first instance to the government were dispersed in the form of direct *per capita* equal grants to private individuals, in recognition of their individual private ownership of the value of the society's natural resources.[9]

The thesis under examination in this article is that distributive justice requires equality in the ownership of the value of natural resources, and that this equality might be achievable by the individualization, rather than the collectivization, of the value of the resources.

The Feasibility Objection

Even if the philosophical, ethical, and economic arguments for an equal sharing of the value of natural resources are deemed to be persuasive or compelling, they will remain as ineffectual speculations if the practical implementation of an equal sharing policy is not feasible. Serious consideration would have to be given to devising appropriate methods for the distribution of the value of natural resources.

Reformers such as John Stuart Mill and Henry George have proposed that an equitable division of the value of natural resources can be achieved by means of taxation. The feasibility of that method must depend on whether it is economically possible to distinguish between the value of the natural resources and the value of the human labor and capital engaged in their utilization, given that commodities and services are produced by the joint contribution of labor, capital, and natural resources. If the value of the human contributions cannot be separated with a reasonable degree of accuracy from the value of the nonhuman resources, then an equal division of the value of natural resources must remain an impossible dream. Its impossibility is gladly asserted by those who currently benefit from unequal sharing, and is reluctantly admitted by many who dearly wish it were not so. Certainly, disentanglement of the value of resources and the value of human input would depend on the existence of an appropriate degree of development in valuation procedures and statistical information, as well as a willingness to implement the procedures and to change the taxation system. Some countries currently claim that the value of land and other natural resources can be successfully separated from the value of the improvements and developments built on the land or sunk into it, and proceed to make use of the separated valuations in their taxation system. Other countries are currently adamant that it cannot be done.

Other important administrative questions also need to be addressed. Would the taxation authority be the central government or local government? If local governments are each free to set the percentage for the tax, there could be wide differences in the percentages and hence in the proportion of value collected, with the result that the goal of an equal sharing would not be realized. The political willingness of a democratic electorate to accept the principle of equal sharing of the value of land and other natural resources will depend on satisfactory decisions being made to such questions of collection and dispersal.

A possible objection to any government-sponsored equal redistribution of the value of land and other natural resources is that some of the recipients might squander their newly acquired wealth in orgies of dissipation or unwise investments.[10] This could be a serious objection if the redistribution took the form of a once-for-all grant. The inequalities of wealth that existed before the redistribution would soon reappear. But it would be a less serious problem and less likely to occur if the redistribution took the form of ongoing, periodical (say, monthly or yearly) grants.

Conclusion: Ownership of Nature and the Evolution of Democracy

Some nations today are perceived to be democratic, and others undemocratic. Inhabitants of the democracies generally have a complacent, self-assured vision of their own political maturity, coupled with a condescending attitude towards those they regard as undemocratic and unenlightened. In the minds of the democratic, a stark either-or antithesis exists between the democratic and the undemocratic peoples of the world. The former are confident they have attained their full democratic goal.

From the perspective of equal rights to Earth, the self-indulgent hubris of the democratic nations is premature. Admittedly, they have progressed along the way to democracy, but the rights proclaimed in their constitutions make no mention of a right to own an equal share of the nation's natural resources. Insofar as this right remains unrecognized and unrealized, it could be argued that the democratic evolutionary process is seriously incomplete. The failure of society to take this further step toward democratization is evidence of the retentive power and persistence of the institution of unequal rights to Earth's resources, and to the power—whether political, economic, or cultural—of those who continue to benefit from a more than equal share and who continue to enjoy the opportunity of exploiting those who have less than an equal share.

Central to this inertia in the evolutionary democratic process is the view that democracy is a fixed set of concepts, and a set that is already fully displayed in the so-called democratic countries of today. An alternative view is that democracy is a fluid concept, in a state of continual transition, and currently lacking at least one essential ingredient of true democracy—the equal right to Earth's resources.

There is no doubt that acceptance of the principle of equal rights to the value of natural resources would require a radical, and one might say revolutionary, transformation of the institution of property as it is currently practiced. It would amount to a redefinition of our proprietorial relationship with Earth.

Notes

1. This distinction between a restricted and a fuller meaning of natural resources, or the distinction between "humans and "nature," or between "made by humans" and "provided by nature" is discussed more fully in Pullen (2005: 179–180).

2. The distinction between equal and common rights is discussed in Pullen (2004). As a referee notes, it is possible that some form of communal or collective ownership of natural resources could exist independently of a formal government. However, communal systems do not necessarily ensure equal shares for all members. Mechanisms would be required to prevent the more powerful members from controlling more-than-equal shares. The

regular rotation of sections of arable land, as practiced in medieval commons and elsewhere, gave some rough-and-ready measure of equality, but diminished the efficiency incentives associated with long-term private ownership.

3. An interesting example of equal distribution of the value of a nation's resources was recently suggested by Paul Bremer, the U.S.-appointed administrator of Iraq. He was quoted as saying that "Iraq's resources cannot be restricted to a lucky or powerful few . . . Iraq's natural resources should be shared by all Iraqis"; and he proposed that "some of the oil revenue be shared with Iraqis through a system of dividends, or a national trust fund to finance public pensions" (*Washington Post*, Reuters; quoted in *Sydney Morning Herald*, July 24, 2003). Mr. Bremer did not recommend that a similar annual distribution of the value of land and other natural resources should be applied to the United States, although a similar allocation of oil revenue already occurs in Alaska.

4. Quoted in Philp (1989: 89). As Philp notes, Paine sees private wealth "as the outcome of social co-operation, rather than something generated wholly by the natural right to the fruits of one's labour," and provides a reasoned defense of the state's right to redistribute private wealth by taxation (Philp 1989: 87, 91).

5. It is arguable that in wartime or other emergencies when the life of society is threatened, society's survival supersedes the right of the individual to self-ownership.

6. In *The Rights of Man* (1791–1792) Paine's redistribution program was to be financed by a progressive tax on property, but his tax did not distinguish between land and developments on the land, and therefore could not be described as a tax specifically on natural resources. But in *Agrarian Justice* (1797) the focus of his reform proposals shifted to land.

7. See Dwyer (2005: 197, 199). Dwyer has also shown how George's views on equal rights to natural resources are relevant to modern debates about the regulation of natural monopolies.

8. "We ourselves . . . adopted this appropriation of land rent by the state among numerous other *transitional measures*" (K. Marx, letter to F. A. Sorge, June 20, 1881. In Marx and Engels [1955] 1965: 342, original emphasis).

9. The distribution of the value of natural resources by means of equal grants to individuals would bear some similarity, in its effects if not in its theoretical basis, to the concepts of "citizen's dividend," or "national dividend," or "basic income," or "guaranteed income," or "public grants." Terms such as "citizen's dividend" did not appear in George's writings and lectures, but the concepts are clearly there—as discussed in Pullen (2004: 130–131).

10. G. A. Cohen: "left-wing libertarians are themselves frequently unaware of how unstable the initial equality they favour would be" (Cohen and Graham 1990: 31).

References

Burke, E. ([1790] 1969). *Reflections on the Revolution in France.* Harmondsworth: Penguin Books.

Christman, J. (1991). "Self-Ownership, Equality, and the Structure of Property Rights." *Political Theory* 19(1): 28–46.

Cohen, G. A., and K. Graham. (1990). "Self-Ownership, Communism and Equality." *Proceedings of the Aristotelian Society, Supplementary Volumes* 64: 25–61.

Dwyer, T. (2005). "Equal Rights, Competition and Monopoly: Henry George's Insight into Current Debates on Regulation of Common Use Infrastructure." In *Henry George's Legacy in Economic Thought.* Ed. J. Laurent, pp. 196–215. Cheltenham, UK: Edward Elgar.

Field, R. D., and H. George. (1885). "Land and Taxation: A Conversation." *North American Review* 151(344): 1–14.

George, H. ([1879] 1956). *Progress and Poverty.* New York: Robert Schalkenbach Foundation.

Hayek, F. A. von. (1979). *Social Justice, Socialism and Democracy.* Sydney: Centre for Independent Studies.

Locke, J. ([1764] 1952). *The Second Treatise of Government* (First edition, 1690). Ed. T. P. Peardon. New York: Liberal Arts Press.

Marx, K., and F. Engels. ([1955] 1965). *Selected Correspondence.* Trans. I. Lasker, ed. S. Ryazanskaya. Moscow: Progress Publishers.

Mill, J. S. ([1848] 1909). *Principles of Political Economy.* Ed. W. J. Ashley. London: Longmans, Green, and Co.

Nozick, R. (1974). *Anarchy, State and Utopia.* Oxford: Blackwell.

Paine, T. ([1791–1792] 1948). *The Rights of Man*, reprinted in *Life and Major Writings of Thomas Paine*, ed. A. S. Foner, 2 vols. Secaucus, NJ: Citadel.

Philp, M. (1989). *Paine.* Oxford: Oxford University Press.

Pullen, J. (2001). "Henry George's Land Reforms: The Distinction Between Private Ownership and Private Possession." *American Journal of Economics and Sociology* 60(2): 547–556.

——. (2004). "Henry George on Property Rights in Land and Land Value: Equal and Private, or Common and Public." In *History and Political Economy. Essays in Honour of P.D. Groenewegen.* Eds. T. Aspromourgos and J. Lodewijks, pp. 118–138. London: Routledge.

——. (2005). "The Philosophy and Feasibility of Henry George's Land-Value Tax." In *Henry George's Legacy in Economic Thought.* Ed. J. Laurent, pp. 177–195. Cheltenham, UK: Edward Elgar.

Rawls, J. ([1971] 1972). *A Theory of Justice.* Oxford: Clarendon Press.

——. (1999). *The Law of Peoples.* Cambridge, MA: Harvard University Press.

Degraded Work, Declining Community, Rising Inequality, and the Transformation of the Protestant Ethic in America: 1870–1930

By Jon D. Wisman† and Matthew E. Davis*‡

Abstract. The Protestant ethic has been depicted as declining in America between 1870 and 1930, due to new consumer durables and less rewarding work. This study finds that the Protestant ethic did not so much decline as become transformed. The work ethic remained in force, while frugality weakened. This transformation is traced to three dynamic social forces: degradation in the quality of work due to industrialization, the decline of community with urbanization, and a dramatic increase in inequality. Consequently, social respect and social standing came increasingly to be sought through consumption, which became a proxy for hard work, entailing a weakening of asceticism.

Introduction

Historians are in general agreement that beginning with European colonization, the Protestant ethic[1] played a critical role in the economic and cultural experience of the United States. There is also broad agreement that the industrialization of America between 1870 and 1930 transformed this ethic, to such an extent that many cultural historians have interpreted it as declining.[2]

Some have linked this transformation/decline to the emergence of consumerism and a weakening of ascetic abstemious behavior (for example, Olney 1991; Bell 1976, 1996). Others have pointed to the fact that industrialization altered the nature and quality of work. Whyte, for instance, claimed that in the larger institutions that came

*The authors are Professor of Economics and Ph.D. Candidate in Economics, respectively, at American University, Washington, D.C. Helpful comments from John Willoughby and an anonymous reviewer are gratefully acknowledged.

†jdwisma@american.edu.

‡davis.matthew@gmail.com.

American Journal of Economics and Sociology, Vol. 72, No. 5 (November, 2013).
DOI: 10.1111/ajes.12038

with industrialization, it became clear that reward and recognition were no longer linked to performance (1956: 16–17). Similarly, Eisenberger (1989) viewed the Protestant ethic in "terminal decline" by the time of the Great Depression due to the inability to take pride in one's work resulting from strenuous assembly-line positions producing low-quality goods. The increased value placed on leisure drove the subsequent increase in demand for consumer products.

Rodgers argues that by the 1920s, the Protestant ethic was "gutted" due to a combination of the above factors: that the opportunities for advancement based on hard work ceased to exist, that the opportunity for creative pride in one's work disappeared, and furthermore, that the new consumer goods created an increased desire for leisure, with the ultimate achievement being freedom from labor (1978: 28–29). Lutz notes that "[h]istorians have been nearly unanimous in interpreting statements like Langdon Mitchell's [1927 work on 'American malaise'] about a lack of work satisfaction as further evidence of what they see as the disappearance of the work ethic by the 1920s" (1996: 260). Zuboff argues that the new mass production systems demanded "a new work ethic that would substitute extrinsic rewards for intrinsic satisfaction" (1983: 163).

Applebaum, in contrast, found that a "work ethic" persisted, although it was transformed from an "artisanal" work ethic into an "industrial" one—where pride in the actual work done became less important, but pride in working and working hard remained (1998: 65, 92–96). Although the above arguments have identified important dynamics in the forces transforming the Protestant ethic, together they do not provide a coherent account or capture the full story. They especially do not ground this transformation in the social dynamics underlying the Protestant ethic, the fact that prior to this period, its social function was due to the fact that hard work and abstemious behavior were highly approved, thereby providing individuals and families with social and self-respect.

This article provides a more comprehensive explanation of what happened to the Protestant ethic between 1870 and 1930 by reexamining it in terms of its social function of providing a behavioral code for acquiring and maintaining social respectability and status. In doing so, it draws upon the general perspective on human behavior developed in the works of Thorstein Veblen, especially his *Theory of the Leisure Class.*[3] Veblen's theory of human behavior views humans as strongly motivated by the need for social approval. Humans do not pursue such ends as wealth, fame, or glory for their own sakes. Instead, they do so because within modern societies attaining these ends gains the approbation of others, which is a requirement for many social rewards. Social approbation is also a requirement for self-respect. When viewed from this behavioral perspective, the character of the transformation of the Protestant ethic between 1870 and 1930 becomes clearer. The two principal components of the Protestant ethic—hard work and ascetic abstemious behavior—were challenged by three interrelated consequences of industrialization: the degradation of work, the decline of community, and rising inequality.

The quality of work was degraded and increasingly unavailable for observation as craft industries and independent farming declined and ever-more workers entered into industrial occupations where the worker's skill and diligence were not clearly visible. A critical source for social and self-respect was thereby weakened. As this industrialization led to greater urbanization, communities within which the actual performance of work might be observed also declined, making it more difficult for others to know how hard or well someone worked. Thus, combined with the degraded quality of work, rising industrial urbanization made it more difficult to find social certification in community. Consequently, individuals increasingly began to seek social certification through consumption, which could serve as an observable consequence, or gauge, of hard work, since presumably, harder work permits greater consumption.[4] It should also be noted that compared to work, consumption is a more efficient way of showing success to large numbers of people; while hard work is visible only to those who can see or know of one's workplace, much consumption is visible to a great number of people with whom there is contact.

Growing inequality between 1870 and 1930—especially after World War I—put pressure on households to consume more to maintain their relative social status or social respectability. As noted above, such consumption served as a proxy for how hard one worked. Although the emergence of consumerism was in part due to the technologically-driven durable goods revolution, this revolution was itself fueled by the rising demand for such goods as a consequence of the degradation of work, declining community, and rising inequality.

Within this context, the depiction of a consumer society as representative of a decline in the Protestant ethic between 1870 and 1930 is only partially correct. It is true that the ascetic abstemious behavior of Protestantism weakened during this period. So too did pride in the quality of work. But hard work did not become less important. Instead, consumption evolved as the predominant viable means by which the virtue of hard work could be socially communicated. Consumption became a proxy for hard work. The Protestant ethic was transformed from a behavioral code that favored both hard work and asceticism in consumption to one that continued to privilege hard work, but needed visible consumption to socially communicate this, and thus, ascetic behavior in consumption was sacrificed in order to maintain the high value placed on work.

Work, Social Respectability, and Self-Respect

The bourgeoisie in Europe owed its status not to birth, as was the case of the aristocracy, but to work. It is not surprising, then, that the new expressions of Christianity that arose in support of the institutions and behavior of this new class would especially honor work.[5] The pursuit of material success had been negatively viewed by Catholicism. Consequently, the hard work that enabled the bourgeois to improve their status needed to be ideologically expressed in religious terms that saw it as a "calling," an utter devotion to one's vocational duty, as opposed to a means of getting rich (Weber 1904: Ch. 3). Work was a worldly way to serve God, and thus it had a divine dignity. Ascetic behavior not only augmented the material success resulting from hard work, it also made clear that this wealth was not for pleasure or sensual ends, thereby making its accumulation more seemingly consonant with traditional Christian values that disapproved of wealth seeking.

Thus, the earliest Protestants were hostile to secular acquisitiveness or anything else that might draw attention away from God. The idea of a "calling" provided a bridge to worldly affairs and thus the centrality of work. It was also a duty to God not to take too great enjoyment in this world, and thus excessive consumption was to be shunned. Nevertheless, accumulating wealth was evidence of hard work, and came to be viewed, especially among Calvinists, as a sign of eternal salvation.[6] However, this wealth was valued not as wealth per se, but rather as evidence of merit, and ultimately it belonged to God, not the individual. As Buchholz notes: "The more possessions one had, the greater was the obligation to be an obedient steward and hold these possessions undiminished for the glory of God by increasing them through relentless effort" (1998: 873). Individuals should not consume this wealth, but be caretakers of what is God's bounty, to be used, as Carnegie (2006) insisted, for the betterment of society.

The Protestant ethic served as a code of conduct for individuals, guiding their pursuit of social approbation, social respectability, and social status. Its general thrust was that status is to be derived from hard work, not the taking of pleasure in consumption.[7] This ethic is grounded in the fact that social status is critically important to people and thus strongly affects their behavior, where social status is meant in the broad sense whereby an individual is motivated, as Polanyi put it, "to safeguard his social standing, his social claims, his social assets. He values material goods only in so far as they serve this end" (1944: 46). The human preoccupation with status or relative social position is understandable from an evolutionary perspective. Those with higher status, whatever its source, would possess disproportionate access to resources and members of the opposite sex, thus permitting more and better-cared-for progeny. A proclivity for seeking status would thus be naturally selected.

How people are judged by others constitutes the foundation for self-esteem, which John Rawls claimed to be "perhaps the most important primary good," such that without it nothing else has much value (1971: 440). As Sayer, drawing on the work of Gilligan (2000) and Sedgwick and Frank (1995), notes: "The vulnerability of individuals consists in their dependence on others and not only for material support but for ongoing recognition, respect, approval and trust . . . sometimes individuals may value respect more than their own lives" (2005: 54).[8]

The Protestant Ethic and U.S. Economic Development

For the initial European settlers of the New World, hard work was not so much a choice as a necessity. For the vast majority, life was mainly one of self-sufficiency and subsistence, and the relationship between hard work and personal success was clearly evident. The Protestant sects that accompanied these colonialists legitimated these values of hard work and limited consumption, which permitted greater saving and investment, thereby providing an impetus for economic growth.[9]

The Protestant work ethic promoted community values. Weber noted that "the usefulness of a calling, and thus its favour in the sight of God, is measured primarily in moral terms, and thus in terms of the importance of the goods produced in it for the community" (1904: 162). The special force of the Protestant ethic that caught Weber's attention may have been due to a number of factors, most notably the character of those who immigrated to America and perhaps especially to the strong belief in vertical social mobility. The vital importance of religion in American life had been earlier noted by de Tocqueville: "There is no country in the world where the Christian religion retains a greater influence than in America" (1945, vol. 1: 314). The Protestant ethic served to nurture the rise of economic growth as a social value, where economic success (measured by growth) served to indicate whether a society is on a morally correct path (Powers 1976: 31).

Making the work ethic especially forceful in the United States was the fact that since colonial times, due to weak class demarcations, there has been a relatively strong belief that vertical mobility was readily possible.[10] Where the potential for vertical mobility is relatively high, class distinctions are blurred.[11] Although individuals in the United States may have had a general sense of where they fell in terms of their society's distribution of income or wealth, they had little sense of belonging to a class. Because of a strong belief in the potential for vertical mobility, Americans generally felt responsible for their own social status. Through adequate dedication and effort, anyone could move up, even to the very highest levels of social status. It was the individual's responsibility and depended upon the individual's willingness to study and work hard.[12] One's social status was not given, but earned.[13]

It should be noted, however, that in spite of the strength of the Protestant ethic in America, the attitude toward work was not without ambiguity. This was made clear by Veblen's studies of the various ways in which people struggled to exhibit leisure status, that is, to be viewed as above work. He noted, for instance, that "wealth acquired passively by transmission from ancestors or other antecedents presently becomes even more honorific than wealth acquired by the possessor's own effort." And, "[t]he leisure class stands at the head of the social structure in point of reputability; and its manner of life and its standards of worth therefore afford the norm of reputability for the community" (1899: 29, 84). The reason for this, he claimed, is that "[d]uring the predatory culture labour comes to be associated in men's habits of thought with weakness and subjection to a master" (1899: 36).[14]

Industrialization and the Degradation of Work

In the wake of the Civil War, the U.S. economy launched into a process of rapid industrialization, transforming practically all aspects of American society. However, three aspects stand out that have critical relevance for the Protestant ethic: the degraded nature of work, the decline of community, and greater inequality. The result of industrialization was that it became progressively more difficult for people to achieve their social identity and status from work and community, prompting them to seek it ever more in consumption. Growing inequality meant that households had to struggle ever harder to maintain their relative status. This section will address the manner in which industrialization changed the fundamental character of work. The following two sections will detail sequentially the accompanying changes in the character of community and the rise of inequality.

In 1870, over half of all adults were self-employed, either in agriculture, crafts, or small proprietorships as owner-workers (Carter et al. 2006 2: 110, 120). And even those who became wage workers retained substantial control over the workplace as late as the 1880s. Production was relatively small scale and technology relatively uncomplicated. Indeed, it was not uncommon for the "boss" to simply

Figure 1

Proportion of Labor Force Engaged in Agricultural Work

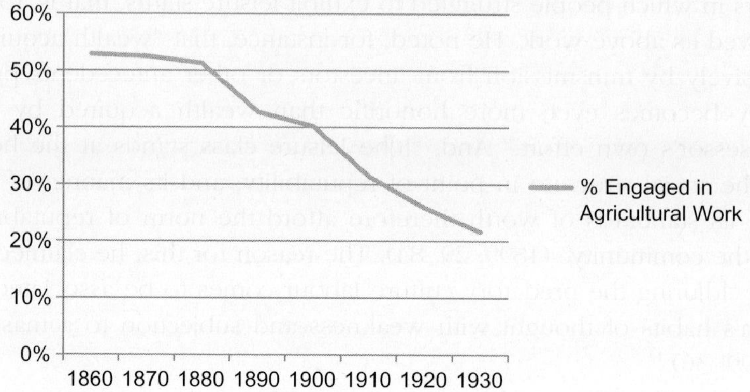

Source: Carter et al. (2006 2: 110).

purchase the equipment and allow the workers to determine how to produce a given amount of output and how to divide among themselves the payment received (Montgomery 1983: 110–111).

But the increasing maturity of industrialization radically changed the labor process. Over the period 1870–1930, farming ceased to be the livelihood of the majority of Americans, declining from over 50 percent of the workforce at the end of the Civil War to slightly over 20 percent by 1930 (see Figure 1). During the latter part of the period, due to productivity gains, which in turn were largely due to labor-saving technology such as the tractor, the number of which increased from 1,000 in 1910 to 920,000 by 1930 (Carter et al. 2006, 4: 80), the actual number of farmers declined. Spending on manufactured inputs over this period grew by 282 percent, while spending on hired labor increased by only 56 percent (Carter et al. 2006, 4: 197). Hatton and Williamson (1991), examining data on Michigan in the 1890s, find that farmers earned about half what unskilled urban workers earned (in nominal terms). After controlling for living costs, payment in kind, and personal characteristics of the laborer, they find that the wage gap shrinks to between 9 and 13 percent.

Figure 2

Proportion of Labor Force Self-Employed or Engaged in Unpaid Family Work (Including Agriculture)

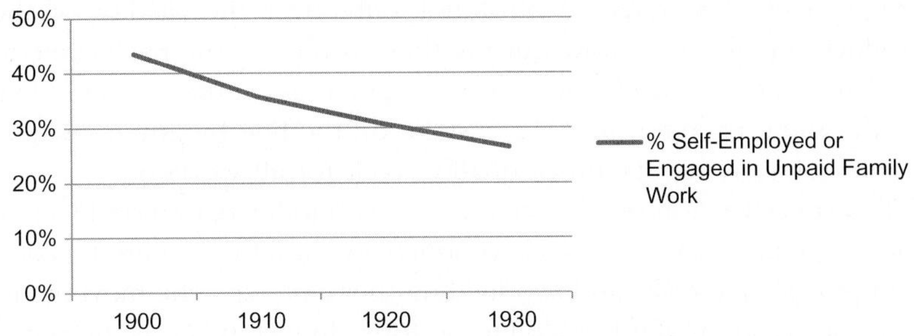

Source: Carter et al. (2006 2: 110; 120).

The percentage of the labor force that was self-employed or engaged in unpaid family work also declined by nearly half (see Figure 2). Even when agricultural labor is excluded, this rate fell from 23 percent in 1900 to 14 percent in 1930 (Carter et al. 2006, 2: 120). Not only did the type of nonagricultural employment shift, but the work environment changed from predominantly small shops to increasingly large factory manufacturing. By 1929, 71 percent of manufacturing workers worked in factories of 100 or more workers, an increase from 61 percent in 1904, the earliest year for which data are available. Over the same time, the proportion of workers in establishments of 20 or fewer workers shrank from 13.6 percent to 9.8 percent (Granovetter 1984: 326).

Workers were both pushed and pulled into industrial work. They were pushed by declining relative incomes due to falling agricultural prices brought on by productivity gains, or because their craft work was underpriced by factory output. They were pulled by higher relative standards of living as industrial workers. Accompanying industrialization and urbanization were rapid declines in transportation costs, creating regional and even national markets for output. Thus whereas earlier workers' output was consumed by neighbors and other members of the community, increasingly workers' output was to be consumed by distant unknown consumers.

As more and more work was done in urban factories, some quite large, with the final product coming from the combined efforts of many individuals who performed small tasks, the diligence and hard work of individuals became less and less visible to others. Individuals progressively lost direct control not only over the quality of the product, but also over how quickly they worked as the pace came to be determined by machinery.[15] The eventual rise of the assembly line set the same pace for all. One mistake on the line by any individual would ruin any reputation of quality work for all workers.

The specialization of labor that came with industrialization brought with it dramatic increases in productivity. It also required taking complex, skilled tasks and subdividing them into specific movements and tasks requiring far less skill to perform. In fact, this was the stated goal of the new "scientific management," as exhibited in Taylor's *Shop Management*: "All possible brain work should be removed from the shop and centered in the planning or laying-out department" (Taylor 1912: 98–99). Any creative participation by the worker was to be forbidden: "Under our system the workman is told minutely just what he is to do and how he is to do it; and any improvement which he makes upon the orders is fatal to success" (Taylor 1907, cited in Sohn-Rethel 1978: 152).

The first jobs to become mechanized were frequently the most skilled, where the high fixed costs of installing machinery were quickly recouped by the savings in labor costs from the wage difference between an unskilled machine operator versus a skilled artisan (Rodgers 1978: 66). As the jobs became uniformly deskilled, wages also equalized among the workers, who thereby lost their ability to showcase their hard work relative to others by their higher salaries. Everyone worked at the same speed to produce the same number of units and everyone worked the same number of hours. The extent of de-skilling was frequently extreme. Bright measured the overall skill level in manufacturing during this time of mechanization and surmised that, on average, the maximum skill required was equal to that necessary to operate a hand-controlled power tool. Increasing mechanization decreased the required skill contributions, particularly in key categories that were used to determine wages (1958: 45, 186–187).

Workers had a hard time adjusting to this new style of production, and turnover was very high.[16] For instance, by the end of 1913, to add 100 men to the labor force, the Ford company was required to hire 963 (Sward 1948: 49). The wife of one of Henry Ford's assembly line workers wrote him in 1914: "The chain system you have is a *slave driver! My God!* Mr. Ford. My husband has come home & thrown himself down & won't eat his supper—so done out! Can't it be remedied?" (cited in Lacey 1986: 129).

As early as 1883, the Episcopal clergyman R. Heber Newton addressed the concern of a failing work ethic as false, declaring that discontent among laborers was symptomatic of the new factory system. The typical factory employee, he wrote, "makes nothing. He sees no complete product of his skill growing into finished shape in his hands. What zest can there be in the toil of this bit of manhood?" (recorded in *Report of the Committee of the Senate* 1885: 549).[17] Applebaum notes that as a result of the shift from a craft ethic to an industrial ethic during the early 20th century, "[w]orkers generally gave up hope of intrinsic satisfaction from factory work since the routinization and subdivision of work tasks rendered factory work monotonous and meaningless for most workers" (1998: 148).[18] Concern over the mental degradation of work[19] led to the rise of the "industrial betterment" movement around the turn of the century, with Jane Addams as a major spokesperson. Although many programs were instituted to boost morale, some with mild success, most labor advocates despaired of achieving more fulfilling work conditions, and pleaded instead for a reduction in working hours so as to enable workers to satisfy life needs outside the job (Rodgers 1978: 88–91). As Bauman has put it: "The true problem which the pioneers of modernization confronted was the need to force people, used to putting meaning into their work through setting its goals and controlling its course, to expend their skill and their work capacity in the implementation of tasks which were now set and controlled by others and hence meaningless for their performers" (2005: 7).[20] To address this problem, by the 1920s "industrial relations" had come forth as a science of motivating workers. It was sold as welfare capitalism (Scase 1992).

For work to provide social certification of personal value and thus be a source for self-respect, how hard and well an individual worked had to be in some sense available for others to appreciate. As Sayer has put this:

> While producing things (including providing services) and hence changing the social world around us can indeed help to create a sense of self-worth, this too depends on others who (a) recognize us as subjects capable of self-determination, and (b) are capable of judging and confirming the worth of our labour. (2005: 56)

But as industrialization proceeded, not only did work cease to be fulfilling, but how well and hard one worked became progressively less directly observable. What more readily caught attention was how much one could consume, which came to stand, more or less, as a signal for how hard one had worked (Scranton 1994: 478). Thus, because Americans believed they were individually responsible for their own social standing, they felt strongly compelled to demonstrate status and hence class identity through consumption.[21]

An attempt to maintain or increase social standing through consumption is what Veblen meant by conspicuous consumption, a critical component of his theory of consumer behavior that is highly useful in understanding the turn toward consumption for social respectability and the influence of rising inequality upon consumption. For Veblen, conspicuous consumption manifests itself in two dimensions. Consumption that permits "invidious comparison" is meant to demonstrate one's status to be above those below. "Pecuniary emulation," on the other hand, refers to the practice of imitating the consumption standards of those of higher status with the intent of appearing also to possess that status. Veblen claimed that "[w]ith the exception of the instinct of self-preservation, the propensity for emulation is probably the strongest and most alert and persistent of the economic motives proper" and "the propensity for emulation—for invidious comparison—is of ancient growth and is a pervading trait of human nature" (Veblen 1899: 109, 110).

Veblen's theory of consumer behavior is founded upon the fact that social status is critically important to people and thus strongly affects their behavior. Participation in conspicuous consumption is strongly socially compelled "though popular insistence on conformity to the accepted scale of expenditure as a matter of propriety, under pain of disesteem and ostracism" (1899: 111).

Industrialization and the Decline of Community

In preindustrial times, most Americans lived on rural farms, in villages, or in small towns, where hard work was directly linked to survival and easily visible to all in the community. Any farmer could tell if another was working hard by the size of the crops he brought in, given easily observable information about size and quality of the fields cultivated. Likewise, the town blacksmith or tanner's work was generally consumed in the very town where it was produced, by the producer's neighbors, and thus served as a key determinant of the respect felt for that producer.

In small communities people generally know who is wealthier, who is more honorable, and whose past actions have been most beneficial to their collective ends. It follows that small and relatively isolated communities are freer of the ostentatious consumption practices that characterize the industrial era. Veblen notes that in such small-scale communities, societies' clothing fashions tend to be more stable and utilitarian (Veblen 1899: 175–176).

Between 1870 and 1930, a tremendous demographic shift occurred, as the urban share of population exploded from 26 to 56 percent (see Table 1). The proportion of Americans living in large cities also increased to the point where by 1930, 30 percent of the population

Table 1

Changing Rural Urban Population Shares

Year	Total Population	Urban Population	Urban Share of Population	Rural Population	Rural Share of Population
1870	38,558,371	9,902,361	0.257	28,656,010	0.743
1880	50,189,209	14,129,735	0.282	36,059,474	0.718
1890	62,979,766	22,106,265	0.351	40,873,501	0.649
1900	75,994,575	30,214,832	0.398	45,779,743	0.602
1910	91,972,266	42,064,001	0.457	49,908,265	0.543
1920	105,710,620	54,253,282	0.513	51,457,338	0.487
1930	122,775,046	69,160,599	0.563	53,614,447	0.437

Source: Carter et al. (2006, 1: 103–104).

Table 2

Growing City Size

Year	Total Population	Number Living in Cities >100K	Proportion Living in Cities >100K
1870	38,558,371	4,129,989	0.107
1880	50,189,209	6,210,909	0.124
1890	62,979,766	9,697,960	0.154
1900	75,994,575	14,208,347	0.187
1910	91,972,266	20,302,138	0.221
1920	105,710,620	27,429,326	0.259
1930	122,775,046	36,463,318	0.297

Source: Carter et al. (2006 1: 103–104).

lived in cities of more than 100,000 inhabitants (see Table 2). In cities of this size, knowing everyone in the community was impossible, and inhabitants would not so frequently come upon or recognize the product of a fellow citizen's labor.

Increased segregation of work and home lives accompanied the rural-to-city migration. In rural life, home and work were typically contingent, the farmhouse on the farm, the living quarters above the shop. The separation of home and work meant that neighbors could no longer so readily witness how hard and well one worked, thereby reducing the potential of work for providing identity and status in one's community.

With the degradation of work and the decline of community, the easiest and most practical way to signal how hard one has worked is through one's consumption. As Veblen noted: "To sustain one's dignity—and to sustain one's self-respect—under the eyes of people who are not socially one's immediate neighbors, it is necessary to display the token of economic worth, which practically coincides pretty closely with economic success" (Veblen 1919: 393). Further:

> One's neighbours, mechanically speaking, often are socially not one's neighbours, or even acquaintances; and still their transient good opinion has a high degree of utility. The only practicable means of impressing one's pecuniary ability on these unsympathetic observers of one's everyday life is an unremitting demonstration of ability to pay. (1899: 86–87)

As the metropolis grew and became more segregated along class, racial, and ethnic lines, the divorce between work and the rest of life became even more pronounced, especially as workplaces were segregated from residential areas. Klein and Kantor describe the process as one whereby

> [t]he larger [cities] grew, the more insulated each of their sections became. Most people no longer lived near where they worked . . . Cut off from all but superficial contact with those different from themselves, they lost their sense of a larger community beyond the neighborhood. (1976: 111)

New transportation means also allowed for further segregation of home and work.[22] The proliferation of streetcars allowed workers to traverse greater distances between home and work fairly rapidly and at low cost. As automobile ownership became more widespread, by the 1920s, the suburbs of the nation's largest cities were growing twice as fast as the cities themselves (Hawley 1956). By 1930, more than half of commuters into medium-sized cities came by car (Jackson 1985: 174).

Industrialization also changed communities in a gender-related manner. In preindustrial work, husband and wife frequently worked as a partnership, whether on the farm, in handicraft industry, or in retail shops. Husbands and wives had similar work and social schedules, as well as some overlap in social circles (Vanek 1980: 429). But when males became wage workers outside the home, wives were left caring for the home and children. The loss of control over work resulted in the segregation of work and leisure/family activites for men, but not for women who continued to work in the house, weakening familial bonds (Vanek 1980: 429). Tilly and Scott (1978) found that women's participation in activities perceived as "economically productive" declined as an economy industrialized (1978: 144–145).[23] Goldin provides evidence that female labor force participation in the United States followed the well-known industrialization "U-shaped function." By Goldin's estimates, the bottom of the U, associated with the lowest level of female labor force participation, occurred in the 1920s (1994: 16).[24] Because husbands earned and therefore more greatly controlled money, women became less empowered, more dependent.

Rising Inequality and the Heightened Challenge to Social Respectability

Historically, it was through work and community that social approval, and thus social status and self-esteem, could be acquired and maintained. But, as noted above, industrialization degraded much work and reduced the percent of population living in traditional communities. Moreover, and pertinent to the Protestant ethic, how hard one worked became less directly observable. What more readily caught attention was how much one could consume, which could stand, more or less, as an indication for how hard one worked. The greater inequality that accompanied this period meant that consumers would have to stretch further to maintain their relative social standing.

Where income and wealth inequality are greater, the amount that must be consumed to create the impression of higher status is greater. But inequality would only have this effect where a belief in the potential for vertical mobility is strong.[25] In societies where relatively little potential for vertical mobility is believed to exist, individuals understand their class status as more fixed and known. Moreover, if an individual were to attempt to show greater status through consumption, it would more readily be viewed as negative, as "show-off" behavior. Rather than signaling virtue, it would signal a character flaw.

Also stimulating consumption is the fact that if identity is less given by inherited status (class membership, community, ethnicity, religion, and even gender), then individuals feel more responsible for their lives and self-identity. There is a greater sense of individuality, and self-identity becomes a project. Consumption acts as a signaling device for identity, a means to define one's self and to project this definition to others. Maintaining if not improving this identity is a never-ending project.

Where there is a strong belief that vertical mobility is possible, a substantial increase in inequality could be expected to prompt households to respond in one or more of three ways: people might consume more of their incomes, forcing them to save less; they might become more indebted to enable greater consumption; and they might increase the hours they work to enable them to increase their income and hence consumption levels. As the evidence presented below demonstrates, as a whole, U.S. households did two, and possibly all three, especially during the last decade of the period 1870–1930 when inequality most dramatically increased.

Available evidence suggests that inequality progressively increased between the Civil War and World War I, and then exploded during the 1920s (Lindert 2000: 186ff). Part of the reason for this rising inequality was the shift away from farming, an occupation that had traditionally had less inequality.

Rising inequality after 1870 in the United States fits the hypothesis set forth by Simon Kuznets in a landmark article (1955), contending that the earlier stages of economic development were characterized by rising inequality. The reason is that "[s]ince . . . the intrasectoral distribution of income is necessarily wider in the urban sector than in the rural sector, a major shift in population from a sector with low inequality to one with greater inequality increases the weight of the unequal sector, thus raising overall inequality" (Moran 2005: 212). Hatton and Williamson (1991) have offered support for this view.

Exploding Inequality in the 1920s

The transformation of the Protestant ethic picked up substantial momentum during the 1920s as war-time production was more fully converted to producing consumer durables for which inequality fueled increased demand.

On the whole, the period leading up to the crisis of 1929 was highly prosperous. Between 1922 and 1929, GNP grew at an annual rate of 4.7 percent and unemployment averaged 3.7 percent (White 1990: 69). However, productivity gains substantially outpaced wages, with important distributional consequences. Accordingly, the share of total income received by the richest 5 percent of the population increased from 24.3 percent in 1919 to 33.5 percent in 1929. By 1928 the richest 10 percent received 46 percent of total income. The disposable income of the top 1 percent of taxpayers rose 63 percent (Livingston 2009: 38). Between 1919 and 1929, the share of income taken by the top one-hundredth of 1 percent soared from about 1.7 to 5 percent (Saez 2009). Phillips estimates that whereas there were about 7,000 millionaires in 1921 or 1922, by 1929 there were about

30,000 (2002: 11). The real prosperity of the 1920s was reserved for those residing in the top of the income scale (Bernstein 1966; Stricker 1983).

Contributing to this heightened inequality were tax reforms that reduced corporate taxes and lowered the maximum personal income tax rate from 75 to 25 percent (Smiley 1998: 218). Holt (1977) notes that per capita income for the lowest 93 percent of the nonfarm working class actually fell by 4 percent from 1923 to 1929.

Automobiles, Houses, Consumer Durables, and Social Status

Rising inequality meant that households had to consume more to maintain their relative status. The advent of automobiles, single-family-dwelling houses, and new consumer durables dramatically fueled this race to keep up. Although inequality increased, household incomes rose dramatically, with real GDP per capita, measured in 1990 dollars, rising from $2,445 in 1870 to $6,899 in 1929 (Maddison 2006).

Furniture always played a role in marking social status. However, it was generally hidden inside and thus only visible to the select few who were invited in. Free-standing houses and automobiles opened up extraordinary potential to flash status because, as Wilkinson and Pickett point out, "research confirms that the tendency to look for goods which confer status and prestige is indeed stronger for things which are more visible to others" (2009: 225). This was especially true of the automobile, since it could accompany its owner (of course, horse-drawn coaches had, earlier, performed the same function, but they were far less convenient in urban environments).

Arguably, no single new consumer good had theretofore more transformed society than the automobile. Not only was the automobile an immediate symbol of status, it also helped fuel a housing boom by making suburban living more viable. Because suburban land was less expensive, housing could be in individual units as opposed to the multi-unit apartment buildings on more expensive in-town land. A detached house has far greater potential for revealing status than units encased within an apartment complex. Automobiles and free-standing houses were not only primary, but also mutually reinforcing, status symbols.

Figure 3

Percentage of GDP Spent on Automobiles and Consumer Durables, 1870–1930

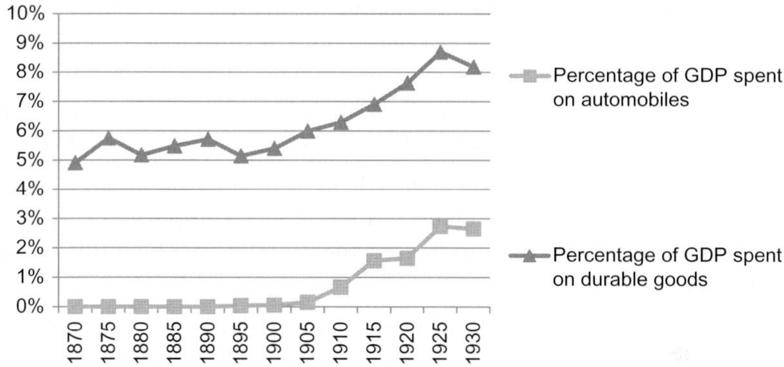

Source: Carter et al. (2006, 3: 24–25, 270–271).

During the 1920s, as the wealthy took ever larger shares of total income, they bought ever-more expensive houses, vacation properties, automobiles, country club memberships, and other luxury items. The rise in durable goods spending is shown in Figure 3, with particular emphasis on the increasing proportion of GDP spent on automobiles. Automobiles made possible the dramatic expansion of private playgrounds for the rich—so-called country clubs. The real estate boom was especially robust in vacation facilities such as hotels, tourist cottages, and motor courts (Grebler, Blank, and Winick 1956). This put intense pressure on all with lower incomes to consume more to maintain their relative social standing.

By the late 1920s, about 80 percent of U.S. households had radios, not only connecting people to a greater world, but also bringing advertising into living rooms. Radio advertising helped erode the historical thriftiness of American families. Debt-shy households were encouraged to buy on the more value-neutral term "credit," as opposed to taking out loans. And to enable them to better do so, installment-plan financing developed.[26] Between 1913 and 1929 the ratio of private credit to gross domestic product nearly doubled.

"Shoestring mortgages" enabled property to be bought on margin. The expansion of such credit instruments unhinged the traditional relationship between income and spending (Olney 1991: 130–131), and thereby increased the potential for conspicuous consumption. This marked a significant change from the 19th century when "[i]nstallment buying wasn't considered quite respectable" (Ayres 1926: 13).

It should be noted that not all of the pressure to consume more falls so clearly within the realm of a struggle to maintain social status. Rising inequality also created externalities that required households to increase spending for the welfare of their families, and especially their children. Robert Frank has addressed the manner in which this works in housing:

> Increased spending at the top of the income distribution has not only imposed psychological costs on families in the middle, it has also raised the cost of achieving many basic goals . . . people cannot send their children to a public school of even average quality if they buy a home in a school district in which house prices are well below average. (2000: 258)

The super-rich households were ever in competition with each other for the very pinnacle of status, with the consequence that "[i]n the consumer race the finishing line always moves faster than the fastest of runners" (Bauman 2000: 72). This put pressure on the lesser rich who also wished to be seen as at the very top. This pressure was reinforced by advertising that increased from $2.28 billion in 1919 to $3.43 billion in 1929 (Olney 1991: 137), and kept the consumption standards of the rich and famous on public display. As Edsforth notes: "In the 1920s, advertising's pictorial images portrayed the comforts and luxuries of the well-to-do while advertising's words promised everyone access to these things . . . [and] corporate elites advertised the 'Democracy of Goods' and urged every citizen to partake of the pleasures offered by the new and exciting mass popular culture" (1998: 260, 266). In *Middletown* (1929), the Lynds argued that workers worked ever harder, not due to a work ethic, but because of their expanding wants, ever stimulated by advertising and films.

As inequality dramatically increased during the 1920s, the struggle by households to maintain their relative status resulted in reduced saving,[27] greater indebtedness, and possibly more work hours for households. Personal saving as a percent of disposable income declined from 6.4 percent in the 1898–1916 period to 3.8 percent in the 1922–1929 period (Olney 1991: 48). However, who continued saving is revealing. Whereas the top 1 percent of income recipients accounted for 49 percent of total saving in 1922, this figure soared to 80 percent by 1928 (Lampman 1962: 236, Table 111). Thus, in their status-driven struggle to consume more, the lower 99 percent were saving very little.

In their struggle to maintain their relative social status in the face of rising inequality, Americans became more indebted, providing further evidence of the significant decline in Protestantism's ascetic component. Debt as a percent of income increased from 4.64 percent in 1919 to 9.34 percent in 1929 (Olney 1991: 88–89). Calder notes that "[b]y 1930, installment credit financed the sales of 60–75 percent of automobiles, 80–90 percent of furniture, 75 percent of washing machines, 65 percent of vacuum cleaners, 18–25 percent of jewelry, 75 percent of radio sets, and 80 percent of phonographs" (1999: 201). Between 1921 and 1929, consumer spending on durables grew 116 percent, whereas spending on nondurables grew by 34 percent (Hall and Ferguson 1998: 19). While some of these durables represented labor-saving technology that enhanced the standard of living, a large quantity were goods that could also serve as indicators of income, and thus, status.

This rise in indebtedness fits the Veblenian hypothesis that in a society in which vertical mobility is believed to be highly fluid, increasing gaps in income all along the spectrum would stimulate everyone to struggle harder to meet their consumption status targets, as those at the very top compete among themselves for the very apex of status.

A third possible response of households in their struggle to maintain their relative social standing in the face of rising inequality would be to work longer hours. Although the work week continued its contraction during the 1920s, Bernstein claims that "[n]ew expectations regarding appropriate family income levels . . . encouraged more women to enter the labor market" (1998: 195). There may also have been increased labor market participation of children. Huberman and

Minns (2007) find inequality to be a strong predictor of average working hours at the national level during this time, whereas in a broad study, Bowles and Park (2005) find that inequality leads to longer working hours. However, because data for total household labor are lacking for this period, any claim of changes in household work hours must remain conjectural.

Rising inequality, especially in a social context of degraded work, weakened community, and new consumer durables, served to exaggerate the devaluation of work and the decline of community resulting from industrialization. Inequality reduces the potential for work to serve as an adequate medium for achieving fulfillment. Because of the way inequality propels households toward consumption to maintain their social standing, where there is a tradeoff between work quality and income, inequality encourages workers to choose the latter. Work becomes more biased toward a means to the end of higher consumption and away from its potential for serving as an outlet for self-expression and creativity.

Inequality reduces the potential for community because, as Irvin reports, it reduces social capital: "Where there is more income inequality, poorer people are more likely to feel out of place participating in community groups, more likely to feel ill at ease and to think that they will make fools of themselves and be looked down upon" (2007: 15). In their survey of studies on trust, Wilkinson and Pickett find that "[w]ith greater inequality, people are less caring of one another, there is less mutuality in relationships, people have to fend for themselves and get what they can—so, inevitably, there is less trust. . . . High levels of trust mean that people feel secure, they have less to worry about, they see others as co-operative rather than competitive" (2009: 56, 57)

In devaluing the potential for work and community to provide social certification and personal fulfillment, inequality fed a material progress vision, the view that ever-greater material abundance is the key to happiness.[28] This change in perception was manifest in the substantial increase in consumption during the early part of the 20th century, particularly in those goods that more ably suggested one's income level, as individuals competed to indicate their worthiness.

Final Reflections

The Protestant ethic was a defining characteristic of America's cultural and economic experience. Just as its birth in Europe toward the end of the Middle Ages was due to evolving socioeconomic conditions, so too was its transformation in the United States between 1870 and 1930. The birth of the Protestant ethic had generated two behavior codes that would favor capital accumulation and economic dynamism, those of ascetic behavior in consumption and the value of hard work. The transformation of this ethic, whereby asceticism greatly weakened as a consequence of industrialization in the United States, heralded the birth of a consumer-driven society.

This transformation of the Protestant ethic has meant that social certification, social status, and self-respect have come to be sought increasingly in consumption as opposed to work and community. Hard work remained critically important, but its social recognition depended increasingly on the level of consumption it permitted. However, the resulting status-driven competitive consumption race now poses an unanticipated challenge—avoiding environmental devastation. Indeed, avoiding devastation of our habitat may be the greatest challenge ever faced by humanity (Wisman 2011).

Although social sciences are turning their analyses toward this challenge, mainstream economic science is ill-equipped for adequately participating. The fundamental reason is its steadfast refusal to examine the manner in which preferences are, at least in part, socially constructed. The pretended queen of the social sciences needs to widen her framework to be able to grasp the social dynamics that heterodox economists such as Veblen so keenly explored. An understanding of the cultural dynamics represented by the Protestant ethic reminds us of the theoretical and social costs of this mainstream stance, and the need for an economic science capable of incorporating sociocultural dynamics into its analytical framework.

Notes

1. Debate surrounding practically every aspect of the Protestant ethic has been vibrant ever since the publication of Weber's seminal work in 1904. Furnham notes that "although the validity of the historical, economic,

sociological and theological hypothesis remains in doubt, and hotly debated, few have denied the validity and accuracy of Weber's specifications of behaviour patterns, goals and values dictated by the PWE, namely asceticism, hard work, postponement of gratification, thrift, frugality, etc . . ." (1984: 88, 100). Bell declares that Weber's book, *The Protestant Ethic and the Spirit of Capitalism* "is probably the most important sociological work of the twentieth century" (1996: 35).

2. Virtually all commentators who see a decline in the Protestant ethic see it occurring either during the period under discussion in this article or in the middle decades of the second half of the 20th century (for a review of those who stress the latter period, see Furnham 1990: 203–206).

3. Veblen's theory of human behavior plays no role in mainstream economics. The principal reason is that it is constructed on the strong assumption that people's preference functions are highly interdependent. Neoclassical economics views them as independent.

4. Davis notes research that concludes that: "Wealth in America is often a symbol of occupational achievement which is in many cases the ultimate criterion of status. But our occupational system includes so many complex skills that popular recognition of them is impossible. Hence income is taken as a least common factor, a rough index of achievement. It is an easy step from there to the emphasis on display and conspicuous consumption which Veblen noted so clearly" (1944: 284).

5. Further evidence that the Protestant work ethic reflected the rise of a commercial bourgeoisie is provided by the fact that a strong Calvin-like work ethic also developed in Japan among merchants as their power and status rose in the 17th century (Landes 1998: 363).

6. A revised appreciation of wealth came to characterize Protestantism in the United States by the early 20th century. Note the following passage in Russell Conwell's *Acres of Diamonds*, a book published in the United States in 1915 that would go on to sell 10 million copies:

> I say that you ought to get rich, and it is your duty to get rich. . . . Some men say, "Don't you sympathize with the poor people?" Of course I do, or else I would not have been lecturing all these years. But the number of poor who are to be sympathized with is very small. To sympathize with a man whom God has punished for his sins, thus to help him when God would still continue his punishment, is to do wrong, no doubt about it. (1915: 17, 21)

7. As Bell put it: "The Protestant ethic as a way of life . . . was one of piety, frugality, discipline, prudence, the strenuous devotion to work, and delayed gratification" (1996: 35).

8. This point was forcefully made by Veblen: "Only individuals with an aberrant temperament can in the long run retain their self-esteem in the face of the disesteem of their fellows" (1899: 39).

9. In the early 20th century, Graeber claimed that "Americans have, since colonial days, been the population least sympathetic to debtors" (Graeber 2011).

10. Alexis de Tocqueville and Karl Marx both noted an exceptionally high degree of vertical mobility in the United States and termed it "American exceptionalism."

11. Vertical mobility became most fully developed first in those capitalist countries that were essentially composed of immigrants who had left behind worlds of more rigid status barriers. Thus not surprisingly, considerable vertical mobility was found in countries populated by immigrants such as the United States, Canada, Australia, and Israel (Tyree, Semyonov, and Hodge 1979: 415).

12. The reverse also might be expected to hold. The less fortunate would more readily be seen as responsible for their economic failures. Therefore, welfare measures would be undeserved, if not corrupting. Criminal conduct would merit stiff punishment.

13. By contrast, in traditional societies in which status was ascribed by birth, high-status individuals felt their status was their right. Indeed, they generally understood themselves to be in fact superior, whereas those below felt themselves to be in fact inferior.

14. Veblen (1899) goes on to argue, however, that as the population becomes more mobile, communities become less close-knit such that people are less well informed of the leisure activities in which other people engage, and so the display of wealth through consumption of goods becomes more important than the display of leisure. It is curious that whereas Veblen viewed much consumption as a resource-wasteful pursuit of higher status, he saw attraction to work as driven by an instinct—the instinct of workmanship—and not as driven by a Protestant ethic.

15. Accompanying this transformation was a decline in paternalism, which, as Collins puts it, "operated through provision of nonwage goods and services, an ideology of beneficence, and the cultivation of deferential relations" (2002: 157).

16. Some workers left their jobs rather than suffer de-skilling, long hours, and loss of control over the workplace (Rodgers 1978: 163–165).

17. Religious views of the changes discussed in this article were varied, and in fact there is some evidence that the Protestant faiths embraced the new consumer culture (Stearns 1997) and were often anti-labor, unsurprising due to the fact that Protestant church membership was heavily concentrated among professional workers and salaried men, while Catholicism was more the religion of the working class and subsequently paid far more attention to the plight of the worker (Hudson 1965: 308).

18. It should be noted that even much of the office work that arose with industrialization was viewed as degraded. In both Gilded Age America and Victorian Britain even the office worker was depicted as a pathetic creature. Note Bartleby the scrivener or Scrooge's assistant, Bob Cratchit.

19. The first recorded recognition of the mental impairment resulting from factory work was ironically Adam Smith, the great champion of the division of labor, which he claimed, over 700 pages into his classic, made workers "as stupid and ignorant as it is possible for a human creature to become" (1776: II: 782).

20. Lane maintains that "[t]here is evidence that exercise of discretion on the job, which is not so much a right as a requirement of complex tasks, has more substantial effect on self-esteem than any exercise of familiar political rights has ever had" (Lane 1991: 198).

21. Riesman suggested yet another reason for the expansion of conspicuous consumption consequent to the changed character of work: "Conspicuous consumption is a form of escape from the regimentation and control of work" (Riesman 1953: 144).

22. New technologies helped alter the definition of "community" for many Americans. The rapid diffusion of technologies such as the telephone and automobile allowed one to maintain contact with those whose approval was needed even while working and living in another community.

23. Interrante points out that "[m]any, if not all, of the village-centered institutions sold goods and provided services . . . which farm women had produced or performed themselves, and over which farm families had retained a close and immediate control. Metropolitanism [accompanying industrialization] interrupted that relationship and thus represented a reorganization of the social relations of consumption" (1979: 158).

24. Although young girls had been working in factories in large numbers since before the Civil War, this was perceived as a temporary situation that would not continue after marriage (Hesse-Biber and Carter 2005: 34).

25. Beyond Veblen, Duesenberry is one of the few well-known economists to have identified a relationship between belief in social mobility and consumption: "recognition of upward mobility as a social goal converts the drive for self-esteem into a desire for high social status [which] requires the maintenance of a high consumption standard" (1949: 31).

26. Bell characterizes "the invention of the installment plan [as] the most 'subversive' instrument that undercut the Protestant ethic . . . [and] Marketing and hedonism became the motor forces of capitalism" (Bell 1996: 38).

27. For an extended discussion of Veblen's theory of consumer behavior applied to more recent U.S. saving behavior, see Wisman (2009).

28. For an extended discussion, see Wisman (2003).

References

Applebaum, H. (1998). *The American Work Ethic and the Changing Work Force.* Westport, CT: Greenwood Press.

Ayres, Milan V. (1926). *Installment Selling and Its Financing: A Report by the Economic Policy Commission to the Executive Council and a Report to the Economic Policy Commission.* Unpublished: American Bankers Association.

Bauman, Zygmunt. (2000). *Liquid Modernity.* Malden, MA: Blackwell.

——. (2005). *Work, Consumerism and the New Poor,* 2nd ed. Berkshire, UK: Open University Press.

Bell, D. (1976). *The Cultural Contradictions of Capitalism.* New York: Basic Books.

——. (1996). "The Protestant Ethic." *World Policy Journal* 13(3): 35–39.

Bernstein, I. (1966). *The Lean Years: A History of the American Worker, 1920–33.* Boston: Penguin Books.

Bernstein, Michael A. (1998). "The American Economy of the Interwar Era." In *Calvin Coolidge and the Coolidge Era.* Ed. John Earl Haynes, pp. 191–213. Washington, DC: Library of Congress.

Bowles, S., and Y. Park. (2005). "Emulation, Inequality, and Work Hours: Was Thorstein Veblen Right?" *Economic Journal* 115(507): F397–F412.

Bright, J. R. (1958). *Automation and Management.* Norwood, MA: Plimpton Press.

Buchholz, R. A. (1998). "The Ethics of Consumption Activities: A Future Paradigm?" *Journal of Business Ethics* 17(8): 871–882.

Calder, L. (1999). *Financing the American Dream: A Cultural History of Consumer Credit.* Princeton, NJ: Princeton University Press.

Carnegie, A. (2006). *The "Gospel of Wealth" Essays and Other Writings,* ed. David Nasaw. New York: Penguin.

Carter, S. B., S. Gartner, M. Haines, A. Olmstead, R. Sutch, and G. Wright, eds. (2006). *Historical Statistics of the United States: Earliest Times to the Present—Millennial Edition.* 5 vols. New York: Cambridge University Press.

Collins, J. (2002). "Deterritorialization and Workplace Culture." *American Ethnologist* 29(1): 151–171.

Conwell, Russell. (1915). *Acres of Diamonds.* New York: Harper & Brothers.

Davis, A. K. (1944). "Veblen on the Decline of the Protestant Ethic." *Social Forces* 22(3): 282–286.

de Tocqueville, A. (1945). *Democracy in America.* Henry Reeve, trans. Vols. 1 and 2. New York: Vintage.

Duesenberry, J. S. (1949). *Income, Saving, and the Theory of Consumer Behavior.* Cambridge, MA: Harvard University Press.

Edsforth, R. (1998). "Made in the U.S.A.: Mass Culture and the Americanization of Working-Class Ethnics in the Coolidge Era." In *Calvin Coolidge and the Coolidge Era.* Ed. John Earl Haynes, pp. 244–272. Washington, DC: Library of Congress.

Eisenberger, R. (1989). *Blue Monday: The Loss of the Work Ethic in America.* New York: Paragon House.

Frank, Robert H. (2000). "Does Growing Inequality Harm the Middle Class?" *Eastern Economic Journal* 26(3): 253–264.

Furnham, A. (1984). "The Protestant Work Ethic: A Review of the Psychological Literature." *European Journal of Social Psychology* 14(1): 87–104.

——. (1990). *The Protestant Work Ethic: The Psychology of Work-Related Beliefs and Behaviors.* London: Routledge.

Gilligan, C. (2000). "Concepts of Self and Morality." In *The Presence of Others*, 3rd ed. Eds. Andrea Lunsford and John J. Ruszkiewicz, pp. 169–178. New York: St. Martin's Press.

Goldin, C. (1994)."The U-Shaped Female Labor Force Function in Economic Development and Economic History." NBER Working Paper No. 4707. http://www.nber.org/papers/w4707.

Graeber, D. (2011). "To Have is to Owe." http://www.canopycanopycanopy.com/10/to_have_is_to_owe (accessed September 8, 2011).

Granovetter, M. (1984). "Small is Bountiful: Labor Markets and Establishment Size." *American Sociological Review* 49(3): 323–334.

Grebler, L., D. M. Blank, and L. Winick. (1956). *Capital Formation in Residential Real Estate: Trends and Prospects.* Princeton: NBER and Princeton University Press.

Hall, T. E., and J. D. Ferguson. (1998). *The Great Depression: An International Disaster of Perverse Economic Policies.* Ann Arbor: University of Michigan Press.

Hatton, T. J., and J. G. Williamson. (1991). "Wage Gaps Between Farm and City: Michigan in the 1890s." *Explorations in Economic History* 28(4): 381–408.

Hawley, Amos H. (1956). *The Changing Shape of Metropolitan America.* Glencoe, IL: Free Press.

Hesse-Biber, S. N., and G. L. Carter. (2005). *Working Women in America.* New York: Oxford University Press.

Holt, C. F. (1977). "Who Benefited from the Prosperity of the Twenties?" *Explorations in Economic History* 14(3): 277–289.

Huberman, M., and C. Minns. (2007). "The Times They Are Not Changin': Days and Hours of Work in the Old and New Worlds, 1870–2000." *Explorations in Economic History* 44(4): 538–567.

Hudson, W. S. (1965). *Religion in America.* New York: Charles Scribner's Sons.

Interrante, J. (1979). "You Can't Go to Town in a Bathtub: Automobile Movement and the Reorganization of Rural American Space, 1900–1930." *Radical History Review* 21: 151–168.

Irvin, G. (2007). "Growing Inequality in the Neo-Liberal Heartland." *Post-Autistic Economics Review* 43: 1–23.

Jackson, K. T. (1985). *Crabgrass Frontier: The Suburbanization of the United States.* New York: Oxford University Press.

Klein, M., and H. A. Kantor. (1976). *Prisoners of Progress: American Industrial Cities 1850–1920.* New York: Macmillan Publishing Co.

Kuznets, S. (1955). "Economic Growth and Income Inequality." *American Economic Review* 45(1): 1–28.

Lacey, R. (1986). *Ford: The Men and the Machine.* Boston: Little, Brown & Co.

Lampman, R. (1962). *The Share of Top Wealth-Holders in National Wealth 1922–1956. A Study by the National Bureau of Economic Research.* Princeton, NJ: Princeton University Press.

Landes, D. (1998). *The Wealth and Poverty of Nations.* New York: W.W. Norton.

Lane, R. E. (1991). *The Market Experience.* New York: Cambridge University Press.

Lindert, P. H. (2000). "Three Centuries of Inequality in Britain and America." In *Handbook of Income Distribution,* Vol. 1. Eds. A. B. Atkinson and F. Bourguignon, pp. 167–216. Amsterdam: Elsevier Science B.V.

Livingston, J. (2009). "Their Great Depression and Ours." *Challenge* 52(3): 34–51.

Lutz, T. (1996). " 'Sweat or Die': The Hedonization of the Work Ethic in the 1920s." *American Literary History* 8(2): 259–283.

Lynd, R. S., and H. M. Lynd. (1929). *Middletown: A Study in Contemporary American Culture.* New York: Harcourt.

Maddison, A. (2006). *The World Economy, Volume 2: Historical Statistics.* OECD Development Centre. E-book. http://www.oecd-ilibrary.org/development/the-world-economy_9789264022621-en (accessed October 27, 2011).

Montgomery, D. (1983). "Workers' Control of Machine Production in the Nineteenth Century." In *The Labor History Reader.* Ed. Daniel J. Leab, pp. 107–152. Urbana, IL: University of Illinois Press.

Moran, T. P. (2005). "Kuznets's Inverted U-Curve Hypothesis: The Rise, Demise, and Continued Relevance of a Socioeconomic Law." *Sociological Forum* 20(2): 209–244.

Olney, M. L. (1991). *Buy Now, Pay Later.* Chapel Hill: University of North Carolina.

Phillips, K. (2002). "Too Much Wealth, Too Little Democracy." Interview. *Challenge* 45(5): 6–20.

Polanyi, K. ([1944] 1957). *The Great Transformation.* Boston: Beacon Press.

Powers, C. W. (1976). "Growth as an American Value: An Ethicist's Point of View." In *Growth in America.* Ed. Chester L. Cooper, pp. 26–38. Westport, CT: Greenwood Press.

Rawls, J. (1971). *A Theory of Justice.* Cambridge: Harvard University Press.

Riesman, D. (1953). *The Lonely Crowd.* New Haven: Yale University Press.

Rodgers, D. T. (1978). *The Work Ethic in Industrial America, 1850–1920.* Chicago: University of Chicago Press.

Saez, E. (2009). "Striking It Richer: The Evolution of Top Incomes in the United States (Update with 2007 estimates)." http://elsa.berkeley.edu/~saez/saez-UStopincomes-2007.pdf (accessed July 22, 2011).

Sayer, A. (2005). *The Moral Significance of Class.* Cambridge: Cambridge University Press.

Scranton, P. (1994). "Manufacturing Diversity: Production Systems, Markets, and an American Consumer Society." *Technology and Culture* 35(3): 476–505.

Scase, Richard. (1992). *Class.* Minneapolis: University of Minnesota Press.

Sedgwick, E. K., and A. Frank. (1995). "Shame in the Cybernetic Fold: Reading Silvan Tomkins." In *Shame and Its Sisters: A Silvan Tomkins Reader.* Eds. Eve Kosofsky Sedgwick and Adam Frank, pp. 496–527. Durham, NC: Duke University Press.

Smiley, G. (1998). "New Estimates of Income Shares During the 1920s." In *Calvin Coolidge and the Coolidge Era: Essays on the History of the 1920.* Ed. John Earl Haynes, pp. 215–232. Washington, DC: Library of Congress.

Smith, A. (1776). *An Inquiry into the Nature and Causes of the Wealth of Nations.* Vols. 1 and II. Oxford: Oxford University Press.

Sohn-Rethel, A. (1978). *Intellectual and Manual Labour.* Atlantic Highlands, NJ: Humanities Press.

Stearns, P. N. (1997). "Stages of Consumerism: Recent Work on the Issues of Periodization." *Journal of Modern History* 69(1): 102–117.

Stricker, F. (1983). "Affluence for Whom? Another Look at Prosperity and the Working Classes in the 1920s." *Labor History* 24(1): 5–33.

Sward, K. (1948). *The Legend of Henry Ford.* New York: Rinehart & Co.

Taylor, F. W. (1907). "On the Art of Cutting Metals: Presidential Address." *Transactions of the American Society of Mechanical Engineers* 28(119): 31–60.

——. (1912). *Shop Management.* New York: Harper & Brothers.

Tilly, L. A., and J. W. Scott. (1978). *Women, Work, and Family.* New York: Holt, Rinehart and Winston.

Tyree, A., M. Semyonov, and R. W. Hodge. (1979). "Gaps and Glissandos: Inequality, Economic Development, and Social Mobility in 24 Countries." *American Sociological Review* 44(3): 410–424.

United States Senate Committee on Education and Labor. ([1885] 1976). *Report of the Committee of the Senate Upon the Relations Between Labor and Capital and Testimony Taken by the Committee.* New York: Arno Press.

Vanek, J. (1980). "Work, Leisure and Family Roles: Farm Households in the United States, 1920–1955." *Journal of Family History* 5(4): 422–431.

Veblen, Thorstein. (1899). *The Theory of the Leisure Class.* New York: Modern Library.

——. (1919). "Some Neglected Points in the Theory of Socialism." In *The Place of Science in Modern Civilization*, pp. 387–408. New York: B.W. Huebsch.

Weber, M. (1904). *The Protestant Ethic and the Spirit of Capitalism.* New York: Charles Scribners' Sons.

White, E. N. (1990). "The Stock Market Boom and Crash of 1929 Revisited." *Journal of Economic Perspectives* 4(2): 67–83.

Whyte, W. (1956). *The Organization Man.* Philadelphia: The University of Pennsylvania Press.

Wilkinson, R., and K. Pickett. (2009). *The Spirit Level: Why More Equal Societies Almost Always Do Better.* London: Allen Lane.

Wisman, Jon D. (2003). "The Scope and Promising Future of Social Economics." *Review of Social Economy* 16(4): 1–21.

——. (2009). "Household Saving, Class Identity, and Conspicuous Consumption." *Journal of Economic Issues* 43(1): 89–114.

——. (2011). "Inequality, Social Respectability, Political Power, and Environmental Devastation." *Journal of Economic Issues* 45(4): 877–900.

Zuboff, Shoshana. (1983). "The Work Ethic and Work Organization." In *The Work Ethic—A Critical Analysis.* Ed. Barbash, pp. 153–181. Bloomington, IL: Pantagraph Printing.

The Making of the Institutional Theory of Social Costs: Discovering the K. W. Kapp and J. M. Clark Correspondence*

By SEBASTIAN BERGER†

ABSTRACT. This article reconstructs the making of the often "overlooked" institutional theory of social costs based on the unexploited correspondence between John Maurice Clark and Karl William Kapp. The reconstruction demonstrates that the institutional argument on social costs was developed as a critique of neoclassical economics and of post-WWII neoliberalism.

Introduction

While most economists feel at ease to identify the boundaries of the discourse on social costs with the views of Pigou and Coase (see, for example, Aslanbeigui and Medema 1998), the distinct institutional argument developed by John Maurice Clark and Karl William Kapp has been largely eclipsed from the discourse (for efforts to revitalize this argument, see Berger 2012; Elsner, Frigato, and Ramazzotti 2012; Berger and Steppacher 2011; Gerber and Steppacher 2011). Therefore, this article has two main aims. Firstly, it reconstructs the making of the institutional argument based on unexplored archival materials, that is, the unpublished correspondence on social costs between Clark and Kapp. The aim is to analyze for the first time their important collaboration, and the development and relation of their arguments. This reveals and corrects imprecisions in the existing literature concerning their use of the term "social costs," sheds new light on how Clark influenced Kapp, and highlights the uniqueness of their institutional argument as a full-fledged theory of social costs. Secondly, this article

*I wish to thank two anonymous reviewers, Rolf Steppacher, and Andrew Farrant for detailed comments. I am grateful to Laurence Shute and Steve Medema for their interesting remarks. All remaining mistakes are my own.

†Currently, Visiting Scholar at the Department of Economics, Harvard University; beginning January 2014, Senior Lecturer in Economics, University of West England.

American Journal of Economics and Sociology, Vol. 72, No. 5 (November, 2013).
DOI: 10.1111/ajes.12040

provides important evidence that the discourse on social costs can only be fully understood as an interaction between neoclassical, neoliberal, and institutional arguments.[1] That is, the institutional argument on social costs was developed not only as a critique of neoclassical economics, but also as a reply to the rise of post-WWII "neo"-liberalism, exemplified in the works of F. A. Hayek and L. Mises. The analysis illustrates how the reaction of leading members of the "neoliberal thought-collective" (see Mirowski and Plehwe 2009 for a sociology of this movement) contributed to the eclipse of the institutional argument on social costs. Thus, the article contributes an important detail to the account of the gradual demise of institutional economics in the period of the great neoliberal transformation of economics (Lee 2009; Rutherford 2011; Mirowski and Plehwe 2009). By reconstructing (Rorty 1984) the making of the institutional argument of social costs in the context of the social costs discourse with members of the "neoliberal thought-collective," this article contributes to the recent sociology of economic knowledge.

The Kapp-Clark Correspondence in Context

The Kapp-Clark correspondence on social costs is situated within the larger context of the demise of institutional economics as the dominant economic theory. Institutional economics is both a critique of neoclassical economics and a full-fledged and influential movement within economics (see Rutherford 2011; Kapp 2011; Dugger 2012). According to Rutherford, between 1926 and 1957 Clark was the leading institutional economist at Columbia, which was the center of institutional economics until the latter's eventual demise. The institutionalist complement that emerged there during the 1920s was given a major boost by the hiring of Clark as Research Professor in Economics. Clark described his work as "social-institutional-dynamic theory," developing a "realist economics" and an approach to social-liberal planning. Before coming to Columbia, he had already critiqued neoclassical theory and called for a more properly scientific economics that was relevant to the issues of its time. The year he arrived at Columbia, he published "Social Control of Business" (1926), which further developed ideas first expressed in "Overhead Costs"

([1923] 1931). His book discussed a large number of market failures that called for additional social controls. Market failure and regulation were key areas of institutional economics at Columbia. Clark agreed with legal realists in viewing law as a key instrument of social control to improve economic outcomes. Clark even co-taught a seminar on law and economics in the 1924 and 1925 terms. Until the late 1930s the institutional program at Columbia was well established. According to Kenneth Arrow, the Veblenian influence was still present at Columbia in the early 1940s; however, things had begun to change and the research program fissured into such a variety of approaches that by the late 1930s, even the leading institutionalists W. Mitchell and Clark would no longer acknowledge a distinct and coherent institutionalism. As elsewhere, the significance of mathematical economics grew and was symbolized by the hiring of George Stigler in 1947. By the early 1950s the department was divided between the prewar institutionalists, such as Clark, and the postwar neoclassical economists, such as Stigler. Clark retired in 1953 (for more details of this account of the situation at Columbia, see Rutherford 2011; for details concerning the development of Clark's economics, see Shute 1997).

Kapp had been a research assistant at the Institute for Social Research at Columbia and an instructor of economics at Columbia between 1937 and 1945 (for a brief biography, see Berger and Steppacher 2011), when institutional economics was still dominant but had entered into its declining stage. When Columbia's postwar hiring strategy favored neoclassical economists, Kapp left for Wesleyan University (CT) (see the accounts of Lee 2003 and Rutherford 2011 on the suppression and demise of institutional economics). The tremendous influence of Clark's work on overhead costs and social economics is acknowledged in Kapp's preface to "Social Costs of Private Enterprise" (1950). Its second—revised and enlarged—edition was entitled "Social Costs of Business Enterprise" (1963), signaling that the core of the institutional argument on social costs had already been stated by Veblen's "Theory of Business Enterprise" (1904). Kapp's work was widely reviewed and translated into many languages worldwide and made a significant impact on such events in the environmental movement in the 1970s as the 1972 UN Conference on Environment and Development, the formation of Ignacy Sachs' Center for Environment and Development, and the Socialist Environment and Resource Association (SERA). Friedrich Pollock—a leading member of the Frankfurt School and close friend of Kapp—invited Kapp to participate in the newly constituted Institut für Sozialforschung in Frankfurt. Kapp's major project, however, to initiate an international association of institutional economists in collaboration with Gunnar Myrdal, eventually failed in the late 1960s due to a lack of funding.[2] After reaching its pinnacle of influence on the social costs discourse in the early 1970s, Kapp's institutional argument on social costs (see below) has gradually been eclipsed from the discourse.

J. M. Clark's Theory of Overhead Costs and Cost Shifting

The following section shows how Clark derived the concept of cost shifting from his argument on overhead costs. This provides the intellectual context for the correspondence on Kapp's institutional theory of the social costs of private enterprise, as it is based on Clark's notion of cost shifting.[3] Clark's earliest letter in the Kapp Archives is dated Feb. 6, 1941 and is a reply to Kapp:

> Dear Dr. Kapp, Your outline and sample chapters are very interesting; and I am naturally interested in your project of developing and applying some of my ideas. . . . Needless to say, I shall be interested in how your study develops.

What was the nature of these "ideas"? Clark developed his ideas mainly in "Overhead Costs" (1931), arguing that "overhead costs" refer to an

> entire family of ideas, but they have one essential thing in common . . . they refer to costs that cannot be traced home and attributed to particular units of business . . . most of the real problems involve one other fact; namely that an increase or decrease in output does not involve a proportionate increase or decrease in cost. . . . the causes are real world complexities . . . unused productive capacity . . . "idle overhead" . . . unused powers of production. (Clark 1931: 1)

> We have a considerable body of economic generalizations, bearing on the facts of that overhead costs are decidedly at variance with the assumptions and conclusions of that type of economics which searches for the conditions of a perfect equilibrium of supply and demand. (Clark 1931 in Gruchy 1967: 364)

Clark argued that the development of the forces of production in the 20th century, characterized by large amounts of fixed capital equipment, a specialized workforce, and disequilibrium, required a corresponding theory of costs (Gruchy 1967: 365–366). Reviewing the conceptual history of costs, Clark concluded that "[t]he entire idea of expenses of production is . . . a rather recent one" (Clark 1931: 1) and that the neoclassical theory of costs was modeled on a long bygone economic reality where "virtually every element which economists now think of as an expense of production was paid for in such a fashion that each item could be directly charged to an item of product" (Clark 1931: 2). Neoclassical cost theory only held true under unique circumstances in which "expenses were virtually all traceable directly to units of product, and overhead costs were virtually non-existent" (Clark 1931: 2). Clark concluded that the "prevalent ideas on expenses of production date back to the domestic system and are not really appropriate to any later stage of industrial development" (Clark 1931: 2). Yet Clark argued that a proper theory of costs was crucial because "the backbone of the science of economics is the balancing of value against cost" (Clark 1931: 17). Clark asked the crucial question how the costs of producing an additional unit of output are determined:

> Is the carload of lumber worth carrying if it covers all the costs that can be attributed to that single carload? . . . Shall we count the costs that would keep on even if the railroad shut down entirely? (Clark 1931: 19)

Clark concluded

> Evidently, "cost" is an ambiguous term and . . . requires a thorough re-examination. (Clark 1931: 19)

> There is no natural system of prices in the old sense. Cost prices do not mean anything definite anymore. (Clark 1931: 32)

What is counted as "costs" is thus a "convention" with "latitude" (Shute 1997: 60). This definition is fully in the tradition of institutional economics that focuses on the effects of habits of thought and institutions in the cumulative causation of the economic process. Clark used the concept of "shifting and conversion of overhead costs" of human labor in the business cycle[4] to elaborate this aspect of institutional theory of costs (Clark 1931: 25–27):

> The cost to society of supporting a group of laborers does not vary with their output, for this cost goes on even though the laborers produce nothing, as is the case in periods of enforced idleness, which comes in the depression phase of the business cycle. (Gruchy 1967: 360)

Clark also extended the concept of overhead costs to mining and farming and called it "an ultimate fact" of human cost that must be maintained in depressions (Gruchy: 361–362). He determined the problem to be that business enterprises did not treat their costs as overhead but as variable costs. The converting of constant overhead costs into variable costs determined the process by which producers judged the profitability of production. Clark observed this, for example, in the business cycle when slowing sales trigger quantity adjustments by the laying off of workers (Clark 1931: 27–30). Clark introduced the terms "shifting and conversion of overhead costs" to describe how businesses make the workers responsible for their own maintenance, or throw the burden on society. These business measures create what Clark called the "accelerator effect" of laying off workers and further reducing purchasing power, leading to a deterioration of productive facilities, i.e., a kind of social damage accelerator. Clark described this in a metaphor: "All of which irresistibly suggests a man on a rock, jumping into the water for fear the tide will rise and wet him" (Clark 1931: 29). According to Clark, this reflected the conflict between social and private interests, since the former required capacity output while the latter sought to maximize revenue over variable costs (Clark 1931: 28–29).

This idea of cost shifting in the conflicting relationship between individual and social interests was a restatement of Veblen's source theme that portrayed social waste as a consequence of the fact that business enterprise did not channel economic activity in ways consistent with public interests (Rutherford 2011: 36). Veblen's pioneering analysis of institutions (including property rights, business-like and finance-like control of industry; see Gerber and Steppacher 2011) focused on social waste and damages. Veblen argued that capital resides in the continuity of ownership and that in a system of business enterprise and absentee ownership the "strong arm intervenes" to shuffle property rights so as to control and increase private pecuniary returns, which includes a subreptitious and predatory shifting of costs and thereby an avoidance of responsibility. Moreover, Veblen argued that this process of realignment of property rights via subreption and predation not only failed to guarantee, but systematically disregarded, the maintenance and efficient use of the material funds of production.

Veblen's examples included natural resource depletion—timberlands, fur-bearing animals, oil fields—next to sabotage of industrial and workers' efficiency, causing unnecessary social waste (Krall and Gowdy 2011).

The rethinking of the notion of costs led Clark to reformulate the notions of efficiency and accounting (Gruchy 1967: 365–367). Clark argued that estimating the efficiency of the total economy could not be undertaken by using data from private accounting because it did not account for all the costs of production. Clark proposed a new form of accounting that would indicate the discrepancies between commercial and community measures of efficiency. He supported a social cost keeping as a "form of economic reckoning which cuts through the sophisms of private financial accountancy and calls social waste by its true name"[5] (Gruchy 1967: 369). This new social accounting would be an effective device for judging the efficiency of the modern economy as a creator of "human values." According to Clark, it was the duty of economists to reveal the shifted and neglected costs of operating our industrial system that were left unpaid by businesses, such as idle men and machinery, destruction of utilities through fashion, waste resulting from competitive advertisement, and private business secrecy. Clark viewed this as a problem of bringing this information to the public's attention and of putting an end to unpaid costs (Gruchy 1967: 369–370). Clark hoped that once it was understood how the legal and institutional matrix produced market values, the discrepancies between market and social valuation could be reduced (Gruchy 1967: 368).

> A knowledge of the laws of overhead costs . . . opens many doors and is one of the indispensable avenues . . . overhead costs are not exceptions to a general economic law: they are the general law. (Clark 1931: 479)

In conclusion, Clark's argument on overhead costs and cost shifting constitute a further development of Veblen's ideas on social waste with a view to justify increasing social controls. In this institutional economics theory, the legal and institutional structure determines the extent to which firms have to pay the costs of production, so that prices based on costs including "mark-up" (Lee 1999) are a function of the institutional framework of society. Without proper legal restrictions and social controls, the latter remains a system of cost shifting, a vicious circle of accelerating social damages. This theory of the institutional causes of cost shifting and social damages was developed by Kapp into the institutional theory of social costs, which is the subject matter of the following correspondence with Clark.

The Kapp-Clark Correspondence on Social Costs[6]

How far did Clark influence Kapp in developing the institutional theory of social costs as a critique of the system of business enterprise and as an argument for social accounting and controls? What was the nature of their interactions? In the above cited letter (February 6, 1941), Clark raised his "chief concern . . . of balancing the emphasis on the negative and the positive side of the critique." Clark contrasted the setting in which "Overhead Costs" was written to the setting of the 1940s:

> [my early work was in a] setting characterized by detail attempts to correct particular defects in the system of private enterprise, involving no serious threat to the evolutionary continuance of the "institution" itself . . . the present setting is different, in that breakdown and radical transformation, which are not intended by the majority of the population and for which we are not prepared, are really threatened.

Clark warned Kapp of the danger of systemic breakdown, reminding him to be aware of his responsibility in writing his book on the social costs of private enterprise:

> therefore it seems to me particularly necessary at present to do justice to the elements of positive value in the institution [private enterprise]—in short to give a balanced presentation. . . . [Your] study seems to judge the system by ideal standards. And the use of ideal standards seems to me justifiable, if one keeps in mind the fact that they are unattainable, and that any actual alternative scheme would have its own imperfections to balance against the ones the existing system reveals. . . . If one of the alternatives is a thoroughgoing transformation to a collectivist system, its imperfections are necessarily conjectural, but might be quite serious; and they need to be recognized.

Additionally, Clark raised serious doubts whether a collectivist system would be inclined to institutionalize a "system of social accountancy," fearing that the imperfections would simply be shifted from the "machinery of the markets" to the "political machinery." This criticism is also the core of the last documented intellectual interaction between Clark and Kapp, via Clark's book review of "Social Costs of Private Enterprise" in the Yale Review entitled "The New Economic Community." In it Clark praised the systematic elaboration of the idea that an " 'enterprise' should reckon with all the costs it occasions, including those the business unit can shift to other members of society." And with regard to neoclassical economics: "if one man's gnat is another man's camel . . . Kapp presents theorists with evidence of the size of the camels they have been swallowing . . . ." However, Clark also raised questions: "has [Kapp] at certain points, charged as costs of private enterprise things that are really costs of modern methods of production under any form of organization [?] . . . is there a sound basis for presuming that a socialist government would treat these matters more justly than they are treated by a state which combines 'private enterprise' with many sided welfare policies? Is a municipality more likely to abolish the smoke nuisance from its own plant than to order a private plant to do the like?" Clark concluded that while questions remained, Kapp's book was important because it brought together ample empirical evidence for the existence of social costs, suggesting the scope and magnitude of the problem (Clark 1950: 173–174).

Both documents show not only that Kapp's critique of private enterprise was too unbalanced for Clark's taste, but also that Clark's own views on the role of private enterprise had changed since the 1920s. Since the draft of the manuscript reviewed by Clark is not available, we do not know in how far Kapp modified his critique. In this context it is of interest that Kapp's letter to Clark on December 12, 1945 referred to a working title that differs from the later book publication: "I am very grateful to you for having read parts of my manuscript on Social Costs and Returns which I submitted to you." We do not know whether Clark's influence was decisive on Kapp's decision not to publish roughly half of his original book manuscript, which contained a discussion of planning for social returns of "utilities which diffuse themselves among all members of society, . . . that are to a large extent inappropriable by individual producers and cannot always be appraised in monetary terms"[7] (Kapp, unpublished ms. III). Kapp had originally developed the interconnected themes of social costs and returns in his dissertation (Kapp 1936). In the unpublished manuscript, Kapp discussed social returns

> derived from the gratification of collective needs; from international economic policies designed to achieve a balanced economy . . . and from the improvement of transportation facilities . . . scientific research, multiple purpose projects (such as TVA), and the maintenance of a social minimum with respect to essential foodstuffs, medical care, housing, and education. (Kapp, unpublished ms. III)

While the issues of social costs and planning for social returns are intimately related, the "returns" portion was not published and remains in the Kapp Archives. Clark's warnings may have caused Kapp to improve and balance his argument on social returns, an improvement evident in his later work. For example, he published the article "Social Costs and Social Benefits—A Contribution to Normative Economics" (1963) in the same year as "Social Costs of Business Enterprise." This article, as well as various others from the late 1950s and early 1960s, resulted from research on the social costs and social benefits in development projects in India and the Philippines, and addressed the social costs and lack of planning for social returns by ineffective public administrations (Kapp 1959a, 1959b, 1960, 1961). These articles display Kapp's openness to balancing his argument, criticizing social costs regardless of whether they were created by private or public entities. Yet, Kapp also maintained that planning for social returns and the minimization of social costs were important goals of economic development policy and that important improvements were achieved. Starting from the interconnected problems of social costs and social returns, Kapp developed a full-fledged theoretical framework of democratic controls of science and technology, socioecological indicators, and social minima (see below for more details; for a full elaboration, see Kapp 2011).

The second half of Clark's letter (February 6, 1941) asked Kapp to consider the question of freedom. Clark saw "value in the device of imagining the setting up of a new community, with our present knowledge." But he asked Kapp to consider

> what sphere would be left to the market process, and what imperfections in that sphere would be tolerated in the interest of minimising central

> regimentation and preserving the prerequisites of liberty, both of thought and expression as well as of consumption and production?

It seems that Clark perceived Kapp's critique not only as too unbalanced, but also with too little focus on the questions of the shortcomings of alternative modes of organization, such as socialism, and the prerequisites of "liberty." Curiously, this criticism is similar to the one levied against Kapp in a book review by the Chicago liberal economist Frank Knight, who had institutional leanings (Knight 1951; Berger 2012; Rutherford 2010: 30–32; Emmett 2010: 282). As an exile from Nazi Germany, an affiliate of the Frankfurt School, and a student of the poet and teacher Ernst Wiechert, Kapp took the issue of integrating freedom with the alleviation of human suffering very seriously. Perhaps due to Clark's criticisms, Kapp published "Economic Planning and Freedom" (1950) the same year as his "Social Costs of Private Enterprise," in which he argued for a substantive understanding of freedom that included planning for social returns. Clark's letter finished on a friendly note: "needless to say, I shall be interested to see how your study develops."

Four years later, on December 4, 1945, Clark wrote down his detailed comments regarding the overall scope of Kapp's draft, as well as its specific arguments. His letter consists of four densely typewritten pages, showing Clark's efforts to further influence and aid in the development of Kapp's institutional theory of social costs. As in the previous reply, the draft upon which the comments were based is not available, so that the basis for interpretation is missing. Yet the letter provides Clark's more general comments as well:

> It is interesting that you are reviving the discussion of extra-market values and costs and putting content into it, with some approach to measurement.

Importantly, Clark addressed the semantic differences of Kapp's concept of "social costs":

> [your definition of] "social" values and costs differs from mine in applying to non-market quantities only, where mine [Clark's] included also the quantities the market "measures".

This shows that Clark defined social costs as nonmarket plus market costs in the neoclassical tradition of Arthur C. Pigou (1929). This may reflect Clark's attempt to improve neoclassical theory rather than repudiate it (Lee 2009: 33), which had led him to dedicate his theory of overhead costs as "a very small contribution toward realizing his [that is, his father's neoclassical] conception of a dynamic economics" (Clark in Gruchy 1967: 357). Throughout his work Kapp roundly rejected neoclassical economics and its conceptual framework in its entirety, criticizing its ineffective and overly conservative reform proposals. Kapp noted in "Social Costs of Business Enterprise" (1963) that Pigou had radicalized his political-economic conclusions by the late 1940s when Pigou (1947) had argued that the social inefficiencies had reached a level that justifies the socialization of the means of production. Yet Kapp maintained that Pigou's neoclassical concept of external costs was imbued with the limitations of the neoclassical theories of price and value, as well as its closed system and equilibrium preconceptions that preclude an adequate understanding of the circular cumulative causation underlying the problem of social costs and its complex value dimensions, as well as its open system character (Kapp 1963, 1976; Berger 2009).

Instead, Kapp distinguished private costs from social costs (social losses, damages, inefficiencies) to emphasize that businesses privatize profits and socialize as many costs as they can. Kapp defined social costs as that part of the costs of production that businesses shift to society to increase their profits, thus avoiding responsibility. According to Kapp, adding social to private costs results in total costs. In the literature, this important difference between Kapp's and Clark's definition of the concept of social costs has been obscured. This may be due to the fact that both agreed on the notion of cost shifting but disagreed on what to call the shifted costs (see Prasch 2005). Thus, it is Kapp's contribution to have elevated the concept of social costs to a stylized fact for a critique of capitalism, the system of business or private enterprise, and formal rationality, further mending and bringing into the open ideas of Marx, Veblen, and Weber.[8] In "The Social Costs of Private Enterprise" (1950) Kapp provides a chapter on the conceptual history of social costs, showing his commitment to engage and acknowledge the large variety of previous contributions and arguments on social costs and returns. It is also Kapp's contribution to have clearly articulated how the institutional theory of social costs differs from neoclassical (see above) and neoliberal approaches (see below).

The significance of Clark's comments is acknowledged by Kapp in his subsequent letter (December 12, 1945):

> Dear Professor Clark: I am very grateful to you for having read parts of my manuscript on Social Costs and Social Returns which I submitted to you. . . . I have studied your comments very carefully and I found them most pertinent . . . I feel that you have called my attention to serious weaknesses in the formulation of my ideas, and in most instances I have found it possible to reformulate my conclusions in a more careful and more satisfactory manner.

However, Kapp's handwritten remarks on the margins of Clark's letter indicate that he did not agree with all of his comments, leading him to reply to Clark:

> The following is a brief reformulation of my ideas—a reformulation which I owe to your challenge and which I shall incorporate in the introductory chapter. . . . The thesis of this book is briefly that the orthodox appraisal and interpretation of the economic process in the unplanned market economy is invalidated by various obstacles to rational conduct and the phenomenon of social costs and social returns.

Clark's remark that the problem of social costs had already been successfully addressed by Oskar Lange and Abba Lerner and that Kapp was "beating a straw-man" challenged Kapp to clarify his aims with regard to developments in economics:

> The presuppositions of classical and neoclassical equilibrium economics continue to determine both the methods and the scope of modern value theory as can be easily ascertained . . . [by] the more recent system of economics which is based upon Keynes' General Theory . . . modern text-books . . . the works of such intransigent economic liberals as Professor F.A. Hayek, L. Mises, and L. Robbins . . . [even] some socialists of the 20th century have so accustomed themselves to the methods of thinking of neoclassical equilibrium analysis that they answer Mises' challenge of socialist planning by proclaiming that the socialist economy would solve the problem of allocating scarce resources among competing ends with the aid of the price mechanism and the competitive calculus. There is no hint that in order to solve the economic problem a planned economy is likely to base its economic decisions upon a social evaluation of total outlays and total benefits which . . . will have to take into account social costs and social returns. In other words, I am not aware of the fact that O. Lange and

> Professor Lerner have any fundamental quarrel with traditional equilibrium theory, and I have the impression that there is no room in the conceptual system of these writers for the phenomena of social cost and social returns. . . . I am also aware that value theory continues to be confined to the search for levels of equilibrium "of the exchange value sort," and not in terms of social value despite the fact that . . . economic decisions of the greatest importance are based on social choices and preferences.

This shows that Kapp aimed at a critique of all economic theories—even the progressive ones by Lange and Lerner—insofar as they adopted core elements of neoclassical economics and ignore the question of social valuation:

> When I said that the search for levels of equilibrium ought to be abandoned, I meant actually that the exclusive preoccupation . . . with problems of exchange value requires supplementation by a study of social value. . . . I like to hope that in the light of this letter there is perhaps a greater area of agreement between your "Preface to Social Economics" and my "Social Costs and Social Returns" than it appeared to you after reading the manuscript. With renewed thanks for your kindness of reading the manuscript, I am Very Sincerely Yours K. William Kapp

Kapp clearly tried to convince Clark that their works were in agreement concerning the importance of social valuation in economic decision making. In the same vein Kapp explains in the unpublished draft versions of the introduction to "The Social Costs of Private Enterprise" that he aimed at a critique of social costs under capitalism, and of neoclassical and neoliberalism theories that do not capture these realities:

> As an analysis of the social inefficiency of the unplanned market economy the study was bound to assume the character of a critique not only of capitalism but also of traditional equilibrium economics. (Kapp, unpublished manuscript I)

> the re-orientation of economics; . . . [exploration of] the possibilities for the setting up of valid criteria for economic planning and the formulation for economic policy, and perhaps to prepare the way for the elaboration of a positive theory of social value are the chief ultimate purposes of this inquiry. (Kapp, unpublished manuscript II)

The final words of Kapp's letter and the unpublished versions confirm that Kapp identified with Clark's project of "Preface to Social Economics" (1936), for which he saw the argument on social costs to be only a preliminary step. Kapp actively pursued this social economics or institutional "foundations project" for the rest of his life (Berger and Steppacher 2011).

Institutionalism vs. Neoliberalism: The Discourse on Social Costs

The above letter to Clark also shows that Kapp was among the economists in the institutional movement who directed his work against the "intransigent" liberalism of Friedrich A. Hayek. Moreover, the unpublished draft version of the preface to "Social Costs of Private Enterprise" (1950) states that the core thesis of the book is directed against a revival of liberalism reflected by the success of Hayek's and Mises's works (for details, see Berger 2012). Unlike Clark's contribution on overhead cost, Kapp's social costs argument emerged less as a critique of neoclassical economics than as a late reply to von Mises's argument in the European socialist accounting debate of the 1920s. Kapp's dissertation "The Planned Economy and International Trade" (1936) developed the social costs argument as a socialist "countervailing impossibility thesis" against Mises's famous neoliberal impossibility thesis. That is, according to Kapp, an accounting system based on market values cannot account for the social value of damages because the latter cannot find "value expression" in exchanges between isolated individuals (Kapp 1936; Berger 2012). Therefore, Kapp concluded, allocation in a pure market economy cannot be rational. Thus, Kapp's theory on social costs was originally motivated by the emerging Austrian neoliberalism in Geneva (Plehwe 2009). At this time, Kapp was also closely affiliated with and influenced by the Frankfurt School, exiled—like Kapp—in Geneva, so that the initial development of his argument on social costs can be seen also as a contribution to the Frankfurt School's post-Weberian project, which Foucault identified as trying to show the "irrational rationality of capitalism" (Foucault 1979: 106).

In this context it is of interest that Clark's book title "Alternative to Serfdom" (ATS) (1948) is a clear reference to Hayek's "Road to Serfdom" (RTS) (1944), and that Kapp's copy of ATS shows intense underlining and three handwritten pages of notes, indicating his agreement with Clark's arguments, in particular the beneficial role of unions and the need to focus economic inquiry on human needs. Kapp's copy of Hayek's RTS likewise shows 10 marks in the margins, including pages 37–39 on social costs and social returns, and contains six newspaper clippings from the debate stirred by Hayek's RTS and Mises's "Bureaucracy" (1944). Hayek's views on social costs evolved after RTS, and his mature point of view on social costs was diametrically opposed to Kapp's. This became especially evident in Hayek's justification of the social costs of Pinochet's dictatorship, which Hayek considered "a necessary evil" in implementing the (neo-)liberal agenda (see Farrant, McPhail, and Berger 2012: 530). Like Hayek, Kapp also contributed to a newspaper debate following the installment of Pinochet's dictatorship. In his article, which the editor of the Swiss newspaper "National-Zeitung" had solicited, Kapp warned of a new "right-wing extremism that puts on the costume of liberalism" (Kapp 1974: 6). Yet Kapp mentioned no names in this article, nor did he direct his final manuscript of "Social Costs of Private Enterprise" or any of his articles against Hayek or Mises. The most probable explanation is that Kapp hoped for a genuine dialogue on the substance of the issue by avoiding an unbalanced ad hominem attack.[9] Kapp's intellectual engagement with neoliberal economics is also evidenced by a book review that critically assessed Eucken's posthumous work on economic policy (Kapp 1953). Kapp noticed the distinct constructivist element in Eucken's work, which, according to Mirowski (Mirowski 2009), is the hallmark of neoliberalism and distinguishes it from laissez-faire neoclassical economics. Kapp's main criticism was that this approach excluded evidence that is contrary to its preconceptions, that is, that Eucken considered social costs as minor exceptions rather than systemic problems that require more substantive controls. Kapp also noted that Eucken's "idealtype" of the exchange economy is too abstract, with no allowance for "less harmonious" facts of economic life, such as systemic social costs.

It is important to note that Kapp's social minima proposal for minimizing social costs (Kapp 2011) is a substantivist reply to minima proposals developed by (neo-)liberal economists, that is, the minima proposal of Walter Eucken (Foucault 1979: 141, 204–206) and Hayek's "non-discretionary rules" argument (for a discussion of Hayek's argument, see Burczak 2011). The difference lies in the extent to which Kapp wanted social minima to control the economic process. That is, he proposed a full-fledged democratic governance of science and technology decisions, including socioecological indicators, to guarantee the maintenance of social minima (Kapp 2011). Contrary to neoliberalism, Kapp's approach endorses a social and democratic dynamic centered on universal and scientifically objectifiable human needs, and the absolute value of human life in the Kantian tradition. The neoliberal approach that turns human life and needs into a means to an end is rejected by Kapp, so that social costs cannot be justified as a "necessary evil" to achieve economic growth, profitable exchanges, or some neoliberal notion of purely formal economic freedom. Kapp dubbed his approach "new rational humanism" (Kapp 1985) based on a theory of integrated social knowledge centered on and derived from a scientific biocultural concept of the human being. In this, Kapp pulled together research on human needs from various humanist scientists and psychologists, for example, Abraham Maslow and Erich Fromm. Kapp placed this approach in the tradition of European substantivist arguments made by Carl Menger and Karl Polanyi (Berger 2008) but also American biocultural approaches of Thorstein Veblen and John Dewey (Kapp 1961; Gerber and Steppacher 2011; Kapp 2011).[10] In sum, Kapp's institutional theory of social costs was part of his larger intellectual project of a new rational humanism and an attempt to counter neoliberal arguments.

The success of Kapp's institutional theory of social costs during the 1950s led various key figures of the "neoliberal thought-collective" to respond or comment directly, for example, Frank Knight (1951), Guido Calabresi (1961), James Buchanan (1962), and Wilfred Beckerman (1972) (for details, see Berger 2012). Post-WWII developments in economics need to be seen as a reaction to institutional economics, with the Chicago School sharply at ideological odds with institutionalism (Rutherford 2011: 351; Mirowski and Plehwe 2009; Van Horn et al. 2011). As Rutherford has pointed out, Chicago economists often modified or reworked existing institutional economics' ideas (Rutherford 2010: 36). In the discourse on social costs, this is best demonstrated by how Coase (1960) and Stigler (1966) contributed to the discourse on social costs. Both remained conspicuously silent on previous institutional arguments and celebrated their argument on the institution of property rights as a "scientific discovery." Stigler's "Coase Theorem" shifted the discourse from the problem of "social costs" to a problem of "transaction costs," corresponding with his lack of interest in actual social damages (see Medema 2011). Instead of seeking ways to prevent social costs ex ante, which was the primary concern of Kapp's theory of social costs, Stigler focused on constructing ex post market-based solutions by minimizing transaction costs and assigning property rights. Stigler did not engage previous institutional arguments concerning the predatory and subreptitious aspects involved in assigning property rights and the impossibility of adequately reflecting social and ecological values in individual market exchanges.

It seems likely that Stigler's contribution to the discourse on social costs was part of his many "demolition derbies" against institutional economics, which he hated: "Institutional economics is dying out at a fantastic rate—though still not fast enough to suit me" (Stigler, in Rutherford 2011: 328).[11] Due to his overt dislike for institutional economics, it seems reasonable to presume that his silence on Clark's and Kapp's well-known arguments on social costs was not an innocent oversight. Clark's work was so prominent that he had received the Francis A. Walker medal by the American Economic Association in 1952, "given to that living American economist who . . . has made over the course of his life the most distinguished contribution to economics" (Shute 1997). Instead of seeking a discourse with institutional economists, Stigler promoted Knight's "Some Fallacies in the Interpretation of Social Costs" (1924) in his publications on price theory (Stigler and Boulding 1952) and in his "Coase Theorem" (1966). Additionally, Stigler was among the "commentators" who encouraged Coase to write "The Problem of Social Costs" (Coase 1960, fn 1; see the "Eureka" event in Medema 2011). Coase refers to Stigler's argument that the problem of social costs should be conceived of as purely "reciprocal nature" (Coase 1960: 2), rather than social or systemic. Much like Stigler, Coase adopted a very disparaging attitude towards institutional economics, describing it as "a mass of descriptive material waiting for a theory, or a fire" (Coase in Rutherford 2010: 25), and also remaining silent on Clark's and Kapp's arguments on social costs.

Conclusion

This article demonstrates that the dominant narrative about the discourse on social costs is incomplete. The findings show that the discourse includes Clark's and Kapp's institutional theory of cost shifting and social costs. The latter reflects a distinct and clearly distinguishable institutional argument on social costs, which further develops earlier ideas by Veblen and Marx. Thus, the institutional theory of social costs is a clearly distinguishable alternative to neoclassical and neoliberal arguments. The Kapp-Clark correspondence shows that Clark was influential in the development of Kapp's institutional theory of social costs and social returns. Throughout their works, both economists harnessed the enormous power of their argument on cost shifting as a rationale for increasing social controls of the economy and the development of a genuine social economics. Yet the archival materials also illustrate that both economists differed on the definition of social costs, and that Clark encouraged Kapp to balance his critique and to consider improving certain weaknesses of his argument. Their correspondence provides further important documentation that Kapp developed the institutional theory on social costs to counter "intransigent [neo-]liberalism," and that leading neoliberal economists sought strategies to undermine and eclipse the institutional argument. Thus, the discourse on social costs cannot be fully understood without appreciating the role of the institutional argument on social costs. This account differs markedly from other recent accounts, ending the hermeneutic "stop play" strategy that fails to acknowledge institutional theories. Thereby, this article contributes to the important advancement of understanding social costs via the "ethics of play" (Vilhauer 2010; Samuels 1990; Arrington 1990).

Notes

1. For an elaboration of Kapp's institutional argument against the return of liberalism and the reaction of leading neoliberal economists, refer to Berger (2012).

2. It is noteworthy that the financial support for institutional economists waned since the 1950s, with the Ford Foundation being the last to quit funding institutional research by the early 1960s (Rutherford 2011). Myrdal's and Kapp's project to start an international association of institutional

economists was denied funding by the Swedish Research Council in 1968 (for details concerning Kapp's intellectual project, see Berger and Steppacher 2011). This may be seen as a consequence of changes in the way economic science was funded with several foundations increasingly supporting neoliberal ideas, for example, the Volcker Fund and the Walgreen Foundation (Mirowski and Plehwe 2009; Nik-Khah 2011).

3. See also Swaney and Evers (1989), who have located this important concept at the core of the institutional theory of social costs.

4. Clark's "Accelerator Principle" is based on the idea of self-reinforcing causation (vicious circle) or circular and cumulative causation, which is one of the key concepts of nonequilibrium economics (Berger 2009).

5. This issue was at the heart of the European socialist accounting debate in the 1920s (Kapp 1936).

6. The Kapp-Clark correspondence—retrieved from the Kapp Archive—contains five letters. Two letters deal with Kapp's article on consumer theory, "Rational Human Conduct" (1943), and three letters concern Kapp's book manuscript "Social Costs of Private Enterprise" (1950). The present analysis only refers to the latter set of letters.

7. The section on social returns was never published. In this, Kapp provides an institutional version of Paul Samuelson's neoclassical "public goods" argument (Samuelson 1954),

8. Leading authors using the institutional argument on social costs in the tradition of Kapp work are Swaney and Evers (1989), Swaney (2006), Sherman et al. (2007), Foster (2000, 2010), and Martinez-Alier (2002).

9. For a similar thesis, see Swaney and Evers (1989) and (Franzini 2006).

10. Today Kapp's approach resembles in important ways Amartya Sen's "capabilities approach" and Max Neef's human needs matrix.

11. Recent archival research has elevated the role played by Stigler as a key protagonist of the Chicago School with a coherent agenda in the areas of law and economics, and science and technology (Nik-Khah 2011), contributing to the demise of the institutional argument on social costs.

References

Arrington, E. C. (1990). "Comment to Raymond Benton Jr.'s 'A Hermeneutic Approach to Economics: If Economics is Not Science, and if it is Not Merely Mathematics, Then What Could it Be?' " In *Economics as Discourse—An Analysis of the Language of Economists.* Ed. Warren J. Samuels, pp. 90–101. Boston/Dordrecht/London: Kluwer Academic Publishers.

Aslanbeigui, N., and S. G. Medema. (1998). "Beyond the Dark Clouds: Pigou and Coase on Social Costs." *History of Political Economy* 30(4): 601–625.

Beckerman, W. (1972). "Environmental Policy and the Challenge to Economic Theory." *Social Science Information* 11(1): 7–15.

Berger, S. (2008). "Karl Polanyi's and Karl William Kapp's Substantive Economics: Important Insights from the Kapp-Polanyi Correspondence." *Review of Social Economy* 66(3): 381–396.

——. (ed.) (2009). *The Foundations of Non-Equilibrium Economics.* London and New York: Routledge.

——. (2012). "The Discourse on Social Costs—Kapp's Impossibility Thesis vs. Neoliberalism." In *Social Costs Today—Institutional Analyses of the Present Crisis.* Eds. Wolfram Elsner, Pietro Frigato, and Paolo Ramazzotti, pp. 96–112. London and New York: Routledge.

Berger, S., and R. Steppacher. (2011). "Editorial Introduction." In *The Foundations of Institutional Economics,* by K. William Kapp, pp. 1–13. London and New York: Routledge.

Buchanan, J. M. (1962). "Politics, Policy and the Pigovian Margins." *Economica* 29(113): 17–28.

Burczak, T. (2011). "A Socialist Spontaneous Order." In *Hayek, Mill, and the Liberal Tradition.* Ed. Andrew Farrant, pp. 130–147. London and New York: Routledge.

Calabresi, G. (1961). "Some Thoughts on Risk Distribution and the Law of Torts." *Yale Law Journal* 70(4): 499–553.

Clark, J. M. ([1923] 1931). *Studies in the Economics of Overhead Costs.* Chicago: University of Chicago Press.

——. (1926). *Social Control of Business.* Chicago: University of Chicago Press.

——. (1936). *Preface to Social Economics: Essays on Economic Theory and Social Problems.* New York: Farrar & Rinehart.

——. (1948). *Alternative to Serfdom.* New York: Alfred A. Knopf.

——. (1950). "The New Economic Community." *Yale Review* 40(1): 171–174.

Coase, R. (1960). "The Problem of Social Costs." *Journal of Law and Economics* 3: 1–44.

Dugger, W. M. (2012). "Book Review—The Foundations of Institutional Economics by Karl William Kapp, edited by S. Berger and R. Steppacher." *Journal of Economic Issues* 46(3): 817–819.

Elsner, W., P. Frigato, and P. Ramazzotti (eds). (2012). *Social Costs Today—Institutional Analyses of the Present Crisis.* London and New York: Routledge.

Emmett, R. B. (2010). "Frank H. Knight." In *The Elgar Companion to the Chicago School of Economics.* Ed. Ross B. Emmett, pp. 280–286. Cheltenham and Northampton: Edward Elgar.

Farrant, A., E. McPhail, and S. E. Berger. (2012). "Preventing the 'Abuses' of Democracy: Hayek, the 'Military Ursurper' and Transitional Dictatorship in Chile." *American Journal of Economics and Sociology* 71(3): 513–538.

Foster, J. B. (2000). *Marx's Ecology: Materialism and Nature.* New York: Monthly Review Press.

——. (2010). *The Ecological Rift: Capitalism's War on Earth.* New York: Monthly Review Press.

Foucault, M. (1979). *The Birth of Biopolitics.* Palgrave-Macmillan.

Franzini, M. (2006). "Social Costs, Social Rights and the Limits of Free Market Capitalism: A Re-Reading of Kapp." In *Social Costs and Public Action in Modern Capitalism—Essays Inspired by Karl William Kapp's Theory of Social Costs.* Eds. Elsner Wolfram et al., pp. 56–71. London and New York: Routledge.

Gerber, J., and R. Steppacher. (2011). *Towards an Integrated Paradigm in Heterodox Economics—Alternative Approaches to the Current Eco-Social Crises.* London: Palgrave-Macmillan.

Gruchy, A. G. ([1947] 1967). *Modern Economic Thought—The American Contribution.* New York: A.M. Kelly.

Hayek, F. A. (1944). *Road to Serfdom.* Chicago: University of Chicago Press.

Kapp, K. W. (1936). *Planwirtschaft und Aussenhandel.* Genf: Georg & Cie.

——. (1943). "Rational Human Conduct and Modern Industrial Society." *Southern Economic Journal* X(2): 136–150.

——. (1950). *The Social Costs of Private Enterprise.* Cambridge, MA: Harvard University Press.

——. (1950). "Economic Planning and Freedom." *Weltwirtschaftliches Archiv* 64: 29–54.

——. (1953), "Eucken's Posthumous Work on Economics Policy." *Kyklos* 6(2): 165–169.

——. (1959a). "River Valley Development Projects: Problems of Evaluation and Social Costs." *Kyklos* 12(4): 589–604; also in Kapp (1963c).

——. (1959b). "River Valley Projects in India: Their Direct Benefits." *Economic Development and Cultural Change* 7(1): 24–47; also in Kapp (1963c).

——. (1960). "Economic Development, National Planning and Public Administration." *Kyklos* 13(2): 172–204.

——. (1961). "The Transition from a Bullock to a Tractor Economy in India: Some Indirect Effects and Benefits (with P. N. Mathur)." *Weltwirtschaftliches Archiv* 87: 333–350.

——. (1961). *Toward a Science of Man in Society—A Positive Approach to the Integration of Social Knowledge.* The Hague: Martinus Nijhoff.

——. (1963a). *The Social Costs of Business Enterprise.* London: Asia Publishing House.

——. (1963b). "Social Costs and Social Benefits—A Contribution to Normative Economics." In *Probleme der normativen Ökonomik und der wirtschaftspolitischen Beratung.* Eds. E. V. Beckerath and H. Giersch, pp. 183–210. Berlin: Duncker & Humblot.

——. ([1967] 1985). "Economics and Rational Humanism." In *The Humanization of the Social Sciences.* Eds. J. E. Ullmann and R. Preiswerk, pp. 99–120. Lanham and London: University Press of America.

——. (1974). "Environmental Indicators as Indicators of Social Use Value." Published as "Substantive vs. Formal Rationality." In *The Foundations of Institutional Economics*. Eds. Sebastian Berger and Rolf Steppacher, pp. 159–169. London and New York: Routledge.

——. (1974). "Die Zentrale Frage" ["The Central Question"]. *National-Zeitung* October 5: 6.

——. ([1975] 2011). "Science and Technology in the Light of Institutional Analysis." In *The Foundations of Institutional Economics*. Eds. Sebastian Berger and Rolf Steppacher, pp. 203–244. London and New York: Routledge.

——. (1976). "Economics in the Future: The Open System Character of the Economy and its Implications." In *Economics in the Future: Towards a New Paradigm*. Ed. Kurt Dopfer, pp. 90–105. London: MacMillan.

——. (undated). Introduction to book manuscript "Social Costs of Private Enterprise" (draft). Unpublished.

——. (undated). Introduction II to book manuscript "Social Costs of Private Enterprise" (draft). Unpublished.

——. (undated). Introduction III to book manuscript "Social Costs of Private Enterprise" (draft). Unpublished.

Knight, F. (1951). "Review—The Social Costs of Private Enterprise." *Annals of the American Academy of Political and Social Science* (273): 233–234.

——. ([1924] 1952). "Some Fallacies in the Interpretation of Social Costs." In *Readings in Price Theory*. Eds. George J. Stigler and Kenneth E. Boulding, pp. 160–179. Chicago: Homewood, Illinois.

Krall, L., and J. Gowdy. (2011). "An Institutional and Evolutionary Critique of Natural Capital." In *Towards an Integrated Paradigm in Heterodox Economics—Alternative Approaches to the Current Eco-Social Crises*. Eds. Julien-Francois Gerber and Rolf Steppacher, pp. 127–146. Palgrave-Macmillan.

Lee, F. S. (1999). *Post-Keynesian Price Theory*. Cambridge: Cambridge University Press.

——. (2009). *A History of Heterodox Economics—Challenging the Mainstream in the 20th Century*. London and New York: Routledge.

Martinez-Alier, J. (2002). *Environmentalism of the Poor—A Study of Ecological Conflicts and Valuation*. Cheltenham: Edward Elgar.

Medema, S. G. (2011). "A Case of Mistaken Identity: George Stigler, 'The Problem of Social Costs,' and the Coase Theorem." In *European Journal of Law and Economics*.

Mirowski, P. (2009). "Postface: Defining Neoliberalism." In *The Road from Mont Pèlerin—The Making of the Neoliberal Thought Collective*. Eds. Philip Mirowski and Dieter Plehwe, pp. 417–456. Cambridge and London: Harvard University Press.

Mirowski, P., and D. Plehwe. (eds). (2009), *The Road from Mont Pèlerin—The Making of the Neoliberal Thought Collective.* Cambridge and London: Harvard University Press.

Mises, L. (1944). *Bureaucracy.* New Haven: Yale University Press.

Nik-Khah, E. (2011). "George Stigler, The Graduate School of Business, and the Pillars of the Chicago School." In *Building Chicago Economics—New Perspectives on the History of America's Most Powerful Economics Program.* Eds. Robert Van Horn et al., pp. 116–150. Cambridge: Cambridge University Press.

Pigou, A. C. (1929). *The Economics of Welfare.* London: Macmillan & Co.

——. (1947). *Socialism vs. Capitalism.* London: Macmillan.

Plehwe, D. (2009). "Introduction." In *The Road from Mont Pèlerin—The Making of the Neoliberal Thought Collective.* Eds. Philip Mirowski and Dieter Plehwe, pp. 1–44. Cambridge and London: Harvard University Press.

Prasch, R.. (2005). "The Social Costs of Labor." *Journal of Economic Issues* 39(2): 439–445.

Rorty, R. (1984). "The Historiography of Philosophy: Four Genres." In *Philosophy in History.* Eds. Richard Rorty et al., pp. 49–76. Cambridge: Cambridge University Press.

Rutherford, M. (2010). "Chicago Economics and Institutionalism." In *The Elgar Companion to the Chicago School of Economics.* Ed. Ross B. Emmett, pp. 25–39. Cheltenham and Northampton: Edward Elgar.

——. (2011). *The Institutionalist Movement in American Economics, 1918–1947.* Cambridge: Cambridge University Press.

Samuels, W. J. (1990). "Introduction." In *Economics as Discourse—An Analysis of the Language of Economists.* Ed. Warren J. Samuels, pp. 1–14. Boston/Dordrecht/London: Kluwer Academic Publishers.

Samuelson, P. A. (1954). "The Pure Theory of Public Expenditure." *Review of Economics and Statistics* 36(4): 387–389.

Sherman, H. J., E. K. Hunt, R. F. Nesiba, and P. A. O'Hara. (eds.) (2007). *Economics: An Introduction to Traditional and Progressive Views.* Armonk and London: M.E. Sharpe.

Shute, L. (1997). *John Maurice Clark—A Social Economics for the 21st Century.* London: Macmillan.

Stigler, G. J. (1966). *The Theory of Price (3rd edition).* New York and London: Macmillan Company and Collier-Macmillan Ltd.

Stigler, G. J., and K. E. Boulding. (1952). *Readings in Price Theory.* Chicago: Homewood, Illinois.

Swaney, J. A. (2006). "Policy for Social Costs: Kapp vs. Neo-classical Economics." In *Social Costs and Public Action in Modern Capitalism—Essays Inspired by Karl William Kapp's Theory of Social Costs.* Eds. W. Elsner,P. Frigato, and P. Ramazzotti, pp. 106–125. London and New York: Routledge.

Swaney, J. A., and M. A. Evers. (1989). "The Social Cost Concepts of Kapp and Polanyi." *Journal of Economic Issues* 23: 7–34.

Van Horn, R., P. Mirowski, and T. Stapleford. (eds). (2011). *Building Chicago Economics—New Perspectives on the History of America's Most Powerful Economics Program.* Cambridge: Cambridge University Press.

Veblen, T. B. (1904). *The Theory of Business Enterprise.* New York: Charles Scribner's Sons.

Vilhauer, Monica. (2010). *Gadamer's Ethics of Play—Hermeneutics and the Other.* Lexington: Lexington Books.

The Problem of Epistemic Cost: Why Do Economists Not Change Their Minds (About the "Coase Theorem")?*

By ALTUG YALCINTAS, PHD‡

ABSTRACT. Errors in the history of economic analysis often remain uncorrected for long periods due to positive epistemic costs (PEC) involved in allocating time to going back over what older generations wrote. In order to demonstrate this in a case study, economists' practice of the "Coase Theorem" is reconsidered from a PEC point of view.

Introduction

Ronald Coase's classic 1960 article, "The Problem of Social Cost," which is celebrating its semi-centenary, deserves special attention in the history of economic analysis. "The Problem of Social Cost" is not only one of the most cited articles in (evolutionary) economics; it has been, ironically, an occasion for economists to discuss one of the most obvious facts in a market economy that has been well-known since Adam Smith: the consequences of *zero* transaction costs. (See McCloskey 1998: 239–240; Medema 2009: 111.) Was the assumption of

*This article was funded by the Council of Higher Education in Turkey and the Scientific and Technological Research Council of Turkey. Earlier versions of the article were presented at the Annual Workshop of the Turkish Initiative for Economic Thought (Istanbul, 2009), Annual Conference of the European Society for the History of Economic Thought (Amsterdam, 2010), and Annual Conference of the History of Economic Society (Syracuse, 2010). The author was one of the Young Scholar Awardees both in Amsterdam and Syracuse. The author would like to thank the participants of these conferences, editor of this journal, and two anonymous referees for their useful remarks. Selma Telalagic helped the author edit the article. The remaining errors are the author's.

‡Assistant Professor, Department of Economics, Ankara University, 06590 Cebeci Ankara Turkey, altug.yalcintas@politics.ankara.edu.tr; altug.yalcintas@gmail.com.

American Journal of Economics and Sociology, Vol. 72, No. 5 (November, 2013).
DOI: 10.1111/ajes.12037

zero transaction costs the "real" message of the article? According to Coase, as well as many others, it was not. "The world of zero transaction costs has often been described as a Coasian world," Coase reports (Coase 1988: 174), "nothing could be further from the truth." The question lingers then: Why is it that the assumption of zero transaction costs has been presented as the central message of "The Problem of Social Cost"?

This article argues that economic scholarship remains locked into the assumption of zero transaction costs even though it has long been reported, clearly and repeatedly, by Coase himself (Coase 1981, 1988: 174, 1992, 1995: 247) as well as many others in a number of publications (Medema 1994, 1999, 2002; McCloskey 1998; Usher 1998; Fox 2007), that the central message of "The Problem of Social Cost" is to show that carrying out transactions in a market economy is not costless. In order to account for the scholarly process in which Coase's contribution has evolved into the "Coase Theorem," a simplified model of intellectual path dependence is introduced. It is argued that the second-generation models built upon the "Coase Theorem" have failed to replicate the results of the previous generation (that is, Stigler 1966) and, as a consequence, the misrepresentation of the original message of "The Problem of Social Cost" has been reproduced time and again.[1]

Such controversies in the history of economic analysis do not resolve easily (if at all). In this article, it is asserted that the effects of several errors in analyses often remain uncorrected for long periods due to high "epistemic costs" of replicating old findings. In a nutshell, epistemic costs refer to the costs involved in operating the various scholarly arrangements (researching, finding funds, going to conferences, writing articles and submitting them to journals) as well as the costs involved in allocating time to reconsider what older generations wrote (Radnitzky 1987; Wible 1998; Fallis 2005). This suggests that the scholarly world of economists is a world of positive epistemic costs (PEC) in which negative externalities are not always and perfectly self-corrective. Perfect solutions do not come about so easily. The "market for ideas" (Coase 1974, 1977) does not operate or fail like competitive markets for goods and services. A consequence of the failure in the market for ideas, on which this article focuses attention, is that errors and misrepresentations frequently remain uncorrected.

The article is arranged in two main sections and a conclusion. In the first section, where the central research question of the article is posed, it is argued that assuming a scholarly world without the costs of undertaking the duty of reconsidering the main findings of past research (including the misrepresentations involved in the methodologies of earlier studies) is, in Coasean terms, "unrealistic." As a matter of fact, there *are* epistemic costs in the global market for ideas. Such costs are often high and have significant consequences for the way researchers pursue science. In the second section, economists' practice of the "Coase Theorem" is reconsidered from a PEC point of view. It is shown that Stigler's misrepresentation of Coase's contribution could have been corrected long ago, but the "theorem" remained as Stigler introduced it in 1966 because the economics of this particular case has prevented correction from happening. In other words, the reason why the "Coase Theorem" has not been corrected for so long has principally been economical. Finally, it is concluded that some ideas in history exist in such institutionalized environments that we cannot easily eliminate the consequences of epistemic failures. The course of events in scholarly life often feeds itself endlessly in such ways that early events in the course generate intellectual pathways that last well into the future.

Failure in Academic Economics

How much would our view of the intellectual history of economics have broadened if we had introduced a PEC viewpoint to the ways in which economists pursued scientific research? To put the question in terms of social costs: How can we interpret the history of economics when the practice of economists inflicts harm upon others?

Theories and ideas are not only selected or rejected by ways of abstract reasoning, sophisticated argumentation, and additional evidence. Academic scholarship is economically constructed as well, in the sense that processes of production, distribution, and use of academic knowledge are so complex that intellectual history should be accounted for on institutional grounds, too. This article is particularly interested in the consequences of (positive) epistemic costs on the evolutionary history of economic analysis. It is argued that an economic critique of academic scholarship based on the principles of evolutionary political economy should in the first place be able to account for a simple question: Why do scholars not change their minds in the face of negative evidence and refuting argumentation?

Epistemic Costs in Academic Scholarship

This simple question is significant because the main reason why scholars do not change their minds has a lot to do with the epistemic costs of starting to use new theories. Epistemic costs are "epistemic resources forgone, resources which would have been available if one had opted for the competitor of the theory" (Radnitzky 1987). Epistemic costs are primarily the costs of scarcity of the most valued element in academic production: time. Epistemic scarcity overwhelmingly dominates the evolution of scientific research in such a way that when researchers start off a new research project, they allocate time between replicable and unreplicable research. It is through replication that theories and research programs are checked in terms of their defensibility, consistency, and coherency. Although replication should be an essential component of scholarly work, such an endeavor is not frequently handled by researchers because "an economist might allocate a larger proportion of time to producing new publishable results devoting relatively less time and effort to the tasks required for replication" (Wible 1998: 25). Replication of results is time consuming and there is no reward for scholars in repeating others' work. No significant research devotes time and effort to replicating the findings of earlier theories and research programs without compensating their economic loss. Instead, researchers rely on the results of papers published in academic journals and they simply "reproduce" their findings without examining their significance and validity (Mirowski and Sklivas 1991: 154).

A PEC view of decision-making processes in an open and homogeneous society holds that adoption of a new model of behavior such as selecting a novel theory or abandonment of an old one depends on whether the benefits of a new behavior exceed the associated epistemic costs. If the new model is attractive to the majority of the scholarly population and it does not significantly differ from the old patterns, new behavioral innovation spreads among the population gradually. Individuals would reject behavioral innovations that are (re-)presented by a minority only and not reinforced by "internal" and "external" factors. Sometimes individuals are constrained by one or all of these factors and such constraints narrow their choice set. Whether individuals will benefit from the constraints and whether constraints will yield profitable results depend on the factor that is reinforced (North 1990: 96). The result will principally be determined on the basis of "subjective perception of the costs and benefits of an institutional alternative which might have its cause in changes in the related cost structures or social learning accompanied by changing mental models that lead to a new evaluation of the behavioral alternatives" (Stahl-Rolf 2000: 281).

Epistemic costs in academic economics are positive because academic research is a time-consuming activity. This conclusion has already been made in Coase's works as well as by many other mainstream economists doing research on cost-benefit analysis. However, Coasean economics as we know it has certain limitations over understanding the life of ideas, especially when there are spillover effects (or "externalities") that do not occur to those who exchange ideas in seminars, conferences, and elsewhere. PEC of academic research suggests that social costs (and social returns) of knowledge production are sometimes significantly higher than the private costs (and social returns) of doing research. Social costs of knowledge production involve "direct and indirect losses suffered by third persons or the general public" (Kapp 1950: 13) such as committing intellectual vices and academic wrong doings, including plagiarism, fraud, and deterioration of data. Individual scholars are occasionally able to shift parts of the consequences of their behavior onto the general scholarship. Scholarly mechanisms, such as refereeing and reviewing as well as the ethics of scholarly behavior and certain codes of act, including the issue of liability, that help increase the productivity of scientific processes, cannot fully correct or cure the harmful consequences of individual scholarship.

Negative spillover effects in academic scholarship are endogenous to academic scholarship primarily because productivity losses are often the consequence of the lack or impossibility of a common law or custom against irresponsible acts of individual scholars.[2] Academic scholarship is a social as well as an economic activity that often requires interaction and cooperation of universities with "pecuniary employments" (Veblen 1932: 279–323) and "thought collectives" (Plehwe 2009; Mirowski 2009). Individual scholars and research institutions interact and cooperate with business enterprises in such ways that salaries, research monies, and academic and social facilities are financed and maintained by these businesses. Scholars working in the advisory companies and funding opportunities largely in control of corporate enterprises have significant influences on the scholarly community as to which direction new research is conducted in.

Such interactions and cooperations have far-reaching consequences for scholarly production. At organizational levels, universities are institutionalized and managed in similar ways to corporate businesses. "Competitive (or business) calculus," which simply covers the cost-benefit analysis within a business enterprise, is not the best way to assess the worthiness of academic work and allocation of research monies in certain fields, the results of which are socially significant but not always applicable or able to contribute to the ways in which profit-making businesses operate. As Kapp argues, "[n]either social costs nor social returns enter into the cost-price calculations of the private firms unless special provisions to this effect are made by law and by the systematic application of the principles of social insurance" (Kapp 1950: 8–9). The risk here is that academic scholarship might fail in similar ways to business enterprises.

Epistemic costs come about as a consequence of ideological risks that are placed on the shoulders of those who pursue research. In fact, ideologies help people understand and explain the events taking place around them insofar as ideologies provide the epistemological tools of understanding to analyze the world. In some sense, ideologies are inevitable. In fact, most epistemological tools are formed via the past experiences of individuals that proved to be useful in certain circumstances in earlier periods. However, ideologies may have further consequences for the advance of human understanding:

ideologies may also set borders and rules that would regulate the pathways of scientific progress. When ideologies operate so as to set borders and rules, they regulate the scientific advancement towards an abstract systematic. That is to say, ideologies set off to organize the scholarly activity in order to achieve specific goals or manners in which individuals or groups view "reality." Instead of providing advantages against uncertainty, in particular, ideologies impose habits and exist by virtue of aged (epistemological) institutions.

Path Dependence in the Intellectual History of Economics

Insofar as habits are the primary codes of behavior among scholars and the entire function of scholarly activity is to produce more habits of conduct, scholarly life is under the risk of ideologization, that is, getting locked into a set of ideological judgments about scientific method. The more intellectuals consult ideologies for more answers the more it becomes difficult (that is, costly) to change viewpoints, methods, and paradigms. Although "new" does not necessarily mean "better," lock-ins amount to irreversibility, which may easily turn out to be undesirable, especially in the long run. This is one of the sources of intellectual path dependence in which scientific markets operate in the absence of an invisible hand that could have prevented errors from happening or corrected them in the long run. Seeds of intellectual lock-in are stored in the scholarly market due to the epistemic costs organically attached to pursuing scientific research.

Intellectual path dependence is the application of the theory of path dependence to the evolutionary history of ideas. The theory of path dependence refers to dynamic processes in the evolution of social institutions, generating consequences often irreversible and sensitive to initial conditions of the process (David 1985; Arthur 1989). Under conditions of path dependence, several self-reinforcing mechanisms, such as network effects or increasing returns, lock in the evolutionary pathway of a system to a number of possible suboptimal states where (negative) externalities prevent systems from moving towards more efficient states (for a longer discussion, see Yalcintas 2012).

In evolutionary political economy, the conception of path dependence is preceded by another notion: cumulative causation.

Path dependence and cumulative causation have a number of similarities, one of the most important of which is perhaps that both conceptions have been argued by heterodox social scientists. Cumulative causation, too, accounts for the processes that do not converge towards a predefined end-point. Such processes operate in non-teleological manners in which causal relationships between social and economic events are continual. Both conceptions aim at explaining long-term social evolution where causal nexus among events are accounted for.

However, path dependence and cumulative causation might refer to different circumstances, in which the evolution of social institutions follows different trajectories. Firstly, cumulative causation claims that equilibrium is "irrelevant" in social processes whereas path dependence accounts for the "multiplicity of locally stable equilibria" featuring properties of suboptimality (David 2007). Secondly, cumulative causation accounts for the dominance of "ceremonial encapsulations" in capitalist societies resisting technological innovations (Hall, Lacasa, and Günter 2011). Path dependence, on the other hand, is about the costs of switching to more efficient technologies, therefore emphasizing lock-ins that come about as a consequence of "technical interrelatedness, economies of scale, and quasi-irreversibility of investment" (David 1985). Thirdly, path-dependent processes are outcomes of positive feedback mechanisms magnifying the significance of several historical accidents or chance events (Yalcintas 2006) whereas cumulative causation accounts for social processes in which social factors other than historical accidents and chance events as well as negative feedbacks are at play (Berger and Elsner 2007; Berger 2008).

Intellectual path dependence might come about as intellectual institutions impose costs on individuals, which individuals should seriously consider in case they attempt to explore decisions alternative to what institutions already provide them with. Actors then basically have two options: they are either going to be content with the consequences of their actions that have evolved out of ideological judgments, or they are going to exchange the risk that the current uncertainty creates with the risk that exploring a new path of evolution could lead to. What they only possess in exploring a new path is their faith in getting free of the path that has been doomed to yield nothing more than it yielded in the past. Exploiting the same path of evolution, actors would rid themselves of the risk of a worse consequence of their action but would be left without the pay-offs from exploring alternatives. Switching among different paths is worth considering because pay-offs from the curiosity of exploring a new path could significantly outweigh the cost that such an exploration would create. Disregarding new paths will only lead to "widening the candidate's field of ignorance while it intensifies his effectiveness within his specialty" (Veblen 1918: 286).

The Mechanism: Replication Failure

What are the scholarly mechanisms through which a scholar's field of ignorance is widened? There are many mechanisms that cause scholars to stick to specific explanations despite the fact that these explanations might be erroneous. "Replication failure" is one of the mechanisms in which either a norm spreads widely and quickly in an academic community or a selected small change in the behavioral system of the community escalates further change and drives the system away from equilibrium.

Replication failure operates in the following way: while a theory or research program spreads among scholars due to its intellectual merit, there is also an economic side to the progress of every research program. This economic side has to do with the costs arising out of the time necessary to replicate the results in the scope of other scholarly works. Economic development of a theory examines the dynamic relations among scholars as well as their products (such as publications and conference meetings) that positively feed back upon each other in mutual support with further evidence and further argumentation. The qualitative resonance among scholars is unique: a small achievement or a small error in scholarly theorizing may spread quickly and broadly. The reason why replication rarely takes place in scholarly life is that "science is more complex than mechanical reenactments of simple experiments" (Wible 1998: 28). Many factors play important roles: for instance, processes of inference and judgment are not totally individual but rather a social phenomenon. It is difficult to replicate certain experiments without the specialized knowledge of earlier researchers. Sometimes, derived results of earlier works can be unreplicable: data may be lost, technical possibilities may not allow researchers to set up identical experimental environments, there may be informational asymmetries, and so on and so forth. Moreover, attempts by rival scientists and graduate students to criticize and publish new findings on older data as part of their routine scientific doings are construed as hostile acts (Wible 1998: 30). The issue is not that all research fails to replicate earlier findings. A considerable amount of time is in fact devoted to the replication of results. And yet a certain proportion of findings are used without being tested by a significant method.

Academic scholarship is often based on (political) intentions and sophisticated reasoning in the sense that "errors" and "misinterpretations" are sometimes part of established ideologies (for further discussion on "error," see Yalcintas 2011). In such cases, initial changes in interpretation and theory selection can hardly be comprehended as small events because harmful consequences of scholarly behavior are not "external" when they are systematic and intentional. When "negative externalities" are systematic and intentional (and therefore "big"), one of the tasks of intellectual history should be the tracing and accounting of ways in which scholarly mechanisms operate so as to sustain harmful effects. The intellectual causation between the individual and scholarly production of errors, misinterpretations, and distortions would then explain the ways in which individual costs are shifted to third parties. This article argues that harmful effects of individual scholarship are intrinsic and institutionalized in the structure of today's academic scholarship even though some of these harmful effects come about as chance events or on contingent bases. These two views are not necessarily rivals because processes that start off with small events eventually turn into processes that keep producing larger significant consequences as the processes become more and more complex. The size of events should not be an issue of discussion here because the more important question is the extent to which economic factors, be they small or large in terms of the magnitude of their causal powers, give rise to significant consequences for academic scholarship.

Market for Ideas Reconsidered

For an intellectual historian willing to shed light on the market failure that financially costs the economics profession an intellectual fortune, there is a sense in which to interpret the operation of academic economics as though economists are exchanging theorems in a market for ideas. The metaphor of market for ideas (and its failure) is certainly a helpful one. But it is also not a "nothing but" argument and not without possible disadvantages (see Dyer 1986; Mirowski 1987; Mirowski and Sent 2002). Most of all, it might be distasteful for the social and political opponents of the current capitalist market system on the grounds at least that knowledge should not be commercialized in the hands of a group of captains of industry. Demands of private sectors to build up partnerships with research universities are not the only, and certainly the not the best, ways of financing and organizing scientific research. On the other hand, skeptics of the metaphor of the market for ideas are concerned, agreeably, with the fact that most (if not all) of the economists of scientific research have mainstream (or "neoclassical") inclinations insofar as their political ideologies are concerned. However, there is no reason to comprehend the history of economic thought in terms of "neoclassical markets" in which agents with perfect information are able to make optimal decisions in their own interests, which are intellectually desirable as well. The metaphor of market for ideas is not necessarily a claim that ideas could and should be bought and sold in the same way as goods and services. There are no demand and supply curves in intellectual history, at least in the sense that "buyers" and "sellers" of ideas come together not to determine the "price of an idea," but to help (or at least unintentionally cause) an idea to get sophisticated. Universities are not business enterprises; it is a fact, however, that knowledge production suffers highly from power relations and surplus appropriation at various levels in research institutes and elsewhere. Finally, the metaphor is not equal to saying that governments should take part in the processes of scientific research although certain codes of behavior should be implemented in the processes of producing and distributing knowledge. Despite the significance of their argument, the skeptics' concern is based on one unrealistic assumption: that the only possible way to analyze academic scholarship is to use the conception of mainstream economics and conceive intellectual history in the ways in which the members of the neoliberal thought collectives conceive global markets. This is not necessarily the case. First, arguing that some of the traditional problems of epistemology have economic aspects, alongside philosophical ones, does not amount to saying that the only relevant way to analyze the market for ideas is to justify the operations of the intellectuals in academic scholarship. Second, debating on the consequences of market failure in the market for ideas is not due to the failure of markets for goods and services in providing funds for academic research in universities. Funding is a crucial issue that should be considered seriously for setting up and sustaining a research program. However, the market for ideas might fail irrespective of the success or failure of the market for goods and services. The reasons of failure in academic scholarship are internal to academic processes in which scholars operate according to certain rules. The theme of this article has so far been that academic scholarship might fail due to the realization of risks involved in conducting research. Markets for ideas are institutionalized processes in which contingencies and chance events cause theorems to lock in to certain pathways. Moreover, certain pathways that come about as an outcome of ideologies and belief systems can collide with other pathways generating even bigger consequences for science in general. In fact, the metaphor of market for ideas is an opportunity to account for the harmful consequences of the power of research funds in specific scholarly activity. Academic scholarship has become such a system that private vices of intellectuals never turn into public virtues of scholarship. In other words, markets for ideas are not able to self-regulate themselves so as to "clear off" or "endogenize externalities."

Failure in the market for ideas is one of the reasons for the destabilization of the growth process of knowledge. Human ideas do not always spread in ways in which better theories outperform others given sufficient time for intellectuals to complete the processes of "shooting for the truth." Scholars compete to win scientific authority that would allow them to speak about and act on scientific matters legitimately in authorized and authoritative ways. Legitimacy in scholarly life can be gained only when social capital accumulates (that is, producers, due to the value of their products, become respected scholars). The amount of social capital possessed by competitors in the market determines the strategies of investment and disinvestment in the research market. Research conducted by the winners of the Swedish Bank Prize and scholars at powerful institutions with which the winners of the Swedish Bank Prize are affiliated, such as the Rand Corporation, Cowles Commission, and the Mont Pélerin Society (Mirowski 2002: 153–231; Horn 2009; Plehwe 2009), are highly credited and further research is often directed by the outcomes of such authors' work. This gives rise to a struggle among competitors for reputation, prestige, authority, and competence.

One might think that monopolization can thus limit epistemic costs. However, economists worry about monopolization particularly when an economic actor, say, a firm, achieves a monopolistic power that lasts for a long time and uses it unfairly in the market. For instance, "cultural standardization" can seriously limit the diversity of solutions and approaches found and developed by scientists to deal with the intellectual problems of scholarly life. Cultural standardization, while making it possible for intellectual actors to interact and exchange ideas on a global scale, "induces a global dilution of the standards of social protection" (Pagano 2007). Different distributions of intellectual assets among academic circles and even nations affect the pathways of scholarly advance, in which the overall outcome of interaction and exchange of ideas can end up with inequalities among intellectual actors. Initial endowments of property rights, as a result of self-reinforcing mechanisms, transform into a dominant system of rights. In this way, the ownership of intellectual assets does not go to those who make use of them in the most efficient ways. Second best solutions, that is, unequal distribution of property rights, resulting from the tendency of standardization and monopolization in "intellectual capitalism," are likely.

The academic community is not powerful enough to fight against shifting epistemic costs onto the shoulders of intellectually weaker individuals and communities. Political commitments, sociological backgrounds, personal and group interests as well as rent seeking and concerns about reputation and power are all constituents of producing "real intellectual income" in the processes of academic scholarship.

When unequal endowment of social capital diminishes opportunities for gaining access to scientific problems and tools (Bourdieu 1999), academic scholarship becomes more restricted (that is, the costs of entry increase) to competitors who are able to produce criticism and discredit established beliefs in the market. Lack of pluralism dominates scholarly life in such a way that there is only one game left in town for scholars to play.

Can failure in the market for ideas also mean then that the operations of scholarly institutions are not satisfactory in correcting replication failure, fraud, or plagiarism? It seems to me that institutions in the market for ideas play a double role here. The primary function of universities is to run together with, if not replace, institutionalized processes in which ideas and theories are debated and exchanged among scholars whereas universities are also part of scholarly mechanisms, producing further costs to which academic scholarship can find a solution only by way of designing further institutions. Cumulative consequences of institutional design generate an entropy effect in the academic environment. Such consequences are irreversible: processes in academic scholarship are not always able to follow the same courses phase by phase in reverse order (Georgescu-Roegen 1971: 196). Plagiarized texts, fraudulent research, and nonreplicable data and findings are of no use for further research but rather a product of the scholarly mechanisms that threaten the epistemic stability and sustainability. Remedies are not impossible. And yet there is no guarantee that the costs of epistemic resources foregone, used in the processes of institutional design, would not exceed the benefits of the operation of new institutions in the long run. Had there been an "economic barometer" or "economic clock" available to intellectual historians, such as the one in which Nicholas Georgescu-Roegen was interested in 1930s, measuring how much harm scholars inflict upon others, this device would have given us scores, in increasing fashions, of the amount of epistemic costs produced as results of implementing (newer and better) institutional solutions to the problems of academic scholarship.

Academic environment is not gratis because neither scholars nor scholarly institutions are isolated. Universities, departments, academic journals, and research programs, including PhD programs, are now "islands of conscious power" (Coase 1937), coordinating scholarly activities in which scholars collaborate and negotiate ideas within and with the help of scientific institutions. However, such collaborations and negotiations can (and do) cause further epistemic costs in terms of, for instance, organizational problems within and among academic teams, learning how to communicate with each other, and not being individually credited for contribution to a collaborated project (Fallis 2005). Further, there is the dominance of high-ranking postgraduate programs and mainstream curricula, such as the Chicago PhD program and Chicago School of Economics curricula (Horn 2009; Horn and Mirowski 2009), over several other postgraduate programs elsewhere in the United States and Europe in the postwar period. Institutionalization and standardization of education techniques (such as requirements of mathematical and statistical courses before admission to PhD programs in economics), homogeneity of dissertation topics (such as exclusion of post-Keynesian, institutionalist, and Marxian issues), and ideologization in the policies of hiring new PhDs and promoting senior members of the academy, all of which have in fact happened or taken place, especially in the United States, since the 1980s (Lee 2009: 66–77), make it less and less likely for pluralism of method, interests, and intellectual and ideological concerns to disseminate among academic economists. All of this suggests, at least to the extent that epistemic costs are concerned, that economic aspects of academic scholarship are embedded within the institutions of scholarly life such that academic scholarship is constructed, operated, and limited by factors other than philosophical and intellectual factors only. A substantial question, which might help the "black box" of (mainstream) economic science to open up, is as follows: How do such institutions operate in a PEC world of academic economics? Or, turning back to the original question, how come economists hesitate to change their minds when they have to face challenges toward their belief systems and ideologies? Is it just "natural" that economists are inclined to defend their "intellectual" position or is there an internal logic, a hidden set of rules, or a social ontology operating in more sophisticated (evolutionary) manners than naïve verificationism or critical rationalism?

Reconsidering the "Coase Theorem"

Revisiting the original works of Ronald Coase, who stated that market mechanisms always worked at a cost, one might even conclude that academic economics has failed to apply, spread, and be proud of one of the most innovative and powerful ideas in the history of economic analyses in its very original and authentic form. Interestingly enough, this idea is also the theoretical source from which the PEC viewpoint originates. Can the evolutionary history of the "Coase Theorem" be an example of intellectual path dependence in which PEC causes the market for economic ideas to fail?

The specificity of the "Coase Theorem" is the following: although Coase had the concept of transaction costs already in mind in the 1930s,[3] the "Coase Theorem" is known to originate from "The Problem of Social Cost." Why was the "Coase Theorem" coined after "The Problem of Social Cost," not after one of his earlier works, and why was it established differently from how Coase proposed?

The "Coase Theorem" first appeared in economic theory in Stigler's third edition of *The Theory of Price* (1966). In a famous passage, Stigler said: "The Coase theorem thus asserts that under perfect competition private and social costs will be equal. It is a more remarkable proposition to us older economists who have believed the opposite for a generation, than it will appear to the young reader who was never wrong, here" (Stigler 1966: 113). The "Coase Theorem" has since been understood as referring to the conditions under which transaction costs are "non-positive" (Medema 2011a).

The "theorem" is now an important topic of investigation in the economic literature. Many of the most cited articles on the "Coase Theorem" (such as Kahneman, Knetsch, and Thaler 1990; Jolls, Sunstein, and Thaler 1998; Hoffman et al. 1994; Elhauge 1991) as well as many dictionaries and textbooks of economics published in the United States and Europe (such as Rutherford 1992: 75; Varian 2002: 542–543; Harrison 1995: 56–60; Cooter and Ulen 1995: 79–84) still describe the "Coasian world" as a world of zero transaction costs. This rich literature focuses a lot of attention on the "Coase Theorem" rather than what Coase "really" said in 1960.

In fact, "The Problem of Social Cost" had received the attention of economic scholarship before Stigler. R. Turvey (1963: 309–313), S. Wellisz (1964: 347–354), G. Calabresi (1965: 729), and E. J. Mishan (1965: 10–11) are among the authors who considered and reviewed Coase's article in their contributions to economic theory in the early 1960s.[4] Most of these articles were interested in the debates regarding the divergence between private and social costs and none of them strayed away from the assumption of positive transaction costs. It must also be stated that a great score of institutionalists, including Veblen (1904) and Kapp (1950), stressed the fact that the significance of social costs was that social costs as well as spillovers were intentional and systematic. Articles published between 1960 and 1966 helped "The Problem of Social Cost" to become known among economists. Books published before the 1960s pointed out that harmful effects of individual production were in fact internal to the capitalist system. However, insofar as the problems with social costs in market economies are concerned, none of these works were as influential as Stigler in getting a "theorem" established in the literatures of economics and law.[5] Today, publications citing "The Problem of Social Cost" and applying positive transaction costs in their economic analysis, such as Nicita and Pagano (2008), Robson and Skaperdas (2008), and Medema (2011a, 2011b), are still a minority. This controversy has evolved into such a state that, in a number of publications, including Williamson (1985) and many others such as Hojman and Hiscock (2010), authors clearly express the controversy on the meaning and implications of the "Coase Theorem" whereas most of these authors nevertheless keep applying the assumption of zero transaction costs in their analysis. This perspective does not help the literature to move away from the sin of Stigler's ideologization.[6]

In his *Memoirs* (1988: 75) Stigler says that "in 1960, Ronald Coase criticized Pigou's theory *rather casually* . . ." (italics added). What Stigler means by "rather casually" is not clear. Does Stigler intend to say that welfare economics and the economics of law are two different fields of research and Coase's critique of the Pigouvian welfare system has become a significant contribution to the economic analysis of law? Or does he mean that Coase's critique lacks the ideological element that would state that markets could actually work and the condition for markets to work is to assume that there are no transaction costs? It is more likely that Stigler had the intention of using Coase to show that competitive markets could work. Stigler did in fact not have much to do with the "truth" that the market operated under positive transactions. Stigler never claimed that markets with positive transaction costs never existed. But neither did he abstain from asking for financial support from corporations and conservative foundations (Nik-Khah 2010). All in all, Stigler achieved an ideological twist that helped mainstream economics ignore markets where transaction costs were high by assuming perfect competition in which private costs were equal to social costs. Coase's critique of the Pigouvian system was thus transformed into a theoretical tool of promoting the ideology of mainstream economics. Had Stigler not manipulated Coase's idea of positive transaction costs, Coase would not have been known as one of the most influential economists of the 20th century, making a chief "contribution" to the intellectual history of the neoliberal thought collectives at the London School of Economics (Tribe 2009) and Chicago School of Economics (Horn and Mirowski 2009) from the 1960s onwards. Chicago economics was (and still is) the dominant paradigm that challenges critical streams of thought in economics. It may not come as a surprise that Coase owes much of his success to the Chicagoans, a group to which he later belonged.[7]

So how has this process of ideologization run? Figure 1 shows the intellectual formation of the "Coase Theorem" in graphical terms.[8] In this scenario, first-generation models include influential articles whose findings, by virtue of innovative research programs, are (re-)formulated in original ways. Second-generation models often take the form of textbooks and secondary or follow-up research, the findings of which are primarily borrowed from first-generation models and strengthen the ideological power of the "contribution." Replication failure works as the engine of this process of positive feedback, which causes the significance of the first-generation model to increase and transform a "contribution" into a constitutive part of the mainstream ideology in economics.

Every time a second-generation model cites Stigler on the "Coase Theorem" the (mis-) interpretation is reinforced and smoothing out

Figure 1

The Intellectual Formation of the "Coase Theorem"

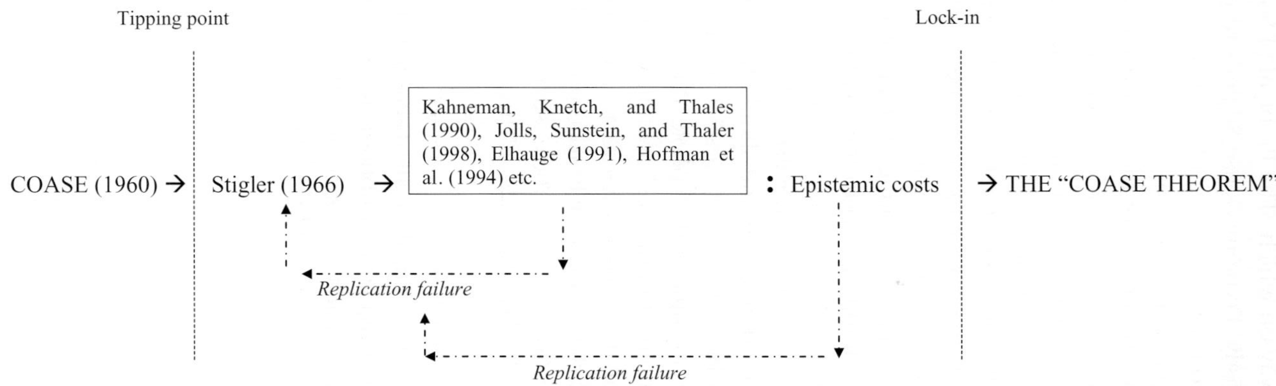

The diagram indicates that inputs in the market for economic ideas such as errors in interpretation, via the mechanism of replication failure, lead to intellectual path dependence. The diagram, by way of using symbols representing sequential stages and mechanisms between stages in the most simplistic form, depicts the transmission mechanism in the market for economic ideas in which scholarly processes of decision-giving authors after Stigler's 1966 article transform into the "Coase Theorem." Arrows with dots (-·-·▶) correspond to replication failure in which second-generation models (Kahneman, Knetch, and Thales 1990; Jolls, Sunstein, and Thaler 1998) do not test the findings of the first-generation model (Stigler 1966) and principally rely on (that is, reproduce) available results in the market. Column (:) signifies the costs generated during the transaction between second-generation models and Stigler (1966). In the case of the "Coase Theorem," epistemic costs disallow intellectuals to retest the result of Stigler (1966) and lock them into a particular research program—the "Coase Theorem." Bold arrows between stages (→) show the direction of the working mechanism. Tipping point is where the erroneous interpretation of Stigler was published in 1966. Lock-in is the stage in which the "Coase Theorem" is accepted as the established message of Coase (1960).

the irregularity in the pathway on which "The Problem of Social Cost" is locked becomes more costly. Economists use Stigler's results, build upon his work, and seek out recognition and prestige among their peers. In this way, the economic literature overinvests in Stigler's *The Theory of Price.* The growing popularity of the "Coase Theorem" and second-generation models increasingly reinforce each other. Epistemic costs involved in the formation of the "theorem" decrease the chances of replicating the findings of the original article. Scarcity of resources (for instance, time) plays the most important role here: researchers' limited time does not allow them to reexamine the results of the models in previous generations. Had economists replicated Stigler's 1966 interpretation by way of simply revisiting "The Problem of Social Cost" for themselves, the assumption of zero transaction costs would perhaps not have had such an impact on the way economists understood Coase's original contribution. Economists who believed that Coase's contribution was important could and should have rechecked the "theorem" in "The Problem of Social Cost" instead of simply reproducing the conclusions in Stigler's 1966 book. Yet economists did not do so until recently. Empirical findings show that whereas almost all the articles on or about the "Coase Theorem" cite Stigler 1966, some of the most cited articles most heavily focused on the "Coase Theorem" do not even cite Coase's 1960 article, such as Kahneman, Knetch, and Thaler (1990).[9] Today, the "Coase Theorem" has turned into a case of intellectual path dependency in which a small event—a (mis) interpretation of an original contribution—grew so large—the "Coase Theorem"—that it has dominated all discussion of Coase's contribution and caused his original contribution to be entirely lost until recently. If the researchers had (economic) incentives to replicate Coase (1960), the "Coase Theorem" could have been "corrected" long ago.

Concluding Remarks

"I would not wish to conclude," reported Coase (1981: 187),

> that, while consideration of what would happen in a world of zero transaction costs can give us valuable insights, these insights are, in my view, without value except as steps on the way to the analysis of the real

> world of positive transaction costs. We do not do well to devote ourselves to a detailed study of the world of zero transaction costs, like augurs divining the future by the minute inspection of the entrails of a goose.

Coase is right: it is questionable how well economists would do, devoting themselves to the "Coase Theorem." But still, economists "stick to their guns" (Jolink and Vromen 2001) especially when they are charged about issues on which they already have strong opinions. Perhaps it is the "nature" of economic scholarship that scholars refuse to change their minds about the ideological consequences of their models. More sophisticated accounts of the evolutionary social ontology of academic scholarship, such as the one tried in this article, might be needed to resolve the complications in the life history of ideas. In fact, ideas do not come out of nothing. Scholarship has a life. It evolves, it transforms, and sometimes it gets stuck. Scholarship cannot overcome every difficulty. Such difficulties are easily visible to an eye that has not been blinded by the once-powerful idea of "progression" or "growth" of knowledge in scholarly life. A PEC worldview may help us explain why some views have survived in academic scholarship yet are inefficient and have not yielded as desirable outcomes as expected. The question now is the following: Is it possible to avoid mis-readings, overemphases, and errors? According to the PEC worldview of science, it is not. However, what is more important than preventing such failures from happening is discovering institutional remedies that uncover and correct errors as soon as possible. In order to be able to do this, one should be knowledgeable about the epistemic costs of scholarly life and the consequences that such costs give rise to.

Notes

1. The "Coase Theorem," used in quotations and with capitals, refers to Stigler's 1966 interpretation of "The Problem of Social Cost" (1960). This interpretation, as this article argues, amounts to a different version from what Coase wanted to prove or argue in his 1960 article.

2. In a letter endorsed by many heterodox economists and sent out to the President of the American Economic Association, Robert E. Hall, it was stated that "[e]conomics is unusual among the social science professions in that it lacks professional ethical codes or guidelines" (January 3, 2011). As a

response to the concerns of heterodox economists as well as many others in the economics profession, the Executive Committee of the American Economic Association "adopted extensions to its principles for authors' disclosures of potential conflicts of interest in the AEA's publications" (January 5, 2012). Will such measures hold academic economics liable for inflicting harm upon others? Time will tell.

3. The notion of transaction costs had been present in his earlier works (see Coase 1937, 1959). Coase also said: "In 1932, when, in a lecture in Dundee, I introduced the concept of transaction costs into economics analysis, I was 21, and if economics was my field, I had only just entered it. However, at first sight, it is not easy to understand why the inclusion of transaction costs in economic analysis was an 'original' idea" (Coase 1995: 246).

4. ISI Web of Science reports that "The Problem of Social Cost" was cited 12 times between 1960 and 1966 whereas it was cited 72 times in the next six years (from 1966 to 1972) and 734 times until Coase was awarded the Swedish Bank Prize in 1991. As of December 2011, "The Problem of Social Cost" has been cited 3,217 times (and counting).

5. Having introduced the "new" conception into economic theory, Stigler, in his later career, did not seriously return to any other original publication of Coase but cited Coase (1960) in his more recent works a number of times. Neither Stigler nor Coase debated any other author, other than Pigou, who proposed alternative/heterodox accounts of social costs caused by private enterprises. See Stigler (1972, 1983, 1989, 1992). It is not implausible to argue that "the discourse of social costs" would have evolved in a novel pathway if the perspectives of Kapp and Veblen on social costs and business enterprises had been taken seriously and not intentionally ignored by these authors.

6. An example of this is the following: "It is noteworthy that this important and influential paper ["The Problem of Social Cost"] is in two parts. The first part features frictionlessness; the second qualifies the earlier discussion to make allowance for frictions. Much of the follow-on literature, including franchise bidding, is largely or wholly preoccupied with frictionlessness or deals with frictions in a limited or sanguine way" (Williamson 1985: 348, 22nd footnote). Williamson might be right. But this is not an excuse to analyze "franchise bidding" as if there were no friction in the market.

7. "I persuaded [Stigler, Friedman, Harberger, McGee, and others] that I was right," reported Coase in his autobiographical essay, "and I was asked to write up my argument for publication in the *Journal of Law and Economics* . . . Had it not been for the fact that these economists at the University of Chicago thought that I had made an error in my article on 'The Federal Communications Commission,' it is probable that 'The Problem of Social Cost' would never have been written" (Coase 1997: 10).

8. For a detailed description of this model, see Sydow, Schreyögg, and Koch (2005) and Schreyögg and Sydow (2010).

9. In a recent study, in which the most cited and the latest articles mentioning the "The Problem of Social Cost" are closely examined in order to see whether (and in what ways) economists have used the "Coase Theorem" in their works, it is found that three-quarters of the articles examined still misrepresent "The Problem of Social Cost" (Yalcintas 2009: 3–23). Such empirical studies suggest that the "Coase Theorem" has a long past but a short history: the "theorem" has been around for 40 years (perhaps more) but Coase's actual contribution is not as old.

References

Arthur, B. (1989). "Competing Technologies, Increasing Returns, and Lock-In by Historical Events." *Economic Journal* 99(394): 116–131.

Berger, S. (2008). "Circular Cumulative Causation (CCC) a la Myrdal and Kapp-Political Institutionalism for Minimizing Costs." *Journal of Economic Issues* 42(2): 1–9.

Berger, S., and W. Elsner. (2007). "European Contributions to Evolutionary Institutional Economics: The Cases of 'Circular Cumulative Causation' (CCC) and 'Open Systems Approach' (OSA)." *Journal of Economic Issues* 41(2): 529–537.

Bourdieu, P. (1999). "The Specificity of the Scientific Field and the Social Conditions of the Progression of Reason." In *The Science Studies Reader*. Ed. M. Biagioli. pp. 19–47. New York and London: Routledge.

Calabresi, G. (1965). "The Decision for Accidents: An Approach to Non-Fault Allocation of Costs." *Harvard Law Review* 78(4): 713–745.

Coase, R. (1937). "The Nature of the Firm." *Econometrica* 4(16): 386–405.

——. (1959). "The Federal Communications Commission." *Journal of Law and Economics* 2(1): 1–40.

——. (1960). "The Problem of Social Cost." *Journal of Law and Economics* 3(1): 1–44.

——. (1974). "Market for Goods and Market for Ideas." *American Economic Review* 64(2): 384–391.

——. (1977). "Advertising and Free Speech." *Journal of Legal Studies* 6(1): 1–34.

——. (1981). "The Coase Theorem and the Empty Core: A Comment." *Journal of Law and Economics* 24(1): 183–187.

——. (1988). *The Firm, the Market, and the Law*. Chicago and London: University of Chicago Press.

——. (1995). "Ronald H. Coase." In *Lives of the Laureates: Thirteen Nobel Economists*. Eds. W. Breit and R. W. Spencer, pp. 227–248. Cambridge, MA: MIT Press.

——. (1997). "Biography of Ronald H. Coase." In *Nobel Lectures in Economic Sciences (1991–1995)*. Ed. T. Persson, pp. 3–20. Singapore: World Scientific Publishing Co. Pte. Ltd.

Cooter, R., and T. Ulen. (1995). *Law and Economics.* Massachusetts: Addison-Wesley.

David, P. (1985). "Clio and the Economics of QWERTY." *American Economic Review* 75(2): 332–337.

——. (2007). "Path Dependence—A Foundational Concept for Historical Science." *Cliometrica* 1(2): 91–114.

Dyer, A. W. (1986). "Veblen on Scientific Creativity: The Influence of Charles S. Peirce." *Journal of Economic Issues* 20(1): 21–41.

Elhauge, E. R. (1991). "Does Interest Group Theory Justify More Intrusive Judicial Review." *Yale Law Journal* 101(1): 31–110.

Fallis, D. (2005). "The Epistemic Costs and Benefits of Collaboration." *Southern Journal of Philosophy* 44: 197–208.

Fox, G. (2007). "The Real Coase Theorems." *CATO Journal* 27(3): 373–396.

Georgescu-Roegen, N. (1971). *The Entropy Law and Economic Process.* Cambridge, MA: Harvard University Press.

Hall, J., I. D. Lacasa, and J. Günter. (2011). "Path Dependence and QWERTY's Lock-In: Toward a Veblenian Interpretation." *Journal of Economic Issues* 45(2): 457–464.

Harrison, J. (1995). *Law and Economics.* Minnesota: West Publishing Co.

Hoffman, E., K. Mccabe, K. Shachat, and V. Smith. (1994). "Preferences, Property Rights, and Anonymity in Bargaining Games." *Games and Economic Behavior* 7(3): 356–380.

Hojman, D. E., and J. Hiscock. (2010). "Interpreting Suboptimal Business Outcomes in Light of the Coase Theorem." *Tourism Management* 31(2): 240–249.

Jolink, A., and J. Vromen. (2001). "Path Dependence in Scientific Evolution." In *Evolution and Path Dependence in Economic Ideas.* Eds. P. Garrouste and S. Ioannides, pp. 205–224. Cheltenham: Edward Elgar.

Jolls, C., C. R. Sunstein, and R. Thaler. (1998). "A Behavioral Approach to Law and Economics." *Stanford Law Review* 50(5): 1471–1550.

Kahneman, D., J. L. Knetsch, and R. Thaler. (1990). "Experimental Tests of the Endowment Effect and the Coase Theorem." *Journal of Political Economy* 98(6): 1325–1348.

Kapp, W. K. (1950). *The Social Costs of Private Enterprise.* Cambridge, MA: Harvard University Press.

Lee, Frederic. (2009). *A History of Heterodox Economics: Challenging the Mainstream in the Twentieth Century.* London and New York: Routledge.

McCloskey, D. (1998). "Good Old Coase Theorem and the Good Old Chicago School: A Comment on Zerbe and Medema." In *Coasean Economics: Law and Economics and the New Institutional Economics.* Ed. S. G. Medema, pp. 239–248. Boston: Kluwer Academic Publishers.

Medema, S. G. (1994). "The Myth of Two Cases: What Coase is Really Saying." *Journal of Economic Issues* 28(1): 208–217.

——. (1999). "Legal Fiction: The Place of the Coase Theorem in Law and Economics." *Economics and Philosophy* 15(2): 209–233.

——. (2002). "George Stigler and the Coase Theorem." *American Journal of Economics and Sociology* 61(3): 638–641.

——. (2009). *The Hesitant Hand: Taming Self-Interest in the History of Economic Ideas.* Princeton: Princeton University Press.

——. (2011a). "A Case of Mistaken Identity: George Stigler, 'The Problem of Social Cost', and the Coase Theorem." *European Journal of Law and Economics* 31(1): 11–38.

——. (2011b). "The Coase Theorem: Lessons for the Study of the History of Economic Thought." *Journal of the History of Economic Thought* 33(1): 1–18.

Mirowski, P. (1987). "The Philosophical Bases of Institutional Economics." *Journal of Economic Issues* 21(3): 1001–1038.

——. (2002). *Machine Dreams: Economics Becomes a Cyborg Science.* Cambridge: Cambridge University Press.

——. (2009). "Postface: Defining Neoliberalism." In *The Road from Mont Pélerin: The Making of the Neoliberal Thought Collective.* Eds. P. Mirowski and D. Plehwe, pp. 417–455. Cambridge, MA: Harvard University Press.

Mirowski, P., and E. M. Sent. (2002). *Science Bought and Sold: Essays in the Economics of Science.* Chicago: University of Chicago Press.

Mirowski, P., and S. Sklivas. (1991). "Why Econometricians Don't Replicate (Although They Do Reproduce)." *Review of Political Economy* 3(2): 146–163.

Mishan, E. (1965). "Reflections on Recent Developments in the Concept of External Effects." *Canadian Journal of Economics and Political Science* 31(1): 3–34.

Nicita, A., and U. Pagano. (2008). "Law and Economics in Retrospect." In *New Institutional Economics: A Guidebook.* Eds. E. Brousseau and J. M Glachant, pp. 409–24. Cambridge: Cambridge University Press.

Nik-Khah, E. (2010). "George Stigler." In *The Elgar Companion to the Chicago School of Economics.* Ed. R. Emmett, pp. 337–341. Cheltenham: Edward Elgar.

North, D. (1990). *Institutions, Institutional Change, and Economic Performance.* Cambridge: Cambridge University Press.

Pagano, U. (2007). "Cultural Globalisation, Institutional Diversity, and the Unequal Accumulation of Intellectual Capital." *Cambridge Journal of Economics* 31(5): 649–667.

Plehwe, D. (2009). "Introduction." In *The Road from Mont Pélerin: The Making of the Neoliberal Thought Collective.* Eds. P. Mirowski and D. Plehwe, pp. 1–42. Cambridge, MA: Harvard University Press.

Radnitzky, G. (1987). "Cost-Benefit Thinking in the Methodology of Research: The 'Economic Approach' Applied to Key Problems of the Philosophy of Science." In *Economic Imperialism: The Economic Approach Applied Outside the Field of Economics.* Eds. G. Radnitzky and P. Bernholz, pp. 283–331. New York: Pargon House Publishers.

Robson, A., and S. Skaperdas. (2008). "Costly Enforcement of Property Rights and the Coase Theorem." *Economic Theory* 36(1): 109–128.

Rutherford, D. (1992). *Dictionary of Economics.* London: Routledge.

Schreyögg, G., and J. Sydow. (2010). "Understanding Institutional and Organizational Path Dependencies." In *The Hidden Dynamics of Path Dependence: Institutions and Organizations.* Eds. G. Schreyögg and J. Sydow, pp. 3–12. New York: Palgrave Macmillan.

Stahl-Rolf, S. R. (2000). "Persistence and Change of Economic Institutions: A Social Cognitive Approach." In *Technology and Knowledge: From the Firm to Innovation Systems.* Eds. P. P. Saviotti and B. Nooteboom, pp. 263–284. Cheltenham: Edward Elgar.

Stigler, G. J. (1966). *The Theory of Price.* 3rd Edition. New York: Macmillan Co.

——. (1972). "The Law and Economics of Public Policy: A Plea for Scholars." *Journal of Legal Studies* 1(1): 1–12.

——. (1983). "Nobel Lecture: The Process and Progress of Economics." *Journal of Political Economy* 91(4): 529–545.

——. (1988). *Memoirs of an Unregulated Economist.* New York: Basic Books.

——. (1989). "Two Notes on the Coase Theorem." *Yale Law Journal* 99(3): 631–633.

——. (1992). "Law or Economics." *Journal of Law and Economics* 35(2): 455–468.

Sydow, J., G. Schreyögg, and J. Koch. (2005). "Organizational Paths: Path Dependency and Beyond." Paper presented at the 21st EGOS Colloqium, June.

Tribe, K. (2009). "Liberalism and Neoliberalism in Britain, 1930–1980." In *The Road from Mont Pélerin: The Making of the Neoliberal Thought Collective.* Eds. P. Mirowski and D. Plehwe, pp. 98–138. Cambridge, MA: Harvard University Press.

Turvey, R. (1963). "On the Divergence Between Social Cost and Private Cost." *Economica* 30(119): 309–313.

Usher, D. (1998). "The Coase Theorem is Tautological, Incoherent, or Wrong." *Economic Letters* 61(1): 3–11.

van Horn, R. (2009). "Reinventing Monopoly and the Role of Corporations: The Roots of Chicago Law and Economics." In *The Road from Mont Pélerin: The Making of the Neoliberal Thought Collective.* Eds. P. Mirowski and D. Plehwe, pp. 204–237. Cambridge, MA: Harvard University Press.

van Horn, R., and P. Mirowski. (2009). "The Rise of the Chicago School of Economics and the Birth of Neoliberalism." In *The Road from Mont Pélerin: The Making of the Neoliberal Thought Collective.* Eds. P. Mirowski and D. Plehwe, pp. 139–178. Cambridge, MA: Harvard University Press.

Varian, H. R. (2002). *Intermediate Microeconomics.* 6th Edition. New York: W. W. Norton.

Veblen, T. (1904). *The Theory of Business Enterprise.* New York: Mentor Books.

——. (1918). *The Higher Learning in America: A Memorandum on the Conduct of Universities by Businessmen.* New York: Huebsch.

——. (1932). *The Place of Science in Modern Civilisation and Other Essays.* New York: Viking Press.

Wellisz, S. (1964). "On External Diseconomies and the Government Assisted Invisible Hand." *Economica* 31(124): 345–362.

Wible, J. (1998). *The Economics of Science: Methodology and Epistemology as if Economics Really Mattered.* London: Routledge.

Williamson, O. (1985). *Economic Institutions of Capitalism.* New York: Free Press.

Yalcintas, A. (2006). "Historical Small Events and the Eclipse of *Utopia*: Perspectives on Path Dependence in Human Thought." *Culture, Theory, and Critique* 47(1): 53–70.

——. (2009). *Intellectual Paths and Pathologies: How Small Events in Scholarly Life Accidentally Grow Big.* PhD Dissertation. Rotterdam: Erasmus University Rotterdam.

——. (2011). "On Error: Undisciplined Thoughts on One of the Causes of Intellectual Path Dependency." *Ankara University SBF Review* 66(2): 215–233.

——. (2012). "A Notion Evolving: From 'Institutional Path Dependence' to 'Intellectual Path Dependence'." *Economics Bulletin* 32(2): 1091–1098.

Financialization and Income Inequality in the United States, 1967–2010

By BRADFORD M. VAN ARNUM† and MICHELE I. NAPLES*‡

ABSTRACT. This article presents a historical overview of the late 20th-century advent of financialization, that is, the unprecedented growth of the financial sector. We summarize its origins and consequences, particularly greater income inequality. An econometric model quantifies the relationship. We conclude that along with higher unemployment and an eroding minimum wage, the growth of the U.S. financial sector has contributed to the exacerbation of inequality in recent decades.

Introduction

The decades before the financial crisis of 2007–2009 were characterized by a widening income gap. The distributive share between labor and capital moved towards property incomes, while wages stagnated. There was also an associated hollowing out of the middle, as the strength of such labor institutions as unions and the minimum wage declined with higher average unemployment and a policy shift towards neoliberalism.

An acceleration of indebtedness propelled the financialization of economic activity, with the associated speculation, layered financial activity, and weak growth of the real sector. With millions of the working and middle class employed in the real sectors of the economy, and many of the wealthiest individuals employed by large investment and banking firms in the financial sector, it is little surprise that financialization may have contributed to an increase in income inequality.

This article argues that U.S. income inequality has reached its highest level in decades in part due to the sweeping changes brought by increased debt leveraging and the associated financialization. The

*Corresponding author.

†van28@tcnj.edu, The College of New Jersey.

‡naples@tcnj.edu, The College of New Jersey.

American Journal of Economics and Sociology, Vol. 72, No. 5 (November, 2013).
DOI: 10.1111/ajes.12036

article delineates the emergence of financialization, traces its links to greater income inequality, and develops an econometric model of the U.S. Gini coefficient for household income, an inequality measure. We explore empirically the extent to which financialization has contributed to the increase in income inequality over the last four decades.

Financialization: Definitions and History

At the most basic level, the term financialization refers to the increasing role of financial motives, financial markets, financial actors, and financial institutions in an economy (Epstein in Epstein 2005: 3). Specifically, financialization entails the increased accumulation of profits through financial means, such as interest, dividends, and capital gains, as opposed to through trade, the production of commodities, or nonfinancial services (Krippner 2005: 174). Financialization is often reflected in an increased share of the financial sector in GDP, an increased emphasis on current shareholder returns, and rising household debt (Stockhammer 2013: 513). The term also encompasses the greater reliance of nonfinancial corporations on the financial sector, both in terms of access to capital as well as investments made in financial assets and subsidiaries (Orhangazi 2008: 14).

Starting in the late 1960s, a series of challenges began to undermine the prosperity of the Golden Age of Capitalism, a period of restrained financial growth that had followed the regulations of the 1930s and 1940s (Crotty in Epstein 2005: 77). The inflationary pressures of the late 1960s, associated with government spending for social programs, the Vietnam War, and union wage gains in oligopolistic industries, brought an end to the low inflation environment on which banks had come to depend. The decline in real interest rates hurt the profitability of many commercial banks, and monetary policy of the late 1960s and early 1970s remained expansionary, further compounding the inflation problem (Bernanke 2003).

In response to these developments, banks undertook a number of innovations to improve their profitability. The encouragement of nontransaction Eurodollar accounts provided a vehicle for banks to circumvent the Fed's reserve requirements on U.S. deposits. The growth of one-bank holding companies in the late 1960s and early

1970s allowed commercial banks to evade the Bank Holding Company Act of 1954 and enter nonbanking lines of business. In addition, as branch banking became available in select states throughout the 1970s, commercial bank branches could escape regulation by not accepting deposits that would have otherwise subjected them to banking laws (Markham 2002: 135). Dorene Isenberg (2003: 239) describes the large commercial banks as "the major supporter[s] of financial liberalization" in this period.

The 1970s witnessed not only new lines of activities for commercial banks, but also the rise of nonbank and hybrid lenders, which led to the growth of a financial industry increasingly beyond the scope of regulation. Just as General Motors and Ford had established financial subsidiaries in previous decades, many nonfinancial corporations began doing the same during this period in response to changing economic conditions (Orhangazi 2008: 32). General Electric was just one of several companies whose financial unit would grow to become extremely profitable, confirming the ever-growing importance of a nonfinancial corporation's establishing its own financial arm (Markham 2002: 243). By blurring the line between banking and finance and thus exploiting loopholes in regulations, both commercial banks and nonfinancial firms realized greater profitability at a time of uncertain returns, but in doing so increased the risk inherent in the financial sector and economy at large.

Although inflation did much to undermine the basis of the Treasury-Federal Reserve Accord[1] and the Golden Age of Capitalism, the declining profit rate of the 1960s and 1970s proved equally disruptive. From 1965 to 1973, the profit rate in manufacturing fell by nearly 41 percent while that of the private business sector declined by 30 percent (Brenner 2006: 57). The emergence of Germany and Japan in global markets was one example of growing international competitive pressure on prices that prevented producers from marking up their products to protect previous rates of return (Sylos-Labini (1979: 8) similarly argued that global exposure constrains markups). The emergence of increased competition abroad led to excess capacity for many U.S. producers, and with it, a lower profit rate.[2] Not surprisingly, domestic firms began shifting from expanding production capacity to investing in financial assets (Krippner 2005: 182). This increasing movement of capital away from the real economy into the financial sector marked the beginning of financialization in the United States, as lower profits were reflected in higher debt levels, financed by those with funds.

The energy crisis in the early 1970s exacerbated the plight of many U.S. firms by further squeezing profits and increasing uncertainty. The profit rate for manufacturing firms, already in steep decline since the late 1960s, fell 25 percent from its low of 1973 during the oil crisis and recession of 1974–1975 (Brenner 2006: 168). The oil crisis produced significant wealth for oil-producing countries at the expense of many U.S. firms, which gave further rise to financialization; flush with funds from the increased price of oil, producing countries began to put their so-called petrodollars in U.S. and European banks (Orhangazi 2008: 34). Through these Eurodollar accounts, U.S. banks suddenly found themselves with more funds to lend and invest.

The experience of the 1970s paved the way for a new series of priorities on the part of not only U.S. firms, which increasingly looked to financial markets for profits, but the government as well. Some policymakers were disillusioned by the failure of Keynesian measures to alleviate the economic crisis of the 1970s, while the accelerating inflation of the Carter years under Federal Reserve Chairman George Miller appeared to abrogate the terms of the Treasury-Federal Reserve Accord. The ensuing negative real interest rates soon triggered accelerating capital flight and the "coup of 1979," wherein financial interests were reassured by appointment of Monetarist Paul Volcker as chairman of the Federal Reserve Board (Epstein and Schor 1995: 8).

Fighting inflation became the new sole priority of monetary policy, and as interest rates rose, financial profitability increased (Duménil and Lévy in Epstein 2005: 25). If the inflation of the 1970s indicated the balance of power had tipped in the borrower's favor, then the tight monetary policy pursued by Volcker showed that lenders had reasserted their influence. Volcker's announced plans to keep interest rates high until inflation was eliminated expedited capital inflows, and the dollar rose dramatically through the mid-1980s. This undermined U.S. manufacturing competitiveness abroad and against cheapened domestic imports, reducing capacity utilization and profitability. As manufacturing had above-average union density, this monetary policy was simultaneously an anti-labor policy, as manufacturing jobs were eliminated (Adams 1985: 27). Downsizing in manufacturing led to offshoring and, over time, the erosion of union membership. This decline of manufacturing itself further contributed to a higher economic share for finance.

Financialization in the early 1980s was given an impetus by Ronald Reagan's efforts to remove the obstacles to economic growth posed by labor, high taxes, and government regulations on capital in the United States and abroad (Brenner 2006: 242). This "Washington Consensus" (see Williamson 2004: 196) saw the social structure of accumulation[3] that had helped stabilize postwar capitalism through institutional means as a hindrance. For proponents of the Washington Consensus, nothing short of dismantling these institutions would restore economic growth; little attention was given to the likely increase in uncertainty and instability without such restraints.

Reagan's efforts to downsize government exacerbated excess capacity, contributing to depression-level unemployment in 1981–1983 and a historically low capacity utilization of 71 percent (Federal Reserve Bank of St. Louis 2012a). Brenner points out,

> . . . with low returns on capital stock discouraging long-term placement of funds in new plant and equipment, money went increasingly to finance and speculation, as well as to luxury consumption, the way being paved by an undisguised lurch in state policy in favour of the rich in general and financiers in particular. (2006: 189)

Arguably, the increase in the real interest rate also raised the reference rate of return in other financial markets, including equity, motivating stockholder revolts in the early 1980s that reoriented corporate boards from long-run profits to short-run payoffs and payouts. The result was a shift in power from corporate stakeholders to shareholders (Orhangazi 2008: 35). New strategies of corporate governance attempted to solve the principal-agent problem by aligning the goals of chief executives with those of shareholders through profit sharing and stock option pay structures, further shifting the balance of power to holders of financial assets (Stockhammer 2013: 515). With the stock market boom beginning in the middle of the

1980s, the profits of financial firms began to increase dramatically compared to those of their nonfinancial counterparts. In particular, a class of rentier interests composed of large financial institutions and those owning financial assets captured an increasing share of national income (Epstein in Epstein 2005: 6).

Institutional financial investors were the beneficiaries of the deregulation of securities markets, and not only gained from new innovations such as clearing and settlement systems that drove down the costs of investing, but became increasingly effective in pressuring firms to consider their interests above those of other stakeholders (Zalewski and Whalen 2010: 766–767). At the same time, large financial institutions acted as another source of pressure on nonfinancial firms to report ever-increasing earnings, offer larger payouts to financial agents, and make larger payments as a percentage of their cash flow to financiers. For most of the 1980s and for parts of the 1990s, these payments accounted for over 50 percent of the cash flow of nonfinancial corporations, with financial agents receiving payments peaking at 76 percent of cash flow in 1989 (Crotty in Epstein 2005: 99).

The process of reducing the U.S. exchange rate from its historic highs in the middle of the 1980s was managed by an ad hoc multinational process spearheaded by Secretary of State James Baker. The coordination among finance ministers and central bankers avoided a repeat of the capital flight of 1979, since those representing financial interests, by laying out a schedule for regular exchange rate adjustments, permitted financiers to plan accordingly. The ensuing decline in the exchange rate promoted net capital outflow and arguably contributed to the stock market crash of 1987. Financial duress ensued, which included the failure of Drexel, Burnham, Lambert and the collapse of the junk bond market, accelerating failures of savings and loans, the failure of 10 percent of all commercial banks between 1989–1991, and the need for a federal cash infusion into the FDIC. To repair FDIC vulnerability, FIRREA (the Financial Institutions Reform, Recovery and Enforcement Act) mandated a 33 percent increase in net worth ratios by 1992 for commercial banks, from 6 percent to 8 percent, with the associated contractionary impact on lending.[4]

This financial reckoning further promoted flight from regulations perceived as costly. The deregulatory initiatives of the 1990s included removing restrictions on interstate banking, which expanded into every state by the end of the decade (Markham 2002: 241). Underwriting and securities activities by nonbank subsidiaries were promoted by the lifting of revenue caps (Markham 2002: 299). The decade's efforts in deregulation culminated in the repeal of the Glass-Steagall Act in 1999, which facilitated mergers and acquisitions and enabled financial firms to realize ever-greater immediate profits with little prospect of regulatory intervention. Even the suggestion of greater oversight, as evidenced by the 1998 call by the head of the Commodity Futures Trading Commission, Brooksley Born, to regulate burgeoning derivatives met with strong criticism and derision. Growing financial sophistication and reduced capital controls accelerated international competition and capital mobility, aggravating the already serious problem of downsizing and offshoring by U.S. firms. Regional free-trade agreements (NAFTA, CAFTA) placed further pressure on the wages of many workers, who now competed with labor abroad.

These changing rules promoted further bank consolidation. The number of commercial banks, which had already shrunk 19 percent from 1986–1992, in part due to failures, fell a further 27 percent by 2000 (Federal Reserve Bank of St. Louis 2012b). At the same time, the process of disintermediation, which had begun several decades earlier but accelerated in the 1980s and 1990s, induced banks to explore new financial products, encouraging the dismantling of regulations (Davis 2009: 115). The loosening of Federal Reserve rules and the ensuing variety of commercial bank financial activities led to disperse regulatory supervision across ". . . state insurance commissions, bank and securities regulators, the SEC, the CFTC, the stock and commodity exchanges, the NASD, the NFA, the Comptroller of the Currency, the FDIC, the Fed, the Justice Department, and even the Federal Trade Commission. (Markham, 2002: 364)"

The unprecedented economic expansion of the 1990s led the U.S. stock market to enjoy one of its best decades. Despite the increasingly wide ownership of equities, stock market gains in fact drove income inequality, since the wealthiest 10 percent owned most stocks and were therefore the primary beneficiaries (Markham 2002: 312). Renewed profitability, as compared with the 1980s, did lead to an immediate investment boom, but many companies continued investing in financial products such as mortgage-backed securities and other increasingly complex instruments. Employment experienced relatively slow growth until 1997, when the East Asian Crisis eliminated the outlet for short-term capital expenditure. Capital inflows to the United States in search of better returns fueled the market in collateralized debt obligations and derivatives. This promoted placement of mortgages, making borrowing easier, and contributed to the housing bubble. By the mid 2000s, financial profits accounted for a little over 40 percent of total U.S. business profits, nearly twice the post-World War II average (Johnson 2009). The subsequent financial crisis of 2008, which owed itself partly to the excess borrowing induced by greater income inequality, is well known (Reich 2010: 23); the consequence of financialization for income inequality has drawn less attention.

Many of the trends cited have coincided chronologically, and exacerbated one another, as shown in Figure 1. The correlation among these mutually reinforcing trends presents a challenge for modeling the determinants of increasing income inequality.

Growing Income Inequality: The Financialization Component

Gerald Epstein and James Crotty (both in Epstein 2005) were the first to link financialization and rising income inequality explicitly. Epstein suggested that financialization and neoliberalism squeezed the profits of nonfinancial firms in which many find employment. The result of such pressures on profits was that wages have increased more slowly for workers in these firms. Crotty (in Epstein 2005: 78) agreed, concluding that the pressure on nonfinancial corporations (NFCs) to pay an increasing share of their cash flow to financial agents "forced NFC top management to switch from the long-term goals and 'high-road' labor relations of the Golden Age to short-term 'survivalist' strategies that involved attacks on white- and blue-collar labor and key firm suppliers." International competitive pressures curtailed price increases, intensifying the drive to cut labor costs (Milberg 2010: 122). Epstein and Jayadev (in Epstein 2005: 58) linked the inflation-adjusted rentier share of gross national income to financialization, which rose from an average of about 7 percent

Figure 1

Causal Chart Linking Financialization and Income Inequality

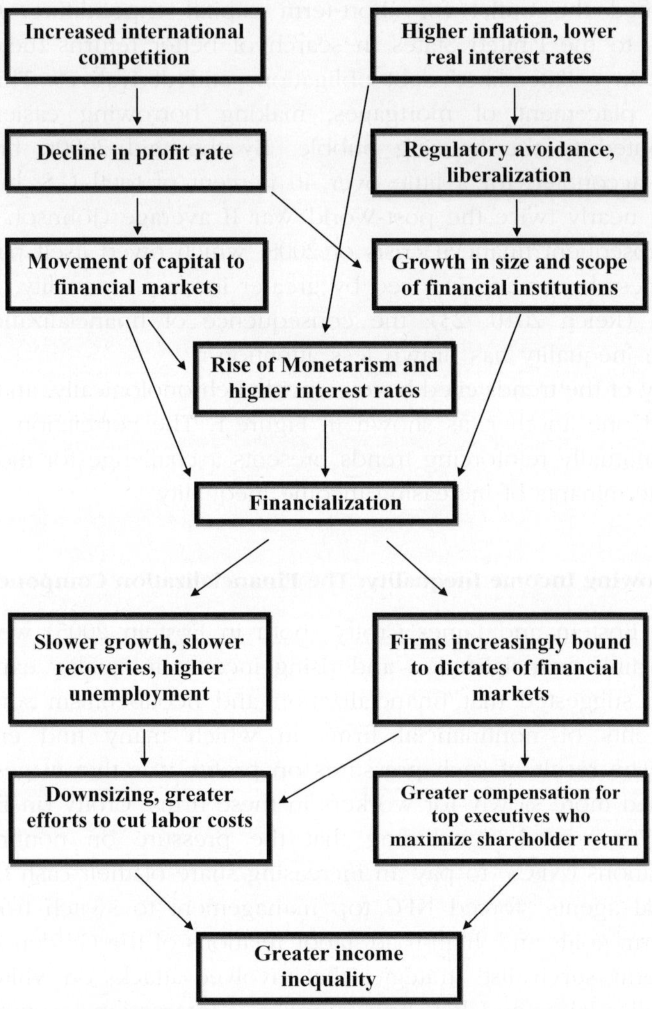

before 1975 to well over 20 percent during the 1980s and 1990s (see also Duenhaupt 2010).

Thomas Palley (2007) noted the disconnect between significant increases in productivity of nonsupervisory workers during the last

20 years and stagnant compensation. He cited multiple reasons for the slow wage growth, including the erosion of unions, the decline in the real purchasing power of the minimum wage, the changes brought about by globalization, the growing demand for skilled as opposed to unskilled workers, and rising CEO pay. Palley observed that only a few who have written about financialization have treated these many factors as being linked and part of the increasingly powerful agenda put forth by the financial sector. Not only have private-sector workers seen the erosion of their wages due to downsizing and outsourcing while public-sector workers have been the victims of a small government agenda, but the shift away from full employment as the main priority of macroeconomic policy has increased income inequality in recent decades.

Ken-Hou Lin and Donald Tomaskovic-Devey (2013) relied on panel data for 35 (40) nonfinancial industries from 1970–1997 (1998–2008) to calculate the decline in labor's share of income induced by financialization. Other significant regressors included union density and college attainment. The two found that during the same period in which labor's share of income fell from more than .7 to about .65, compensation for top executives rose dramatically, owing to processes related to financialization, such as substituting financial investment for production and sales investment (Lin and Tomaskovic-Devey 2013: 1299, 1306).

There have also been a number of panel studies of inequality in high-income countries that addressed global aspects of financialization. Because inequality varies far more across countries than within a country over time, these results may be dominated by cross-section effects.

Engelbert Stockhammer (2009) was perhaps the first to explore the contribution of global financialization to the declining wage share of income for 22 high-income countries from 1979–2007. He found in several different specifications of a nonoverlapping five-year average estimation that the global financialization variable (defined as foreign assets and liabilities as a share of GDP) was statistically significant and negatively correlated with the wage share (Stockhammer 2009: 45–46). In his preferred model, the nonoverlapping five-year average model, this global financial exposure variable was the single most significant, explaining a 4.2 percent decline in the wage share (Stockhammer 2009: 50).

David Zalewski and Charles Whalen (2010) also argued that financialization has contributed to increasing income inequality in 15 European countries, Canada, Japan, and the United States since the 1990s. They used the IMF index of the prominence of arm's-length vs. relational finance (intermediation) in a country. That measure and the Gini coefficient had simple cross-section correlations of 0.184 for 1995 and 0.254 in 2004 (Zalewski and Whalen 2010: 765).

Matthieu Charpe (with Steven Tobin 2011: 60) also studied the impact of this global financialization measure on labor's share in 16 high-income countries from 1981–2005. Regression analysis confirmed that the wage share is negatively impacted by financial globalization when controlling for such factors as union density and trade openness.

These literatures motivate the inclusion of financialization in our time-series analysis of income inequality. They also provide several other potential controls that we explore next.

Econometric Model

To measure income inequality, this article uses annual data for the Gini coefficient for household pretax, pretransfer income as the dependent variable. Since we argue that financialization's negative impact on wages came in large part from its pressure on companies to distribute high current profits, the pretax income measure, reflecting wages paid, is best for our purposes. This Gini ratio, available since 1967, ranges from 0 to 1, with higher values representing greater levels of income inequality. In 1993, a series of data collection changes in the Current Population Survey contributed to a 5.3 percent one-year jump in the Gini ratio; estimates suggest that from one-third to over one-half of the one-year increase reflected purely procedural changes (Ryscavage 1995, 1999; Weinberg 1996). We will explore results for the corrected Gini ratio adjusted for measurement changes.[5]

Since the Gini is a truncated variable, the econometric analysis focuses on its natural logarithm ($LnGini_c$) to mitigate distortion problems at high and low values. Figure 2 is a graph depicting the

Figure 2

Ln of Gini Coefficient (Original and Revised)

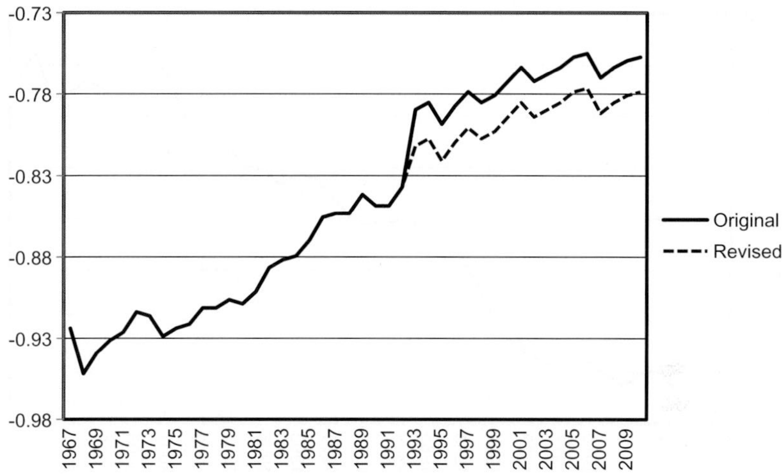

change in the natural logarithm of the Gini coefficient from 1967 to 2010, before and after correcting for the 1993 discontinuity. As shown, income inequality in the United States has risen steadily since 1967, accelerating in the early 1980s.

Among the explanatory variables for the model is a measure representing the growth of financialization in recent decades. This proxy is the percentage of value added to GDP by the FIRE sector, which includes the finance, insurance, and real estate industries as listed in the Bureau of Economic Analysis NAICS tables (see Figure 3).[6] *FIRE* captures the increased prominence of the U.S. financial sector, whose growth has arguably come at the expense of the real economy and wages for many ordinary workers.[7]

The remaining explanatory variables quantify other historical developments in the United States that have led to greater income inequality. Several analysts point to higher unemployment and more severe recessions as contributing to inequality, both because of the direct effect of lost income for those laid off and because of the indirect

Figure 3

Share of Value Added to GDP by FIRE

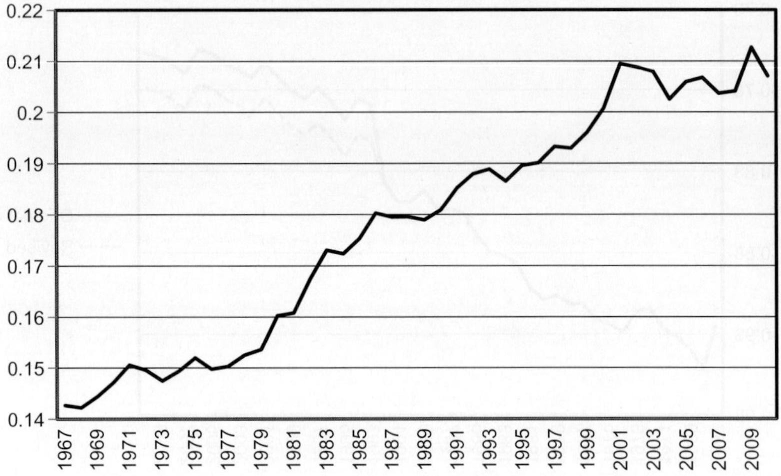

effect of depressed wages for those still employed. However, economic downturns affect capital income as well as labor income, since lower capital utilization drains revenue and profits decline into the downturn. Therefore, income inequality might not perceptibly change as total income declines. It is rather in the early expansion of the subsequent cyclical upturn that incomes diverge and inequality increases, since profits recover quickly while wages stagnate (Naples 2009: 159). Since most years of a business cycle are expansion years (expansions are typically three times as long as recessions), this cyclical pattern will dominate the data. We include the inverse of the unemployment rate (U) to measure this cyclical effect; experiments found that lagging $1/U$ two years ($1/U_{t-2}$) to capture the divergent behavior of profit and wage incomes after a recession was most successful.

The erosion of union strength since the late 1960s has arguably put downward pressure on wages, especially in industries dominated by collective bargaining; see Fichtenbaum's (2011) evidence for labor's share in manufacturing. We would expect that lower rates of unionization have contributed to an increase in income inequality. To measure the decline in union representation since the late 1960s, the econometric model calculates union density as the percentage of nonagricultural wage and salary workers who are union members (*Union*).

The decline in the real value of the minimum wage over time would directly affect income inequality. The decline in that wage relative to the economy's ability to pay (that is to say, relative to productivity) is a more complete measure of its contribution to inequality. For this reason, this model uses the nominal value of the minimum wage in a given year divided by the average nominal private GDP per production and nonsupervisory worker-hours that year (*MinW/Prod*). The minimum wage arguably puts a floor under other low-income wages, and its stagnation permits relative declines in wages for lower-income workers, even those earning above the minimum wage.

In light of the rising college "premium," the increasing level of college attainment (*College*) is expected to contribute to growing income inequality. The majority of U.S. adults with no college degree (about 70 percent of those 25 or older in 2010) have witnessed declining real wages when compared to their college-educated counterparts.

The entry of women into the workforce was most pronounced during the 1960s and 1970s, before income inequality rose significantly in the 1980s. Its effects on income inequality depend on whether upper-income or working-class women had higher increases in labor force participation. Ryscavage (1999: 114–115) suggested that it was higher-income households that experienced an increase in dual earners since poorer married women were already working, so that women's higher labor force participation (*FemaleLF*) exacerbated income inequality.

As the United States moved from being a net exporter to a net importer beginning in the early 1970s, it witnessed the decline of export industries, which were heavily manufacturing based and paid higher wages. Moreover, the increased reliance of U.S. firms on low-cost imports from abroad has arguably enabled cheap foreign labor to compete with domestic labor, putting downward pressure on wages for U.S. workers in lower-wage industries. We include U.S.

imported goods and services as a percent of gross private domestic product (*ImportShare*).

Since the 1930s, the expansion of government expenditures at the federal, state, and local levels has helped provide a stabilizing force for GDP, and thereby helped reduce cyclical fluctuations in inequality. Arguably, this effect would be picked up by the intervening variable, our unemployment measure. However, to the extent the government acts as model employer, its wages and salaries for its low-income workers are relatively high, and those for its high-income employees are below competitive private wages. Moreover, employment patterns for public-sector workers are far less cyclical than those faced by private-sector workers. For both these reasons, a high government share would tend to promote lower inequality. Following Muinelo-Gallo and Roca-Sagalés (2011), we hypothesize a negative impact of fiscal policy on income inequality, and focus on a trend measure of GDP (G/GDP_{trend}) as they did.[8]

With these eight explanatory variables, the multiple regression model to be tested can be written as follows:

$$LnGini_c = \beta_1 FIRE + \beta_2 1/U_{t-2} + \beta_3 Union + \beta_4 MinW/Prod + \beta_5 College + \beta_6 FemaleLF + \beta_7 ImportShare + \beta_8 G/GDP_{trend} + \varepsilon$$

The expected signs of β_1, β_5, β_6, and β_7 are positive, and those of β_2, β_3, β_4, and β_8 are negative.

Econometric Results

Initial regression runs exhibited serial correlation, so results for the Prais-Winston technique for corrected estimates are reported in Table 1. The financialization measure is the only statistically significant regressor at conventional levels. Multicollinearity is confirmed by the simple correlations in Table 2a. Except for lagged unemployment and the fiscal-policy measure, every simple correlation exceeds .9, with associated high VIF scores. The Durbin-Watson statistic indicates no autocorrelation at the 1 percent level. The very high R-squared and the fact that several of these variables are dominated by a time trend suggest the possibility of nonstationarity. Dickey-Fuller tests confirmed that every variable except *FemaleLF* participation was nonstationary.

Table 1

Regression Results for $LnGini_c$

Explanatory Variables	Coefficients	t-Statistics	Regression Statistics	
FIRE	1.4294	2.59⁺	R-Squared	0.9868
$1/U_{t-2}$	−0.0913	−1.47	Adjusted R-Squared	0.9837
Union	−0.3152	−0.93	F-Statistic	325.88
MinW/Prod	−0.2631	−1.13	n	44
College	0.1646	0.59	DW^	2.0134
FemaleLF	−0.1725	−0.91		
ImportShare	−0.0088	−0.06		
G/GDP_{trend}	−0.2927	−1.26		
Intercept	−0.8842	−4.49*		

^Estimation by Prais-Winston method; DW statistic after correction.
*Significant at 1% level.
⁺Significant at 5% level.

Collinearity and stationarity issues were ameliorated by transforming the variables to discrete changes. The simple correlations among regressors were then much lower (see Table 2b), and Dickey-Fuller tests indicated that nonstationarity was no longer a problem. The regression was run again using discrete-change variables (see Table 3); VIF scores were no longer a cause for concern, and the Durbin-Watson statistic again showed that autocorrelation was not an issue at the 1 percent level. However, heteroskedasticity was indicated, so robust estimates are provided in Table 4.

In these estimations, changes in the *MinW/Prod* and $1/U_{t-2}$ emerge as the strongest explanatory variables for the change in $LnGini_c$, with evidence that changes in *FIRE* and *College* contributed to inequality as well (significant at the 7 percent and 11 percent levels, respectively). Experiments showed that the inverse of the unemployment rate lagged two years was the best version of that measure, judging from both t-statistics and AIC-BIC tests. In this specification, the statistically salient contributors to income inequality are those that indicate a lower labor share and reduced wages at the bottom tier of the income

Table 2

2a Correlations, Levels of the Variables

	$LnGini_c$	*FIRE*	*Union*	*FemaleLF*	*MinW/Prod*	*College*	*ImportShare*	$1/U_{t-2}$	G/GDP_{trend}
$LnGini_c$	1.000								
FIRE	0.985	1.000							
Union	−0.975	−0.980	1.000						
FemaleLF	0.935	0.938	−0.978	1.000					
MinW/Prod	−0.939	−0.937	0.965	−0.949	1.000				
College	0.973	0.980	−0.978	0.939	−0.938	1.000			
ImportShare	0.912	0.914	−0.923	0.883	−0.895	0.968	1.000		
$1/U_{t-2}$	−0.066	−0.036	0.181	−0.277	0.277	−0.112	−0.155	1.000	
G/GDP_{trend}	0.662	0.696	−0.736	0.706	−0.689	0.686	0.610	−0.311	1.000

2b Correlations, Discrete Changes in the Variables

	$chLnGini_c$	*chFIRE*	*chUnion*	*chFemaleLF*	*chMinW/ Prod*	*chCollege*	*chImportShare*	$ch1/U_{t-2}$	chG/GDP_{trend}
$chLnGini_c$	1.000								
chFIRE	0.226	1.000							
chUnion	−0.094	−0.100	1.000						
chFemaleLF	0.118	0.000	−0.177	1.000					
chMinW/Prod	−0.476	−0.032	0.241	−0.057	1.000				
chCollege	−0.153	−0.147	0.151	0.054	−0.082	1.000			
chImportShare	−0.164	−0.539	0.072	0.070	0.037	0.201	1.000		
$ch1/U_{t-2}$	−0.354	0.372	0.056	0.020	0.401	−0.098	−0.160	1.000	
chG/GDP_{trend}	−0.063	0.287	−0.380	−0.284	0.175	−0.199	−0.274	0.189	1.000

Table 3

OLS Regression for Change in $LnGini_c$, Discrete Changes in Variables

Explanatory Variables	Coefficients	t-Statistics	Regression Statistics	
chFIRE	0.9445	1.88[&]	R-Squared	0.4071
$ch1/U_{t\text{-}2}$	−0.1287	−2.28[+]	Adjusted R-Squared	0.2675
chUnion	0.2090	0.63	F-Statistic	2.92[+]
chMinW/Prod	−0.4866	−2.23[+]	n	43
chCollege	−0.6929	−1.37		
chFemaleLF	0.2772	0.93		
chImportShare	−0.0093	−0.07		
chG/GDP_{trend}	0.0195	0.07		
Intercept	0.0036	1.13		

Significant at: *1% level, +5% level, &7% level.

distribution. Arguably, these impaired middle-income wages as well by lowering the floor beneath them.

Regressing changes in *FIRE* on the other regressors confirmed some joint collinearity, in particular with changes in *ImportShare* and $1/U_{t\text{-}2}$.[9] In light of that, we also reran the discrete-change regression first without *ImportShare*, then without *FIRE*, not because either should be omitted, but simply to illustrate the collinearity issue. In this alternative estimate, *FIRE* is significant at the 2 percent level, and changes in *College* become significant at the 10 percent level. In the third equation, with *FIRE* suppressed, *ImportShare* is significant at the 13 percent level, *College* at the 8 percent level, and both the unemployment variable and the equation's F-statistic are then only significant at the 6 percent level. These equations confirm the importance of including *FIRE* in the inequality equation.

These results are a reminder that the contributions of orthogonal regressors are most readily perceptible by linear regressions. Both the minimum wage and the unemployment variables have unique determinants, as the former is set by legislation and the latter by the

Table 4

OLS Regression for Discrete Changes, Robust Estimation

Explanatory Variables	Coefficients (t-Statistics) 1	2	3
chFIRE	0.9445	0.9606	
	(1.89)^	(2.54)⁺	
*ch*1/$U_{t\text{-}2}$	−0.1287	−0.1289	−0.0896
	(−2.35)⁺	(−2.42)⁺	(−1.94)^
chUnion	0.2090	0.2105	0.2313
	(0.68)	(0.70)	(0.77)
chMinW/Prod	−0.4866	−0.4874	−0.5699
	(−2.28)⁺	(−2.29)⁺	(−2.57)⁺
chCollege	−0.6929	−0.6977	−0.7140
	(−1.68)	(−1.73)^	(−1.81)^
chFemaleLF	0.2772	0.2769	0.3203
	(1.18)	(1.20)	(1.39)
chImportShare	−0.0093		−0.1286
	(−0.08)		(−1.59)
chG/GDP$_{trend}$	0.0195	0.0222	0.1069
	(0.07)	(0.08)	(0.36)
Intercept	0.0036	0.0036	0.0051
	(1.43)	(1.49)	(2.16)⁺
R-Squared	0.4071	0.4070	0.3457
F-Statistic	2.58⁺	2.87⁺	2.23^
n	43	43	43

Significant at: *1% level, ⁺5% level, ^10% level.

business cycle. The remaining regressors share some strong trends, which makes it difficult to disentangle their independent effects econometrically.

These results do not confirm the role of several variables widely understood to have contributed to increased inequality, including declining union density and increasing labor force participation by women, and provide only weak confirmation for a direct impact from import penetration controlling for other variables, particularly unemployment and college attainment. The insignificance of *FemaleLF* may reflect the fact that its most rapid increases were from the 1960s through the mid 1980s, with relative stagnation thereafter as inequality continued to increase. There may also be contradictory lines of causation, since higher female labor force participation can signal a less gender-stratified workforce and greater gender wage equality. Simultaneously, higher labor force participation by wives in high-income marriages can exacerbate household inequality.

The effects of import penetration may already be picked up by the unemployment measure, but the standard view is that displaced workers ultimately have to take lower-paying jobs. Perhaps the impact of changes in union density and import share are felt over a longer time horizon than one year, which may well be the case for several of the regressors, including the financialization measure.

Conclusion

The picture that emerges from this study is that increases in income inequality over the last several decades derive most clearly from worsening economic conditions and a reduction in the minimum wage relative to the economy's ability to pay (productivity). The results of the econometric model also suggest that financialization should be included in any econometric study of income inequality. That is, rather than following from such demographic changes as college attendance and women's labor force participation, income inequality has resulted primarily from a shift in the balance of power toward rentiers and away from workers. Declining profits and increased financialization led to cost pressures, including downward pressures on wages, decertification of unions, and rising recourse to imports.

The policy implications of this study are twofold. First, reducing inequality requires not just improving the leverage of labor interests, but addressing the growth of the financial sector. Successful regulation of financial activity will reduce the scope and effectiveness of any financial speculation, limiting the profitability and magnitude of such activities. The results presented here suggest that doing so may have the hitherto unexpected consequence of improving U.S. income equality.

However, the interrelationship between financialization and other income variables raises the question as to whether a shift in the balance of power, not just between finance and industry, but between finance and labor interests, may not be a necessary prerequisite to any success in containing the excesses of the financial sector. Hyman Minsky (1975) suggested that short of a catastrophic reckoning that puts an end to financial speculation, financiers' willingness to bear risk simply grows. The question is whether a coalition of business/managerial and labor interests united to clip rentiers' wings could be successful without facing that kind of cataclysm. If not, legislation such as the Dodd-Frank Act may be ineffective in preventing moral hazard. Its unspecified regulatory provisions may permit financial consolidation and risk taking and thereby cause financialization to expand once more, further exacerbating income inequality.

Notes

1. This 1951 accord assured the Treasury that the Federal Reserve would accommodate its expenditures as long as financial sector inflationary concerns were taken seriously (see Epstein and Schor 1995; Hetzel and Leach 2001).

2. Capacity utilization trended downward from the late 1960s through the 1980s, stagnated, then continued its downward trend 2000s-present (Federal Reserve Bank of St. Louis 2012a).

3. The social structure of accumulation refers to the set of institutions comprising the postwar paradigm for managing conflicts between classes of economic actors: finance and industry, nationally-oriented businesses and transnationals, and organized labor and business. That social structure constitutes such class relations by shaping and constraining the acceptable foci and expressions of conflict; see Kotz, McDonough, and Reich (2010: 97) for an expanded discussion of the theory.

4. A bank's net worth or capital ratio is the ratio of its net worth to its assets. It is difficult to raise the numerator of this ratio 33 percent in a recession with low bank profits, or to attract additional investors into existing bank assets, but banks could achieve the same increased ratio by cutting risk-weighted assets by 25 percent. Since loans to nonbank borrowers are weighted most heavily, such lending contracted. The credit crunch of the early 1990s was caused by Congress rather than the Federal Reserve.

5. The econometric results focus on a Gini adjusted downward by one-half of its 5.3 percent increase in 1993. The results were substantially the same without the correction, but the corrected series is theoretically appropriate.

6. Starting in 1998, the Bureau of Economic Analysis switched from its previous SIC system to its current NAICS. The pre-1998 data used for the FIRE variable were corrected by the BEA for comparability to later data. Another potential measure of financialization, financial profits relative to total domestic profits, proved very cyclical and was not significant.

7. Stockhammer (2009) and Charpe (2011) focus on global financialization, specifically a country's exposure to external debt or foreign-owned assets. This specification may be appropriate for small economies, but our argument is different: it is the expansion of the size and influence of the financial sector, whether assets are domestically or foreign owned, that puts downward pressure on labor income in the United States.

8. Muinelo-Gallo and Roca-Sagalés (2011) explored the contribution of public-sector spending on the Gini ratio in 33–35 high- and middle-income countries from 1972–2006. They discovered that higher public expenditures contributed to lower inequality, controlling for other public-sector variables and the growth of GDP. They observed that their study was most suited to explaining cross-country variation since their Gini ratios varied far more between than within countries (Muinelo-Gallo and Roca-Sagalés 2011: 81).

9. $FIRE^{\wedge} = 0.001635 + 0.023593 chUnion + 0.045586 chFemaleLF - 0.088207 chMinW/Prod - 0.022258 chCollege - 0.126294 chImportShare^{*} + 0.041406 ch1/U_{t-2}^{\#} + 0.092508 chG/GDP_{trend}$, $R^2 = 0.4137$, adjusted $R^2 = 0.2965$, $F(7, 35) = 3.53^{*}$, where ^ indicates estimate, * significance at 1 percent level, # at 2 percent level.

References

Adams, L. T. (1985). "Changing Employment Patterns of Organized Workers." *Monthly Labor Review* 108(2): 25–31. Http://stats.bls.gov/opub/mlr/1985/02/art3full.pdf.

Bernanke, B. S. (2003). " 'Constrained Discretion' and Monetary Policy." Federal Reserve Board. Http://www.federalreserve.gov/boarddocs/speeches/2003/20030203/default.htm.

Brenner, R. P. (2006). *The Economics of Global Turbulence: The Advanced Capitalist Economies from Long Boom to Long Downturn, 1945–2005.* New York: Verso.

Charpe, M., with S. Tobin. (2011). "The Labour Share of Income: Determinants and Potential Contribution to Exiting the Financial Crisis." In *World of Work Report 2011.* Ed. R. Torres, pp. 55–73. Geneva: ILO. Http://www.ilo.org/public/english/bureau/inst/download/wow2011.pdf.

Davis, D. F. (2009). *Managed by the Markets: How Finance Reshaped America.* New York: Oxford University Press.

Duenhaupt, P. (2010). "Financialization and the Rentier Income Share—Evidence from the USA and Germany." *Macroeconomic Policy Institute Working Paper.* Http://www.boeckler.de/pdf/p_imk_wp_2_2010.pdf.

Epstein, G. A., ed. (2005). *Financialization and the World Economy.* Northampton: Edward Elgar Publishing.

Epstein, G. A., and J. B. Schor. (1995). "The Federal Reserve-Treasury Accord and the Construction of the Post-War Monetary Regime." *Social Concept* 7(1): 7–48.

Federal Reserve Bank of St. Louis, Economic Research Division (2012a). Economic Data, FRED. "Graph: Capacity Utilization: Total Industry (TCU)." Http://research.stlouisfed.org/fred2/graph/?id=TCU.

——. (2012b). Economic Data, FRED. "Graph: Commercial Banks in the United States." Https://research.stlouisfed.org/fred2/graph/?graph_id=68586&category_id=0.

Fichtenbaum, R. (2011). "Do Unions Affect Labor's Share of Income: Evidence Using Panel Data." *American Journal of Economics and Sociology* 70(3): 784–810.

Hetzel, R. L., and R. F. Leach. (2001). "The Treasury-Fed Accord: A New Narrative Account." *Federal Reserve Bank of Richmond Quarterly Review* 87(1): 33–55. Http://www.richmondfed.org/publications/research/economic_quarterly/2001/winter/pdf/hetzel.pdf.

Hirsch, B. T., D. A. Macpherson, and W. G. Vroman. (2001). "Estimates of Union Density by State." *Monthly Labor Review* 124(7): 51–55. Http://stat.bls.gov/opub/mlr/2001/07/ressum2.pdf.

Isenberg, D. (2003). "The National Origin of Financial Liberalization: The Case of the United States." In *Globalisation, Regionalism and Economic Activity.* Eds. P. Arestis, M. Baddeley, and J. McCombie, pp. 220–244. Northampton: Edward Elgar Publishing.

Johnson, S. (2009). "The Quiet Coup." *Atlantic.* Http://www.theatlantic.com/magazine/archive/2009/05/the-quiet-coup/7364/.

Kotz, D. M., T. McDonough, and M. Reich. (2010). *Contemporary Capitalism and its Crises: Social Structure of Accumulation Theory for the 21st Century.* Cambridge: Cambridge University Press.

Krippner, G. (2005). "The Financialization of the American Economy." *Socio-Economic Review* 3(2): 173–208.

Lin, K., and D. Tomaskovic-Devey. (2013). "Financialization and U.S. Income Inequality, 1970–2008." *American Journal of Sociology* 118(5): 1284–1329. Http://www.kenhouslin.info/lin%20and%20tomaskovic-devey%20 2013%20AJS.pdf?attredirects=0.

Markham, J. W. (2002). *A Financial History of the United States: From the Age of Derivatives into the New Millennium (1970–2001).* Armonk: M. E. Sharpe, Inc.

Milberg, W. (2010). "Pricing and Profits Under Globalized Production: A Post Keynesian Perspective on U.S. Economic Hegemony." In *Money and Macrodynamics: Alfred Eichner and Post-Keynesian Economics.* Eds. M. Lavoie, L.-P. Rochon, and M. Seccareccia, pp. 116–138. Armonk: M. E. Sharpe, Inc.

Minsky, H. P. (1975). *John Maynard Keynes.* Armonk: M. E. Sharpe, Inc.

Muinelo-Gallo, L., and O. Roca-Sagalés. (2011). "Economic Growth and Inequality: The Role of Fiscal Policies." *Australian Economic Papers* 50(2–3): 74–97.

Naples, M. I. (2009). "Labor Demand Under Strategic Competition and the Cyclical Profit Squeeze." In *Heterodox Macroeconomics: Keynes, Marx and Globalization.* Eds. J. P. Goldstein and M. G. Hillard, pp. 151–162. New York: Routledge.

Orhangazi, O. (2008). *Financialization and the U.S. Economy.* Northampton: Edward Elgar Publishing.

Palley, T. (2007). "Financialization: What it is and Why it Matters." *Levy Economics Institute of Bard College Working Paper* 525. Http://www.levyinstitute.org/pubs/wp_525.pdf.

Reich, R. B. (2010). *Aftershock: The Next Economy and America's Future.* New York: Alfred A. Knopf.

Ryscavage, P. (1995). "A Surge in Growing Income Inequality?" *Monthly Labor Review* 118(8): 51–61. Http://www.bls.gov/mlr/1995/08/art5full.pdf.

——. (1999). *Income Inequality in America: An Analysis of Trends.* Armonk: M. E. Sharpe, Inc.

Stockhammer, E. (2009). "Determinants of Functional Income Distribution in OECD Countries." Macroeconomic Policy Institute study commissioned by the Hans Böckler Foundation. Http://gesd.free.fr/stock509.pdf.

——. (2013). "Financialization and the Global Economy." In *The Political Economy of Financial Crises.* Eds. M. H. Wolfson and G. H. Epstein, pp. 512–525. New York: Oxford University Press.

Sylos-Labini, P. (1979). "Prices and Income Distribution in Manufacturing Industry." *Journal of Post Keynesian Economics* 2(1): 3–25.

Weinberg, D. H. (1996). "A Brief Look at Postwar U.S. Income Inequality." *Current Population Reports.* Census Bureau, Report P60-191 (June). Http://www.census.gov/hhes/www/img/p60-191.pdf.

Williamson, J. (2004). "The Strange History of the Washington Consensus." *Journal of Post Keynesian Economics* 27(2): 195–206.

Zalewski, D. A., and C. J. Whalen. (2010). "Financialization and Income Inequality: A Post Keynesian Institutionalist Analysis." *Journal of Economic Issues* 44(3): 757–777.

Appendix

Data Definitions and Sources

Variable	Definition	Source
College	Percentage of those 25 and older with at least a college degree	Census Bureau, Current Population Survey
FemaleLF	Percentage of women in the labor force	Bureau of Labor Statistics
FIRE	Share of value added to GDP by finance, insurance, and real estate industries	Bureau of Economic Analysis, NAICS data
$LnGini_c$	Pretax, pretransfer Gini coefficient	Census Bureau, Current Population Survey
G/GDP_{trend}	Government spending as share of potential GDP	Department of Commerce, Bureau of Economic Analysis; U.S. Congress, Congressional Budget Office
ImportShare	Imports as percentage of private GDP	Bureau of Economic Analysis
MinW/Prod	Minimum wage divided by private GDP per production and nonsupervisory worker-hours	Department of Labor, Bureau of Labor Statistics
$1/U_{t-2}$	Inverse of unemployment rate, lagged two years	Bureau of Labor Statistics
Union	Union density of nonagricultural wage and salary employees	Unionstats; Hirsch et al. (2001)

Conspicuous Consumption as Routine Expenditure and its Place in the Social Provisioning Process

By ZDRAVKA TODOROVA*

ABSTRACT. The article utilizes the framework of social provisioning to argue that conspicuous consumption is an essential process of capitalism, and should be explored as a routine practice rather than an exceptional behavior. The objectives are: 1) to discuss conspicuous consumption as a process within a heterodox social provisioning framework; and 2) to emphasize the need for formulating theoretical concepts and discussions that are consistent with heterodox frameworks such as social provisioning.

Introduction

It is common to credit Thorstein Veblen (1899) with the term conspicuous consumption, while ignoring his theory of capitalism, or "pecuniary culture" and generally his evolutionary framework. While the *term* receives wide attention, the *concept* of conspicuous consumption has been hollowed out to various degrees.[1] Furthermore, Veblen's work is readily defined as a contribution to consumer choice theory, and few outside of original institutional economics see the analytical place of the "conspicuous consumption" concept in his overall analysis of capitalism. Treated as an exceptional and well-defined monolithic behavior, the term has obtained a life on its own—it has an immutable meaning and is used in any type of theoretical framework. As a result, analyses of class, surplus, and capitalism as a system of provision are habitually left out.

The concept of social provisioning has been used to draw elements in a coherent manner from various heterodox approaches[2] that differ in their method, terminology, concepts, and focus, while arguably share a general understanding of economic activity as social provisioning.

*Zdravka Todorova, Associate Professor, Wright State University, zdravka.todorova@wright.edu.

American Journal of Economics and Sociology, Vol. 72, No. 5 (November, 2013).
DOI: 10.1111/ajes.12039

As a result, a common general definition of economics has emerged: the study of the process that provides the flow of goods and services required by society to meet the needs of those who participate in its activities. This particular definition allows for examination of processes and human agency in cultural context and historical time, and enables the exploration of evolution of resources, production, and consumption patterns, as well as of the sociocultural meaning of activities that constitute social provisioning. The structure of the economy—the schema of production and finance and the income flows relative to produced goods and services—are embedded within ecosystems and a historically specific sociocultural framework—including ideology and conventional wisdom (Gruchy 1987; Nelson 1993; Dugger 1996; Power 2004; Lee 2010, 2011; Jo 2011).

The objectives of the article are: 1) to discuss conspicuous consumption as a process within a heterodox social provisioning framework; and 2) to emphasize the need for formulating theoretical concepts and discussions that are consistent with heterodox frameworks such as social provisioning. The first two sections introduce social provisioning, the production and distribution of social surplus, waste, and the class structure of the capitalist economy as the context of consumption analysis. The discussion builds on Veblen's theory, but is not limited to his analysis; as well as on Lee (2010; 2011), adding a greater focus on households and on waste in the Veblenian sense. In the next two sections the article discusses discretionary and routine consumption expenditures, and argues that conspicuous consumption is a routine rather than an exceptional phenomenon and a process embedded within social provisioning. This is followed by a conclusion.

Social Provisioning as a Context for Analysis of Consumption

Any culture has to engage in *social provisioning*—providing for the material means of life resulting in economic activities that generate the flow of goods and services necessary to meet the biological and socially created needs of individuals and to maintain what Veblen called the *collective life process.* This formulation of economic activity is broader and deeper than "market exchange" because it draws connections among production, consumption, and distribution, and encompasses nonmarket activities, culture, and ecosystems.

The social provisioning process is generated and directed by social organizations—business enterprises, the state, and households, and the existing power relations. The concepts of market clearing, relative scarcity, and price mechanism have no meaning in the framework of social provisioning. Prices and output are determined independently of each other, and there is no relation between prices and sales. Prices are not functioning as signals and do not coordinate economic activity, nor do they allocate resources, and particularly they do not drive consumer demand. Managerial price setting, investment projects, and production and employment targets are strategic decisions designed to meet specific goals of the business enterprises (Eichner 1985; Lee 2010).

Business enterprises launch product lines in order to achieve various business goals, which may or may not correspond to the households' need to secure livelihood and sustain the life process. There is a contradiction between production of profits and production of use values, or as described by Veblen (1921), between business (in monetary terms) and industrial (in technological terms) goals. Capitalist social relations ensure the reproduction of business enterprises and capitalist households, but not necessary the survival of all workers. Consequently, social provisioning organized around, and directed by, the decision making within the business enterprise entails conflict rather than harmony.

The social provisioning process is founded on the interdependent production of goods and services that are embedded in social relations and have social meaning. Production is a circular flow and all intermediate capital goods are produced inputs. These are interconnected in a technically specific manner and are not viewed as substitutable relatively scarce factors of production. Some of the outputs replace the goods and services used up in production, and the rest constitutes the *social surplus* to be used for household consumption, private fixed investment, and government services (Lee 2010).

The surplus is generated by the society's usage of tools, skills, and labor. Knowledge is communally generated, but ownership secures individual income streams—hence Veblen's (1919) conceptualization of "free income," or "vested interest." The claim of ownership on communal knowledge is described by Veblen as predation that secures consumption without being engaged in production of the social surplus.

Just like production has industrial (making goods that maintain the life process) and pecuniary aspects (making money), consumption has both instrumental (serviceable) and ceremonial (symbolic) aspects. The instrumental (industrial) attributes of a product enhance the life process, and include durability, instrumental efficiency, safety, and recreational capacity (Sturgeon 2010: 30–31). In Veblen's analysis the ceremonial aspects are demonstrated by "pecuniary emulation," "pecuniary canons of taste and beauty," "conspicuous waste," "conspicuous leisure," and "conspicuous consumption." These processes encompass the activities of business enterprises, households, the state, and other organizations.

Waste is "expenditure that does not serve human life or human well-being on the whole . . . and occurs on the ground of an invidious pecuniary comparison" (Veblen [1899] 1994: 60). Waste can be accounted for only at the level of social provisioning, and not at the level of individual agents. Waste is considered a "necessity" at the individual level because it generates income and secures status to those who engage in its production and consumption. Consequently, conspicuous consumption and waste should be viewed as a broader process—and not just part of individual decision making.

Classes, Power, and Consumption

Demand for consumption goods and services takes place in the described context of the social provisioning process. Expenditure flow generated by consumer demand is just one aspect of the consumption process that is embedded in culture and power relations based on a class structure. There are two broad classes with respect to economic activity: those who do not own or control the means of production, and hence do not receive income flows generated from capital, and those who own and control the means of production and receive such incomes. Veblen's ([1919] 2005: 160) formulation is: "the kept classes" and the "common man." "It is a division between those who control the conditions of work and the rate and volume of output and to whom the net output of industry goes as free income, on the one hand, and those others who have the work to do and to whom a livelihood is allowed by these persons in control, on the other hand" (Veblen [1919] 2005: 161).

The *common men* are common in the respect that they are not vested with the right to "get something for nothing"—or "free income" (Veblen [1919] 2005: 162). The *kept classes* include the leisure class, capitalists, rentiers, elite professionals, and the political elite. These could also be referred to as the *ruling class* that in addition to a superior material standard of living has the power to maintain ownership and control so to continue the directing of the social provisioning process for its benefit. The ruling class actively seeks to preserve its social power and prevalent habits of thought through engaging in various economic, political, social, and academic activities. This is done through the organization of business enterprises, households, and the state, as well through other social institutions such as think-tanks, education, and the media. The ruling class directs the generation and distribution of the social surplus, and shapes public policy. Workers do participate to various degrees in democratic processes, but their political power is very limited in the direction of the social surplus.

Individuals and households who have no choice but to sell their labor power to those who own the means of production are the working class. Unemployment insurance recipients are part of the working class who could not sell their labor power, but have participated and will eventually be engaged in paid production of the surplus. Furthermore, when providing care for their household members these workers are in fact participating in the production of the social surplus. Small family business enterprises are also part of the working class—since they provide mostly subsistence for their households. Finally, some members of the working class receive income flows generated from capital gains—but these are not sufficient to maintain them, so they have to continue on selling their labor power, and thus are clearly categorized as workers.

Members of the working class could not simply decide to not sell their labor and to become part of the capitalist class, for two main reasons. First, their financial positions are not sufficiently liquid, and if they stop selling their labor for wages they could not maintain their households as going concerns. The result will be poverty—financial, social, psychological, and biological—trauma, and death. Second, in order to be able to live without selling their labor, workers would need sufficient collateral or other means to finance the purchase of capital goods. Alternatively, they would need a significant bequest of asset portfolio to join the rentier class.[3]

Children, the disabled, retired persons, and partners who are supported by breadwinners constitute the *financially dependent class* that needs to consume a portion of the social surplus in order to survive, but does not participate currently in monetary production. Some of that population may be part of the future labor force (children), others have contributed to the generation of the social surplus and knowledge in the past (retirees), and yet others are engaged in household activities that support the social provisioning process in the present, but are not wage workers. The commonality among these segments of the population is that at a given point of time they need to be financially supported by those who currently produce the social surplus. The support can be direct—through allotment of workers' wages—or through various transfers. Welfare recipients are part of the working class since they are also required to work for pay. In cases where this requirement is absent—they are part of the dependant class—for example, receiving payments from the state to fund the purchase of inputs needed for providing care for household members such as children.[4] Members of ruling class households who are maintained by another household member's capital gains proceeds are in a different position. They are part of the capitalists' or rentiers' consumption activities (Veblen 1899; Todorova 2009).

The financially dependent class is not to be confused with the *leisure class*. Members of the leisure class could participate in the social provisioning process but they are financially liquid and engaging in labor would be contrary to their desired social standing. An updated formulation would also include those who work but for whom wage earnings are not essential, in other words those who treat work as a consumption activity. Furthermore, Veblen's definition of the leisure class as engaged in acquisition rather than in production can include today's money managers and those who rely largely on income from speculation.

The distribution of social surplus varies within the working class—giving rise to inequities and socioeconomic distinctions within that broad class. These distinctions blur the similarities in position of the various social classes with respect to their place in the social provisioning process and "working class consciousness" is subsumed. Workers live within *working-class households*, and see themselves as being unified or categorized by patterns of consumption, occupations, and social activities, rather than by their common role as wage earners. Thus, members of the working class are represented and/or see themselves as being part of culturally specific and socially constructed categories such as: "middle class," "upper middle class," and "professionals" formulated around *life-styles.* Furthermore, within popular culture as well as public and academic discourse, reference categories have emerged to signify groups of people based on types of activities they are perceived to engage in, places they shop, consumption patterns, education, living quarters, and neighborhoods, such as: "yuppies"[5] and "the creative class."[6] The consumption-based distinction among such sociocultural characterizations disarticulates the fundamental commonality within members of the working class—their common dependence on money wages. As Fine, Heasman, and Wright (1996: 236) put it, "[p]atterns of consumption may serve to obscure the underlying class relations upon which they are based." Consequently, workers participate in stock ownership and do engage in conspicuous consumption, both of which do not undermine the empirical existence of a distinct working class.[7]

Within households, we can conceptualize of goods and services that are produced and consumed, and that contribute to the survival of workers and their dependents. These "outputs" do not generate income flows—and are qualitatively different from market goods and services—yet they are a part of the social provisioning process. The "production" of these "outputs" requires the purchase of commodities. Thus, within the capitalist economy the reciprocal relations within and among households (such as cooking and care for family members) cannot be sustained without access to the available social surplus.

Nonmonetary activities such as domestic work and care activities could serve as a buffer to partially offset worsened households' financial positions, only to some extent. The reason is because households must obtain money through participation in the market process since they do not own the means of production, and have to pay their tax obligation by selling their labor power. Furthermore, labor power is itself a produced "input." Labor power is thus socially produced, that is, it is not produced within a private domain of autonomous households functioning independently from the monetary production process (Todorova 2009). Individual households may be financially responsible for, and emotionally vested in, raising children, and taking care of dependants and workers, but the "produced" labor power is a result of households' activities, social institutions, social stock of knowledge, and the production and distribution of social surplus.

Consequently, even though nonmarket activities exist within the capitalist social provisioning process, households are not self-sufficient—they mostly rely on the output, income, and employment determined by business enterprises and the state. The volume and composition of the social surplus are determined by the desire for surplus goods and services by capitalists and the state, rather than by a price mechanism that embodies consumer sovereignty and labor markets.

The ruling class (leisure class, capitalists, and the political elite) actively seek to preserve their social power through engaging in various economic, political, and social activities. They do so through the organization of business enterprises the media, and through the state, all of which affect the notion of ideal types of household organization and relations, including consumption patterns. The lives of working-class households are directed by the ruling-class households not only by decisions about production and distribution of the social surplus, but also by the cultural effects of the "kept classes." This includes the evolution of reputable consumption patterns and aspirations.

The working and dependent classes demand consumption goods, but they do not command the production of those goods. First, the production of social surplus is not constrained by households' savings. On the contrary, households' activities and their financial positions—ability to save—are constrained by the desire of the business enterprises and the state for social surplus. In the process of accumulation and market expansion business enterprises, particularly their financial branches, and financial institutions, enable households to temporarily circumvent that constraint and to ameliorate the accompanying inequalities. As a result, households become indebted and financially fragile in order to meet socially evolved needs that cannot be supported fully by their incomes (Sullivan, Warren, and Westbrook 2000; Parenteau 2006; Wolf 2007; Brown 2008; Todorova 2009).

Second, households choose out of a given sets of goods and services that have been determined independently of them. Management goals formed in a particular regulatory and cultural context (both influenced by the business enterprises' activities) determine the available goods for consumption. While consumption is not a passive reflection of production (Fine 2002), it is a part of the social provisioning and production of social surplus that is directed largely by the capitalist class. While business enterprises use past consumption patterns in forming their decisions about production and employment, this does not mean that individuals in their roles as consumers are driving production. Business enterprises are actively participating in creating wants and needs through development of new products and marketing campaigns. Satisfaction of consumption needs/wants is a by-product of the business enterprise and the state's activities. Use values emerge only as a coincidence—they are not an end in business activity (monetary production) (Veblen 1919, 1921, 1923).

Within the described social provisioning process, producers do not respond passively to "spontaneous consumer needs"; rather, the accumulation process develops desires for consumption: "If production is to increase, the wants must be effectively contrived" (Galbraith 1958: 129). *Growth of needs* occurs as a result of the accumulation process (Marx [1859] 1973; Veblen 1923; Galbraith 1958; Hamilton 1987, 1989; Lavoie 2004). Furthermore, the principle of *satiability of needs* (Lavoie 1994, 2004) ought to be extended in the context of growth of needs and invidious distinction. Rather than constructing a mirror image to the insatiable needs concept, it is more adequate to use Veblen's notion of "*chronic dissatisfaction*" that encompasses both a natural predisposition (not based on hedonistic terms) and salesmanship effort on part of business enterprises. The manufactured needs are not just for specific products but for maintaining particular lifestyles formed by a system of goods, services, and activities. Needs for maintaining lifestyles are manufactured as an organized element of production, and so is the need to desire more. Baudrillard ([1970] 1998) speaks of a *system of needs* within the larger *system of production.*

> Needs as a system are also radically different from enjoyment and satisfaction. They are produced as *system elements,* not as a *relationship of an individual to an object* (just as labour power no longer has anything to do with—and even denies—the worker's relation to the product of his labour, and just as exchange-value no longer has anything to do with concrete, personal exchange, or the commodity from with real goods, etc.). (Baudrillard [1970] 1998: 75).

Consequently, conceiving of endogenous preferences is not enough—the formulation of the economic process within which this is done is what matters.[8] Within the social provisioning framework the notion of "consumer sovereignty" has no meaning within the described formulation of the social provisioning process. In the *Economics of Imperfect Competition* Joan Robinson ([1933] 1969: xii) stated that consumer sovereignty would require a monopsony of consumers, and that cannot be conceived so long as the initiative lies with producers.[9] The notion of "consumer sovereignty" assumes that given "free markets" producers act in the interests of consumers—any other outcome is defined as "market failure"—where the workings of markets are specified without a notion of social surplus. In the social provisioning framework outlined here, satisfaction of consumption needs is an incidental by-product of the monetary production activity. There is no market mechanism that ensures that the consumption needs/wants of households who do not own means of production will be accommodated.

Routine and Discretionary Consumption Expenditures

Households' consumption baskets are comprised of routine and discretionary goods and services. The distinction between routine and discretionary expenditures does not parallel a distinction between some minimum/biological level of consumption and a level above what is necessary for the biological survival; positional and nonpositional goods; or instrumental and ceremonial needs.

Even when addressing biological needs, consumption is a way of reaffirming households' place within a specific group. Because there is a biological limit to consumption of food, for example, invidious distinction will be manifested not through quantity consumed, but by buying different types of food (for example, more vegetables), and furthermore by quality within a category (organically produced vegetables). Furthermore, the definition of discretionary income varies over time due to the evolution of the definition of what constitutes "primary needs." That is not to say that biology does not matter and that all primary needs are entirely socially constructed, but to emphasize that households' understanding of primary needs is evolving, and that the demarcation between discretionary and routine spending is not a biological one. Consequently, spending of discretionary income above some fixed "primary needs" is not an adequate way to define conspicuous consumption.

No consumption is outside a social context, and all goods and services have ceremonial attributes. In that context, Ann Mayhew's (2003) statement that "all consumption is conspicuous" is correct, since consumption patterns involve ceremonial attributes that are means to invidious distinction. All goods embody ceremonial and instrumental attributes, and ceremonial valuation is present at all levels of consumption. Instrumental attributes may or may not be selected over the ceremonial attributes. Products may be selected primarily for their ceremonial attributes, and may be seen as part of nondiscretionary expenditures.

Furthermore, the notions of "positional" and "nonpositional" are inadequate. If we look at lifestyles comprised by various categories of goods and activities, most of these will be positional—even products that are considered mundane. The higher the incomes the larger is the number of mundane products that can be identified as positional goods. It is more adequate then, to view nonpositional goods as exceptions, and as changing with income levels, which puts under question the positional/nonpositional distinction.

Goods and services demanded by households are specified in terms of a consumption basket that changes with income and the desirable socioeconomic status of households. Goods in the consumption basket are qualitatively distinct and separable, and there is very limited degree of substitutability between goods in different groups. Consequently, the principle of the *separability of needs* (Earl 1983; Lavoie 1994, 2004) can be extended to analyzing a particular product. The attributes of a good are separable into instrumental and ceremonial functions. However, individuals and households do not necessarily conceive of such a separation.

The principle of *subordination of needs* delineated by Lavoie (1994, 2004) also needs an extension. While there is a hierarchy of needs (Drakopoulos 1994), there is no necessity of an immediate perception on part of the households to recognize the consequences of purchasing goods mainly for their ceremonial attributes. Limiting factors such as budget constraint, credit lines, or bodies may not be taken into consideration, and adaptation may be slow. Even if households recognize that they have to give up a good/service that is being consumed for its ceremonial attributes, they may see this as devastating for their social status, and instead give up goods and services that fulfill instrumental functions.

The reason households may not recognize the separability and subordination of needs is not because they are irrational—but because habit adjustment is a process. "Adjustment involves tension—a stretch in the value structure" (Sturgeon 2010: 33). The ceremonial habits of thought ought to adjust, if they do not—the household would cease to exist as a going concern—which is the equivalent of an institution being unable to adapt. The ability to incur household debt allows for ceremonial habits to prevail longer and postpones compelling changes in consumption patterns. Access to credit has the capacity to alter the value structure of households and to enhance the demand for goods for their ceremonial attributes. However, because of biological (and ecological) limitations lack of such recognition is unsustainable, and cannot continue indefinitely. Households and communities are going concerns, and the individuals within them are living human beings ultimately subject to the principle of subordination of needs.

Furthermore, the presence of a hierarchy of needs does not mean that "primary goods," such as food and shelter, are not part of conspicuous consumption. The types of products (food and the activities related to its consumption—type of restaurants, ingredients, cooking, kitchen designs, houses and their locations) differentiate households. Goods (including those that satisfy "primary needs") serve as social symbols or "communication devices" (Duesenberry 1949). This communication may not be necessarily conscious at the moment of purchase or consumption, but nonetheless it is based on reasoning that is grounded in the prevailing habits of thought (Veblen 1899; Bourdieu 1984; Trigg 2001).

Conspicuous Consumption as a Process

I argue that conspicuous consumption is not a trivial and curious phenomenon, or "funny consumption" (Hamilton 1983: 794), but a process—part of the system of social provisioning and evolution of the culture. Social acceptability is a goal that is pursued in households' everyday life, and involves routine expenditures. A household has to plan routinely on maintaining a specific lifestyle by purchasing a particular consumption basket. In the process of maintaining a socioeconomic status and acceptability, conspicuous consumption becomes routine spending for households.

Roger Mason (1981: 28), who has provided a significant discussion of conspicuous consumption outside utility theory, states that "the ability of any person to consume for display will be directly related to the basic level of discretionary wealth which he commands—that is the wealth remaining after all 'primary' living costs have been met." Mason (1981: 31) correctly points out that conspicuous consumption requires first recognition that status is an important element of peoples' lives, which presupposes a broad cultural and economic environment that allows differentiation on the basis of significant variations in economic power. He rightly points out that the variations in economic power give rise to pecuniary emulation and conspicuous consumption that in turn reinforces and stabilizes these very variations. Yet, the notion of "the conspicuous consumer" (1981: 27) that Mason adopts relegates conspicuous consumption to a discrete category of individuals. When treated as part of discretionary spending performed by a "socially sensitive class of consumer" (Mason 1984: 26), conspicuous consumption is in effect reduced to *instances* of exceptional consumer behavior rather than a normal and structural process within capitalist relations. It is worth reading Mason's explanation of why the neoclassical analyses of consumer behavior leave out discussions of conspicuous consumption.

> There is no doubt that the classical general theories of consumer decision processes do not happily accommodate conspicuous consumption—a fact which cannot be considered surprising in view of the exceptional atypical nature of such behaviour. Whilst there is considerable recognition of the importance of the consumer's social psychological environment, status-directed consumption has been neglected primarily because of the necessity to accept two fundamental assumptions when developing a general theory—firstly, that while both rational (economic) and "irrational" (social) elements will both often influence particular purchase decisions, the rational element must be considered dominant; secondly, that product utility in use will be the consumer's prime consideration in product evaluation and purchase. These are necessary assumptions for a general theory of brand selection and purchase. The problem, however, is that the resultant theoretical models will tend to understate or even ignore so-called irrational consumer behaviour. And as conspicuous consumption is predominantly "social" in its motivation and expression it has consequently received little attention within general theory. (Mason 1984: 31)

Disinterest in "irrational" behavior is not at the heart of the problem. The inadequate treatment of conspicuous consumption is not because of its exceptional character, but because it is in fact a normal process of the capitalist economy. Conspicuous consumption is ignored or trivialized and neutralized just like the nature of production, money, or prices. The social nature of consumption can be described in various ways, including by obfuscating real capitalist relations. The starting point of inquiry should be the workings of the capitalist system itself.

Conspicuous consumption is a particular method of invidious distinction that is routinely practiced in different manner across various income, social groups, and regions, involving a variety of goods and consumption activities. Through their patterns of consumption households engage in attaining and maintaining particular lifestyles based on various organizing principles—*habitus* that are based on social class (Bourdieu 1984; Tomlinson and Warde 1993; Fine, Heasman, and Wright 1996). For the purpose they rely on reference groups (Bearden and Etzel 1982; Mason 1981: 25; Eichner 1985: 160). Reference groups, household consumption patterns, and needs are informed by specific *habits of thought* that embody particular "canons of decency" (Veblen

1899). For example, gender is a habit of thought that encompasses proper male and female activities. Generational relations are also habits of thought that embody proper consumption patterns. For example, the expectation to leave the parents' dwelling at a certain age, or independent elderly living rather than co-habiting with off-spring, have evolved as a result of economic changes and affect the consumption basket of households.

Veblen's "canons of decency" are influenced, created, or exaggerated by the marketing and product development activities of business enterprises, as well as by the state's public policy and taxation. There is a synergy between the functioning of the capitalist economy and the fear of deviation from these canons. As Charusheela (2010: 1153–1154) points out, consumption spending occurs as part of people's efforts to meet ideals of a good provider, a good parent, a properly raised child, or adult who shows appropriate race, class, or ethnic markers. The canons of social acceptability generate not only stability in consumption but also the persistence of the capitalist system. By stabilizing household forms, consumption stabilizes both the unit of decision making and the patterns of spending in predictable directions.

Consequently, households' consumption activities are manifestations of the normalization of the prevalent habits of thought, as well as of invidious distinction. Consumption as an evidence of wealth is viewed by Veblen (1899: 69) as "an adaptation to a new end, by a selective process, of a distinction previously existing and well established in men's habits of thought." In Veblen's analysis instinctual drives of human behavior based on biological factors have historically adapted from striving for existence in subsistence societies to striving for status in "predatory cultures," one of which is the pecuniary culture of capitalism. The process of pecuniary emulation permeates all levels of income and wealth, and the goods and services that are part of conspicuous consumption vary across these levels.

> No class of society, not even the most abjectly poor, forgoes all customary conspicuous consumption. The last items of this category of consumption are not given up except under stress of the direst necessity. Very much of squalor and discomfort will be endured before the last trinket or the last pretense of pecuniary decency is put away. There is no class and no

> country that has yielded so abjectly before the pressure of physical want as to deny themselves all gratification of this higher or spiritual need. (Veblen, 1899: 53)

While maintaining their position within a group, households are engaging in routine conspicuous consumption spending and activities. Households use their discretionary income to occasionally purchase goods and services that are routine for higher income groups. Consequently, a distinction can be made between conspicuous consumption as routine expenditure, and as a part of discretionary expenditure. The benefit of such a distinction is to account for: 1) the conspicuous nature of everyday consumption activities that symbolize belonging to a group; and 2) the conspicuous emulation of higher income life-style through occasional purchases as discretionary expenditures.

The establishment of status within a higher income group always entails discretionary income and spending on conspicuous consumption of goods that are higher priced than those that are routinely consumed. Once income (or a credit line) is sufficient and on a more permanent basis those eventually transform into routine expenditures, comprising conspicuous consumption—but one that symbolizes the belonging to a particular group. Aspirations to attain and maintain particular life-styles represent efforts of distinction that are part of everyday lives and routines. Exclusive life-styles preserve ceremonial/pecuniary valuation methods by passing them to the next generations, and by serving as a reference point of emulation. For that reason it is important to see the routine nature of conspicuous consumption. The formation of consumption patterns does not pertain only to the individual but to habit formation.

Maintaining distinctive life-styles involves habit formation. Habit is not simply repetition, nor can it be characterized merely as a "rule of thumb." The *principle of procedural rationality* that is applied in heterodox analysis of consumer choice (Lavoie 2004) can be enriched by the concept of habit. Procedural rationality asserts that agents have designed rules and procedures that allow them to reach decisions quickly and efficiently, despite imperfect knowledge and an overload of information. The "rules and procedures" are habits that adapt in order to deal with changing circumstances and a problem in the context of the whole system of social provisioning. With respect to consumption, habit formation involves adaptation to income growth and transformation of discretionary expenditures into routine expenditures. The available income and the sets of goods and services are a function of the class structure that determines the generation and distribution of the social surplus. To treat conspicuous consumption as a *process* means that distinction and emulation are: 1) part of the social provisioning process—they are systemically connected to the production and distribution of social surplus; and 2) distinction and emulation are habits rather than exceptional phenomena.

Conclusion

Analytical categories emerge, vanish, change meaning, and may become trivialized within specific economic frameworks. A concept cannot be transplanted into a framework based on qualitatively different definition of economics (that is, as allocation of scarce resources) and conceptualization of how economic activity is organized (that is, by "the price mechanism"), while preserving its full meaning and original analytical importance. Uprooting the term of conspicuous consumption and planting it in any theoretical framework inevitably distorts the concept and makes it theoretically unimportant.

The concept of conspicuous consumption has been so readily uprooted from analysis of capitalism through the method of stripping it from its routine nature. Describing conspicuous consumption as an exceptional behavior and as part of discretionary spending obfuscates its stabilizing place in the capitalist economy. Examining routines necessarily involves discussion of habit formation, which prompts the articulation of a specific social structure. On the other hand, conceptualizing of conspicuous consumption independently of distribution and the class structure of the economy is enabled by its definition as an exceptional behavior. Conspicuous consumption develops as a part of habit formation within power relations. It is a process that preserves and enhances these relations. Within the delineated social provisioning framework the starting point of analysis of conspicuous consumption is the logic of production and distribution within a culture of invidious distinction, rather than the individual consumer choice.

Pecuniary emulation is an intrinsic element of capitalism. Accumulation generates distinction and a hierarchy of reference points of emulation. Furthermore, the consumption-based distinction among the working class disarticulates their class position in the production and distribution of the social surplus. The process of conspicuous consumption enables that disarticulation. Workers routinely engage in conspicuous consumption seeking social distancing and belonging by articulating social groups for the purpose of invidious distinction. The resulting segmentation, however, could not transcend the actual class position of workers as the "common man" in the production and distribution of the social surplus.

What distinguishes broadly mainstream vs. heterodox economists is their very different and incompatible articulation of social structures and the nature of provisioning. Consequently, analysis of conspicuous consumption is very different within these two broad paradigms, but that difference can be articulated only when the routine nature of conspicuous consumption is acknowledged. Only then we can see the connection of conspicuous consumption to the rest of socioeconomic process. The implication of this argument is that the starting point for heterodox analysis of conspicuous consumption need *not* be a theory of consumer choice that is formulated in a mirror image of mainstream theory, but the capitalist system itself.

Notes

1. For example, see Leibenstein's (1950) famous formulation of "Veblen, snob, and bandwagon effects" and Frank's (1985) discussion of "positional goods," both based on a marginalist framework where utility functions give the structure of individuals' motivation. Other formulations include equilibrium signaling relation between price and utility derived through status (Bagwell and Bernheim 1996).

2. Heterodox economics has intellectual roots in traditions that emphasize the wealth of nations, accumulation, full employment, social relationships, and economic and social reproduction These elements are emphasized to a different degree in the various traditions (hence the potential benefits of collaboration across heterodox approaches).

3. For analysis of intergenerational and short-term income mobility in the USA, see Tom Hertz. (2006). Understanding Mobility in America. Center for American Progress, available at: http://www.americanprogress.org/issues/

2006/04/b1579981.html. Also see The State of Working America, Mobility, Economic Policy Institute, available at: http://stateofworkingamerica.org/subjects/mobility/.

4. See Abramovitz (1996), Rose (2000), and Mink (2002) on scapegoating single poor women and welfare reform in the United States.

5. Andler (1984).

6. See Florida (2005) and Bourdieu (1984).

7. The notion of class is empirically grounded. See Assena and Wolf (2004) for distribution of wealth in the USA; Wolf (2007) for wealth inequality and rising U.S. household debt; Ajit Zacharias, Wolf, and Masterson (2009) on estimates of income inequality; and Allegretto (2011) on widening wealth gap.

8. Conceptualization of endogenous preferences is not a real break with mainstream theory as long as economic activity is defined as individualist exchange. Incorporating endogenous preferences need not break with the market price adjustment framework and utilitarian value theory. Analysis based on utility theory of value constructs symmetry between production and demand, thus escaping the conceptualization of class (Bharadwaj 1986). The conceptual symmetry between production and demand allows for the construction of "consumer surplus" and "producer surplus" as categories in place of "social surplus."

9. Another way to look at this is that monopoly and oligopoly are the norm of the described social provisioning process.

References

Abramovitz, M. (1996). *Regulating the Lives of Women: Social Welfare Policy from Colonial Times to the Present.* Boston: South End Press.

Allegretto, S. (2011). "The State of Working America's Wealth, 2011." *Economic Policy Institute*, Briefing Paper # 292. http://www.epi.org/publication/the_state_of_working_americas_wealth_2011/

Andler, J. (1984). "The Year of the Yuppie." *Newsweek* December 31: 14–34.

Bagwell, L. S., and B. D. Bernheim. (1996). "Veblen Effects in a Theory of Conspicuous Consumption." *American Economic Review* 86(3): 349–373.

Baudrillard, J. ([1970] 1998). *The Consumer Society: Myths and Structures.* London: Sage.

Bearden, W., and M. Etzel. (1982). "Reference Group Influence on Product and Brand Purchase Decisions." *Journal of Consumer Research* 9(September): 183–194.

Bharadwaj, K. (1986). *Classical Political Economy and the Rise to Dominance of Supply and Demand Theories.* Calcutta: Universities Press.

Bourdieu, P. (1984). *Distinction: A Social Critique of the Judgment of Taste.* London: Routledge.

Brown, C. (2008). *Inequality, Consumer Credit, and the Savings Puzzle.* Cheltenham: Edward Elgar.

Charusheela, S. (2010). "Gender and the Stability of Consumption: A Feminist Contribution to Post-Keynesian Economics." *Cambridge Journal of Economics* 34(6): 1145–1156.

Drakopoulos, S. (1994). "Hierarchical Choice in Economics." *Journal of Economic Surveys* 8(2): 133–153.

Duesenberry, J. (1949). *Income, Saving, and the Theory of Consumer Behavior.* Cambridge: Harvard University Press.

Dugger, W. M. (1996). "Redefining Economics: From Market Allocation to Social Provisioning." In *Political Economy for the 21st Century: Contemporary Views on the Trend of Economics.* Ed. C. J. Whalen, pp. 31–43. Armonk, NY: M.E. Sharpe.

Earl, P. (1983). *The Economic Imagination: Towards a Behavioural Analysis of Choice.* Armonk: M.E. Sharpe.

Eichner, A. (1985). *Toward a New Economics: Essays in Post-Keynesian and Institutionalist Theory.* Armonk: M.E. Sharpe.

Fine, B. (2002). *The World of Consumption: The Material and Cultural Revisited.* London: Routledge.

Fine, B., M. Heasman, and J. Wright. (1996). *Consumption in the Age of Affluence: The World of Food.* London: Routledge.

Florida, R. (2005). *The Rise of the Creative Class.* New York: Perseus Book Group.

Frank, R. (1985). "The Demand for Unobservable and Other Nonpositional Goods." *American Economic Review* 75(1): 101–106.

Galbraith, J. K. (1958). *The Affluent Society.* Bombay: Asia Publishing House.

Gruchy, A. (1987). *The Reconstruction of Economics: An Analysis of the Fundamentals of Institutional Economics.* New York: Greenwood Press.

Hamilton, D. (1983). "Review of Roger S. Mason: 'Conspicuous Consumption: A Study of Exceptional Consumer Behavior'." *Journal of Economic Issues* 17(3): 791–796.

——. (1987). "Institutional Economics and Consumption." *Journal of Economic Issues* 21(4): 1531–1554.

——. (1989). "Thorstein Veblen as the First Professor of Marketing Science." *Journal of Economic Issues* 23(4): 1097–1104.

Hertz, T. (2006). "Understanding Mobility in America." Center for American Progress, http://www.americanprogress.org/issues/2006/04/b1579981.html, accessed 01/05/2012.

Jo, T.- H. (2011). "Social Provisioning Process and Socio-Economic Modeling." *American Journal of Economics and Sociology* 70(5): 1094–1116.

Lavoie, M. (1994). "A Post Keynesian Approach to Consumer Choice." *Journal of Post Keynesian Economics* 16(4): 539–562.

——. (2004). "Post-Keynesian Consumer Theory: Potential Synergies with Consumer Research and Economic Psychology." *Journal of Economic Psychology* 25(5): 639–649.

Lee, F. (2010). "Alfred Eichner's Missing 'Complete Model': A Heterodox Micro-Macro Model of a Monetary Production Economy." In *Money and Macrodynamics: Alfred Eichner and Post-Keynesian Economics.* Eds. M. Lavoie, L.-P. Rochon, and M. Seccareccia, pp. 22–42, Armonk: M.E. Sharpe.

——. (2011). "Modeling the Economy as a Whole: An Integrative Approach." *American Journal of Economics and Sociology* 70(5): 1282–1314.

Leibenstein, H. (1950). "Bandwagon, Snob, and Veblen Effects in the Theory of Consumers' Demand." *Quarterly Journal of Economics* 64(2): 183–207.

Mason, R. (1981). *Conspicuous Consumption—A Study of Exceptional Consumer Behavior.* New York: St. Martin's Press.

——. (1984). "Conspicuous Consumption: A Literature Review." *European Journal of Marketing* 18(3): 26–39.

Marx, K. ([1859] 1973). *Grundrisse: Foundations of the Critique of Political Economy.* New York: Vintage Press.

Mayhew, A. (2003). "All Consumption is Conspicuous." In *Intersubjectivity in Economics.* Ed. E. Fullbrook, pp. 43–55. New York: Routledge.

Mink, G. (2002). "Violating Women: Rights Abuses in the Welfare Police State." In *Lost Ground: Welfare Reform, Poverty and Beyond.* Eds. R. Albelda and A. Withorn. Cambridge: South End Press.

Nelson, J. (1993). "The Study of Choice or the Study of Provisioning? Gender and the Definition of Economics." In *Beyond Economic Man: Feminist Theory and Economics.* Eds. F. Marianne and J. Nelson, pp. 23–37. Chicago: University of Chicago Press.

Parenteau, R. (2006). "U.S. Household Deficit Spending: A Randezvous with Reality." *Levy Economics Institute,* Public Policy Brief # 88. www.levy.org

Power, M. (2004). "Social Provisioning as a Starting Point for Feminist Economics." *Feminist Economics* 10(3): 3–21.

Robinson, J. ([1933] 1969). *The Economics of Imperfect Competition.* London: Macmillan.

Rose, N. (2000). "Scapegoating Poor Women." *Journal of Economic Issues* 34(1): 143–157.

Sturgeon, J. (2010). "Explorations in Institutional Economics: The Kansas City Approach." Evolutionary Social Theory Workgroup Working Papers, http://cas.umkc.edu/econ/_researchcommunity/EVOworkgroup/, (accessed 5 April, 2012).

Sullivan, T., E. Warren, and J. Westbrook. (2000). *The Fragile Middle Class: Americans in Debt.* New Haven: Yale University Press.

Todorova, Z. (2009). *Money and Households in a Capitalist Economy: A Gendered Post Keynesian—Institutional Analysis.* Northampton: Edward Elgar.

Tomlinson, M., and A. Warde. (1993). "Social Class and Change in Eating Habits." *British Food Journal* 95(1): 3–10.

Trigg, A. (2001). "Veblen, Bourdieu, and Conspicuous Consumption." *Journal of Economic Issues* 35(1): 99–115.

Veblen, T. ([1899] 1994). *The Theory of the Leisure Class.* New York: Dover Publications Inc.

——. ([1919] 2005). *The Vested Interests and the Common Man.* New York: Cosimo Classics.

——. (1921). *The Engineers and the Price System.* Kitchener, Ontario, Canada: Batoche Books.

——. (1923). *The Absentee Ownership and Business Enterprise in Recent Times: The Case of America.* New York: Huebsch.

Wolf, E. (2007). "Recent Trends in Household Wealth in the United States: Rising Debt and the Middle-Class Squeeze." *Levy Economics Institute*, Working Paper # 502, www.levy.org

Zacharias, A., E. Wolf, and T. Masterson. (2009). "New Estimates of Economic Inequality in America, 1959–2004." *Levy Economics Institute*, LIMEW Report, April, www.levy.org.

Classical Surplus Theory and Heterodox Economics

By Nuno Ornelas Martins*

Abstract. It has recently been suggested that heterodox economics can benefit from an engagement with classical surplus theory. However, caution is often recommended due to the ideological concepts that are embedded in classical political economy. This article argues that many of the ideological concepts that are often attributed to classical political economy are actually not part of classical political economy, but rather of a "vulgar" form of political economy, a project that emerged after Ricardo. This vulgar project, often termed as "Ricardian economics," is often mistakenly taken to be a development of classical political economy, but it is actually a rupture with the classical political economy of Petty, Smith, and Ricardo, as Marx, and later Sraffa, argued. Once this is acknowledged, the relationship between classical political economy and heterodox economics becomes clearer.

Introduction

Heterodox economics comprises various traditions that have emerged as a group of interconnected perspectives through their opposition to neoclassical economics (Lee 2009). However, the coherence of these perspectives still raises many issues. Frederic Lee and Tae-Hee Jo

*Centro de Estudos em Gestão e Economia and University of the Azores, Rua Capitão João D'Ávila, 9700-042, Angra do Heroísmo, Portugal. E-mail: nmartins@uac.pt.

For most helpful comments on an earlier draft the author is most thankful to Jorge Bateira, Luís Francisco Carvalho, William Davies, John Davis, Gary Dymski, Sheila Dow, Joaquim Feio, Geoffrey Harcourt, Stuart Holland, Tony Lawson, Vítor Neves, the participants of the Coimbra Conference on the Revival of Political Economy 2010, and the editor and anonymous referees of the *American Journal of Economics and Sociology*. The author is also most grateful to Pierangelo Garegnani, literary executor of Piero Sraffa's papers and correspondence, for permission to quote from Sraffa's unpublished papers, and to Jonathan Smith for his help when going through Sraffa's unpublished papers. The references to Sraffa's unpublished writings are those in the catalogue prepared by Jonathan Smith, archivist, at the Wren Library, Trinity College, Cambridge.

American Journal of Economics and Sociology, Vol. 72, No. 5 (November, 2013).
DOI: 10.1111/ajes.12045

(2011) have argued that since the notions of social product and social surplus are a key organizing concept of heterodox economics, fruitful interaction may emerge between heterodox economics and the surplus approach of classical political economists and Sraffian economics, a topic further developed by Lee (2011).

Nevertheless, Lee and Jo (2011) note that while Sraffians prefer to look back at classical political economy (henceforth, CPE), the ideological concepts embedded in it, such as competition and a uniform rate of profit, recommend that heterodox economics use the CPE framework selectively, while combining it with the developments brought by Wassily Leontief and John Maynard Keynes. Lee and Jo (2011) further argue that it is misleading to believe that there is only one surplus approach, namely, the Sraffian one.

I will argue that, as Lee and Jo (2011) suggest, the notion of the surplus can be used as a unifying concept that could contribute to the development of a coherent heterodox framework. I will also argue that many of the ideological elements often attributed to CPE are a result of the juxtaposition of two different approaches that Sraffa, following Marx, clearly distinguishes, namely, "classical" political economy and "vulgar" political economy. Sraffa's unpublished writings show how the CPE of Petty, Smith, and Ricardo, when properly understood, was a step towards Marx and what is now termed heterodox economics, whereas Say, Malthus, and John Stuart Mill were a step towards marginalism and the neoclassical approach. Many of the ideological concepts attributed to CPE are not a characteristic of it, but rather of vulgar political economy, an approach that emerged *after* CPE, which is often conflated with it.

Concerning the relation between heterodox economics and Sraffian economics, Lee and Jo (2011) also note that Sraffians take the level and the composition of the social surplus as given, which leads to the neglect of the concept of agency, a central topic in heterodox economics. Agency requires a dynamic analysis which is absent in the Sraffian scheme. In this regard, I will argue that CPE already contained the essential elements for a theory of agency, which, however, remained underdeveloped.

Vivian Walsh (2000, 2003, 2008) and Hilary Putnam (2002) argue that while Sraffa was concerned with a revival of CPE's basic analytical structure, the contribution of Amartya Sen (1987, 1999) constitutes a revival of CPE's rich philosophical anthropology of authors from Smith to Marx. In this sense, the contributions of Sraffa and Sen are complementary. I will argue that this is true not only concerning the contribution of Sen, but also heterodox economists, who maintained a conception of the human agent, and of human well-being, much closer to the one of classical political economists than to that of neoclassical economists.

Classical Political Economy and the Surplus Approach

Alfred Marshall (1890) argued that his contribution was an attempt to make marginalist theory compatible with CPE, leading to an approach that was thus termed as neo*classical* by Thorstein Veblen (1900), in order to distinguish it (and others) from the approach of Carl Menger (which inspired Austrian economics). Marshall claimed that his approach was in continuity with the CPE of Smith, Ricardo, and Mill.

Piero Sraffa, however, believed that Marshall was not in continuity with CPE. As Pierangelo Garegnani (2005) argues, according to the view Sraffa developed after 1927, there are two fundamental theories of value. According to the first perspective, which became more prominent with authors like Petty, Smith, and Ricardo, there is an objective conception of value, where value depends upon the conditions of production that will determine the natural price. This is the framework that underlies CPE.

Writing within this tradition, Smith defines effectual demand as the demand of those who are willing to pay the natural price, and thus effectual demand is not an independent concept from that of the natural price because it emerges after natural prices are formed by the conditions of production. Thus, conditions of production determine the natural price, which in turn is a determinant of effectual demand. Sraffa's (1960) contribution can be seen as a revival of this perspective, that is, of CPE, as Ronald Meek (1961) argued. Sraffa considered Marx's theory of the prices of production as the more elaborated development of this perspective.

The second perspective on value underpins neoclassical economics and has become the dominant perspective after the marginalist revolution. In it, prices are not explained in terms of costs of production (where the conditions of production determine natural prices, which in turn determine effectual demand), but rather, prices and quantities are determined mutually, by supply and demand—two independent factors. Thus, instead of having natural prices (formed by the conditions of production) as a determinant of effectual demand, demand is seen as an independent factor that, with supply, determines prices and quantities.

For Smith and Ricardo, however, the terms "supply" and "demand" denote the forces that drive the market price away from the natural price, and not a systematic explanation of prices and quantities, as in neoclassical economics:

> [I]n classical theory, demand ("effectual demand") and supply ("quantity brought to market") were only introduced to explain the tendency of a commodity's actual price—or "market price" as the classical economists called it—towards a normal or "natural" level which was itself determined without reference to such a demand and supply. Thus, "effectual demand" was defined by Smith as "the demand of those who are willing to pay the natural price of the commodity" with the "natural" or normal price being therefore a necessary datum for defining that "demand" itself. In fact Smith's "effectual demand" could only be described as a *point*, and not a *schedule*, in the price-quantity space. (Garegnani 1998: 417, emphasis in original).

This does not mean that there was no attempt to understand value in terms of a supply and demand analysis before the marginalist revolution. In his unpublished manuscripts, Sraffa (D3/12/4/10) distinguishes between the "classical" political economists and the "vulgar" political economists. While "classical" political economists developed a theory of the surplus, and of how it is divided between wages, profits, and rent, the "vulgar" political economists were already heading towards the supply and demand analysis that would be developed by Marshall after the marginalist revolution.

Sraffa (D3/12/4/10) considers CPE to be the period from Petty to Ricardo, while vulgar political economy is the period from Malthus to John Stuart Mill. For Sraffa, vulgar political economy was a period dominated by Mill. Sraffa writes about that period: "Marx stands here towering as the last of the classical amongst the vulgar, just as Smith stood isolated among the classical, being the first of the vulgars" (Sraffa D3/12/4/10).

Sraffa (D3/12/4/10) defined "economics" as the stage that came after "vulgar political economy," with the marginalist revolution, and characterized it as "the age of Marshall." But Sraffa saw all these three stages, of "classical political economy," "vulgar political economy," and "economics," as being influenced by Smith. Sraffa (D3/12/4/10) wrote that "A. Smith had stronger 'vulgar' tendencies" and so is "[t]ruly the father of modern economics," who had a significant influence in "Classical Political Economy (Age of Ricardo)," in "Vulgar Political Economy (the age of Mill)," and in "Economics (the age of Marshall)."

The distinction between CPE and vulgar political economy that Sraffa drew is similar to the one we find in a footnote of Marx's *Capital*, where Marx writes:

> Once and for all I may here state, that by classical Political Economy, I understand that economy which, since the time of W. Petty, has investigated the real relations of production in bourgeois society, in contradistinction to vulgar economy, which deals with appearances only, ruminates without ceasing on the materials long since provided by scientific economy, and there seeks plausible explanations of the most obtrusive phenomena, for bourgeois daily use, but for the rest, confines itself to systematising in a pedantic way, and proclaiming for everlasting truths, the trite ideas held by the self-complacent bourgeoisie with regard to their own world, to them the best of all possible worlds. (Marx 1999: 493)

Therefore, according to Marx, as well as Sraffa, we must not see Petty, Smith, Say, Ricardo, Malthus, and Mill as being all engaged in a similar project. Rather, Petty, Smith, and Ricardo developed a surplus approach that ultimately led to Marx's analysis, while Say, Malthus, and Mill (following nevertheless some of Smith's "vulgar tendencies") were the precursors of marginalism and of supply and demand analysis.

The Theory of Value, Theory of Agency, and Theory of Human Well-Being

According to Marx, Smith wrote in a way that rendered his contribution easily accommodated within both versions of political economy (the "classical" version and the "vulgar" version), hence Marx's distinction between the *exoteric* aspects of Smith's writings, which anticipated "vulgar" political economy, and the *esoteric* aspects, which contain the scientific insights of "classical" political economy. We can briefly summarize the differences, between "classical" political economy and "vulgar" political economy, in terms of their theory of value, theory of human agency, and theory of human well-being.

As explained above, in terms of the theory of value, the key difference was that, for CPE, value depends upon the conditions of production (and thus prices converge towards the cost of production, measured in terms of labor), while vulgar political economy was already heading towards a perspective in which value is determined by the interaction between supply and demand, which was only fully achieved later, in neoclassical economics.

Ricardo systematized the classical doctrine, arguing that an increase in production can always offset increases in demand, and thus value will be governed by the conditions of production, unless in exceptional cases such as scarce goods (for example, artistic objects), in which case demand will also play a role. But after Ricardo, vulgar political economy started to see value as *always* being determined by the interaction between demand and supply, even by many who claimed to be followers of Ricardo.

In terms of the theory of agency, for CPE, human action presupposes an existing social structure that is constituted by social classes. Vulgar political economy, on the other hand, adopts methodological individualism, where society can be totally explained in terms of the interaction of self-interested individuals, who make up society through a social contract. While for classical political economists the human individual is already a *social* being, in vulgar political economy the starting point is the *isolated* individual.

In terms of the theory of human well-being, for CPE, there is a multidimensional conception of well-being, where the latter depends upon several activities and the achievements of human beings in various dimensions. This conception appears more clearly in the writings of Smith and Marx. In vulgar political economy, on the other hand, well-being is a one-dimensional notion that is measured in terms of the subjective pleasure, or utility, which is acquired through any activity.

This means that for vulgar political economy, the well-being generated by any activity can be reduced to a common unit, namely, pleasure, or utility, as Jeremy Bentham argued, while for CPE this reduction of various dimensions to a common unit does not occur. Marx's critique of Bentham's reduction of well-being to a unidimensional subjective measure highlights that different activities cannot be adequately compared in a multidimensional conception of well-being.

These different conceptions at the level of the theory of value, theory of agency, and theory of well-being spring essentially from the fact that CPE was grounded in an objective analysis (a point stressed from the beginning by Petty), while vulgar political economy was grounded in a subjective analysis. Thus, for the classical theory of value, value was determined by the objective conditions of production. But for vulgar economic theory, value also depended on demand, and thus on the subjective preferences that shape demand.

In fact, it was the emphasis on subjectivism that led vulgar political economists to take subjective self-interest as the starting point of their theory of agency, and subjective well-being as the starting point of their theory of well-being. For CPE, on the other hand, the starting point for the theory of agency is not the subjective self-interest of the isolated individual, but rather the social classes that have an objective existence. And for CPE, human well-being depends on objective human achievements in various objective activities, rather than subjective preferences.

This does not mean that subjective elements are not taken into account in CPE. In fact, subjective elements always manifest themselves in objective entities. The point to note is that the starting point of CPE consists in these objective entities, and it is from this objective analysis that inferences about subjective aspects can be made. In vulgar political economy, however, subjective elements can also be a starting point of the analysis.

The Marginalist Revolution as a Reaction Against Marx and Classical Political Economy

Subjective preferences came to occupy center stage in economic analysis, and became the starting point for understanding value, with the marginalist revolution, which was brought by Stanley Jevons, Carl Menger, and Léon Walras. As noted above, the move towards a subjectivist economics was already under way with the "vulgar" movement that emerged after Ricardo. But it is only with the marginalist revolution that we begin to find a conscious break with the classical tradition. If vulgar political economists still attempted to find in Smith and Ricardo the sources of their inspiration, the marginalists will explicitly acknowledge a rupture with CPE.

The marginalists focused on exchange between individuals in a competitive market, driven by preferences that were never totally satisfied by scarce resources. In this sense, economic activity was no longer seen as the reproduction of a surplus produced by labor, as in CPE, but as the optimization of individual utility in the context of scarce resources.

The marginalists argued that the source of value is (subjective) marginal utility (not labor as was the case for the classical political economists), which can only be found through exchange in a competitive market. Because the emphasis of the marginalists was on the exchange of a finite set of existing goods, rather than on the *production* of these goods (which, for Ricardo, could be extended), economists started to focus on the inevitability of *scarcity* of existing goods, rather than on the distribution of the *surplus* generated in production. There was a switch from a surplus theory towards a scarcity theory.

While the "vulgar" movement still hesitated between the subjective tendency and the objective analysis of CPE, with the marginalists we find no hesitation, but rather a bold movement towards the subjective camp. John Stuart Mill, who was the central author of what Marx called "vulgar" political economy, claimed to be doing no more than updating Smith's insights in a new century, and was hesitant about the key (economic, social, and ethical) issues dividing "classical" and "vulgar" political economy.

Thus, Mill hesitated about the source of value, debated whether the self-interested individual is the best starting point of analysis, and tried to make utilitarianism compatible with a multidimensional (and indeed classical) conception of well-being by distinguishing between different kinds of pleasure (unlike Bentham). With marginalism, however, we have a definite break with the classical tradition, and none of Mill's hesitations.

According to Sraffa, the marginalist revolution was a reaction *against* Marx, and in particular against the way he developed CPE. Thus, Garegnani (2005: 457) notes that Sraffa saw the " 'immediate and simultaneous success' of the utility-based theory of value of Jevons, Menger and Walras" as a response to Marx, who saw clearly how "Classical P[olitical] E[economy], with its surplus to be arbitrarily divided leads straight to Socialism" (Sraffa as cited in Garegnani 2005: 489).

Effectively, Sraffa summarizes the main failings of marginalism in the following way:

> When reduced to its simplest elements, the errors of the "marginal" theory of distribution consists in saying that the "shares" (i.e. level of wages and profits) depends [sic] upon, is governed by, the methods of production (including proportions of factors). Whereas the opposite is the case, the methods adopted <u>depend upon</u> the shares. (Sraffa D3/12/42/26)

That is, while in marginalism the distribution between wages and profits is determined by the marginal productivity of labor and capital, which is in turn determined by the methods of production, Sraffa argued the opposite, namely, that the distribution between wages and profits is the exogenous variable, which will in turn determine the methods of production.

The Relation Between Distribution and the Mode of Production

Unlike John Stuart Mill (1848), Sraffa did not argue that production and distribution are independent. Marx criticized John Stuart Mill's claims that production is essentially determined by technology, and that distribution is essentially determined by social institutions. Marx noted that socialism cannot be confined to the realm of distribution (as implied in the "vulgar" socialism of John Stuart Mill), since distribution is connected to production, in the sense that the social class that each person will occupy (and the corresponding share of the surplus) will depend upon the role played by this person in the mode of production.

Sraffa's point is simply that distribution, whatever its ultimate cause is, will affect the cost of each method of production, and the choice of techniques. We may want to separate distribution from production, as John Stuart Mill did, or we may want to go further, like Marx, and see how the institutional arrangements that cause distribution were in turn caused by the mode of production and the class structure it generates. But these are issues that Sraffa did not discuss because he was addressing only the technical relation between production and distribution, and not its institutional features. Sraffa simply noted that, in technical terms, it is not the marginal productivity that causes distribution, but rather distribution that leads to a given method of production.

And if production causes distribution in some sense, it is because of institutional factors, and not because of technical factors such as the mathematical marginal productivity of the factors of production. Marx argued that production influences distribution because the mode of production leads to a given class structure that generates a given institutional arrangement for distribution. For Marx, the relation of production to distribution is mediated by social institutions, rather than being merely technical, as in neoclassical economics, or being simply neglected, as was the case for John Stuart Mill.

Sraffa's point is that if we neglect the way in which production affects the class structure, and focus on the technical relation, as neoclassical economists do, then the causal relation is from distribution to production, not the opposite. In this sense, there is no incompatibility between Sraffa's technical analysis of the way in which distribution influences production and Marx's institutional analysis of the way in which production influences distribution.

Furthermore, Sraffa shows how to explain value in terms of labor, and saw Marx as the author who developed the political consequences of this classical theory of value and distribution. Marginalism, in this context, is seen by Sraffa as a reaction to Marx, and an attempt to argue that distribution is not determined by the class structure, but rather by laws of marginal productivity of capital and labor.

Thus, if Lee and Jo (2011) recommend a selective use of CPE given the ideological concepts embedded in it, the distinction between "classical" political economy and "vulgar" political economy that Sraffa does, following Marx, may provide guidance to such a selection. The idea that from a technical point of view, the distribution of the surplus is a cause, rather than a consequence, of the methods of production is an example of a far-reaching idea.

Lee and Jo (2011) argue that by taking the level and the composition of the social surplus as given, Sraffians neglect the topic of agency, a central topic to heterodox economics. On the topic of agency, we find Sraffa defending a view that is opposed to neoclassical economics. While the latter came to portray the human agent as an optimizer responding to subjective preferences, Sraffa stressed that human beings are creatures of habits:

> man learns from experience, or at any rate is changed by it, forms and transforms habits, etc (This is recognized by Marshall . . . but he does not draw the inevitable conclusion that what he draws are historical, not equilibrium, diagrams). (Sraffa D3/12/42/11)

If Marshall did recognize the complexity of the human agent, the neoclassical tradition he left for us came to forget it altogether.

The Cambridge Economic Tradition

Marshall's contribution led to the emergence of what has been termed the Cambridge economic tradition, which was shaped by Marshall's neoclassical approach, and was continued by Arthur Cecil Pigou (1912, 1920)—see Geoffrey Harcourt (2003). Henry Sidgwick (1883), who had a significant influence on Marshall, is also a central figure at the beginning of the Cambridge economics tradition, the methodology of which was systematized by John Neville Keynes. However, the neoclassical orthodoxy in Cambridge soon came to be challenged not only by Sraffa, but also by John Maynard Keynes (1936), leading to significant developments within the Cambridge tradition.

Keynes (1936) criticized the Marshallian theory, which, unlike Sraffa, Keynes considered to be a continuation of the Ricardian classical framework, and not of Malthus's theory. Hence, Keynes argues that he is criticizing classical theory, since he considers Marshall to be essentially continuing the classical Ricardian tradition. Here, Keynes, like Marshall, failed to distinguish between CPE and vulgar political economy, while juxtaposing both, and designating them as "classical theory." Keynes (1936) rejected Marshall's framework and initiated the Cambridge Keynesian tradition (Pasinetti 2005; Harcourt 2006; Harcourt and Kerr 2003; Davidson 2007).

With Keynes's critique of the Marshallian neoclassical framework, and the subsequent emergence of the Cambridge Keynesian tradition, the Cambridge economics tradition, founded by Marshall, became divided into two branches: the Cambridge "welfare" tradition, with Pigou's (1912, 1920) continuation of the Marshallian tradition; and the Cambridge Keynesian tradition (Geoffrey Harcourt 2003).

Keynes (1936), like Richard Kahn (1931), argued that the impact of investment on output is mediated by the investment multiplier. Keynes (1936) also argued that the effect of the investment multiplier depends on the level of income inequality, which affects the marginal propensities to save and to consume, which in turn determine the investment multiplier. Other economists of the Cambridge Keynesian tradition, like Michal Kalecki, Joan Robinson, and Nicholas Kaldor, explained the effects of inequality in terms of the division of the surplus between wages and profits, and connected that analysis to the investment multiplier and the level of output.

There were, of course, differences between the various authors of the Cambridge Keynesian tradition. For example, while Sraffa was concerned with the distribution of the surplus for a given level of output, other authors, like Michael Kalecki, drawing on the principle of effective demand, provided a theory explaining how the distribution of the surplus causes changes in output. In fact, the work of Kalecki and Sraffa led to the formation of other groups within the Cambridge Keynesian tradition—Sraffians and Kaleckians

In general, the authors of the Cambridge Keynesian tradition explained the economy using a "surplus approach," some focusing on the impact of the distribution of the surplus on output and growth (Robinson 1962; Kaldor 1967), others focusing on the distribution of the surplus for a given level of output (Sraffa 1960), and yet others trying to reconcile both (Kalecki 1971). In this sense, the theoretical framework of the Cambridge Keynesian tradition can be best interpreted as a return to the surplus theory of CPE, and a rejection of the scarcity theory that underpins marginalist theory and the neoclassical approach that evolved from it (Cohen and Harcourt 2003).

Luigi Pasinetti (2005: 846) argued that Sraffa had developed, at the level of the "pure theory" of value, a nonneoclassical framework, which, when combined with Keynes's "institutional analysis," or theory of agency, provides the basis for a "coherent, non-reductionist, Keynesian-Sraffian theoretical framework." A key idea within the Keynesian-Sraffian framework is that in technical terms, distribution is a cause, and not a consequence of production.

Thus, for Sraffa it is distribution that determines value, and for Keynes and the Keynesians (Kalecki, Robinson, and Kaldor) distribution (and the level of inequality) is a determinant of the level of output. This does not mean, however, that distribution is independent of production, or of the class structure that the mode of production generates. Rather, it means that if we focus on what Pasinetti (2005) called "pure theory," then distribution becomes an exogenous variable. But if we focus on what Pasinetti called "institutional analysis," then we will find that distribution is in turn generated by the class structure and may find that the latter depends upon the mode of production.

However, the authors of the Cambridge Keynesian tradition were essentially concerned with "pure theory." And their contribution is helpful in addressing many problems raised by Marx at the level of "pure theory," such as the problem of *transformation* of labor-values into prices, or the problem of the *realization* of the surplus-value generated by labor.

Effectively, while Sraffa's theory of value deals with the problem of the transformation of value into prices, the Keynesian theory of employment addresses the problem of the realization of the created value, that is, of the existence of effective demand to absorb production. And both address these problems taking distribution to be a cause, and not a consequence, of a given economic outcome. In this context, the problem becomes no longer the inevitability of scarcity, as in neoclassical economics, but rather the distribution of the surplus.

This approach to the economic problem has significant implications for many contemporary problems. For example, one of the structural problems underlying the current economic crisis is the inequality in distribution, which leads to a lack of effective demand (Martins 2011a). Without a reversal of the current inequality trend, aggregate demand can only be maintained by credit, and by the financial sector.

According to neoclassical economics, the existing distribution is the inevitable consequence of the marginal productivity of the factors of production. Thus, distribution is an endogenous variable, and not an exogenous variable, as is the case for Sraffa and Keynes. But if distribution is seen as a determinant of effective demand, as in Keynesian analysis, then we can address the question of which distribution should be achieved, rather than simply accepting the existing distribution as inevitable. Using a surplus approach, the solution to the crisis lies not in the acceptance of scarcity (and of "austerity"), but instead requires a study of how the distribution of the surplus may have contributed to the crisis, and which alternative distribution of the surplus would lead to a better outcome.

The change from the classical theory of value to a subjective theory of value also led to the widespread belief that prices are ultimately dependent upon subjective preferences, rather than on the objective conditions of production. This leads to the conclusion that the only way to know value is by observing market exchange, where subjective preferences are revealed. As a result, the classical idea that the market price gravitates towards an objective natural (or production) price disappears, and the market price is taken as a final *datum*, which means that it is no longer possible to question market prices. Thus, the market mechanism cannot be questioned, and the outcomes it leads to are seen as the more efficient ones. This, in turn, makes neoclassical theory unable to question the existing market prices, even when they are the outcome of speculation.

We can then see that switching from the neoclassical scarcity approach to the classical surplus approach opens many avenues for economic policy. For in the classical surplus approach the emphasis is no longer on the inevitability of the existing distribution and the need for "austerity" measures leading to the inevitable reduction of the standard of living, as in the neoclassical scarcity approach. Rather, in the classical surplus approach, distribution is an exogenous variable, and thus the emphasis is on how we can change it, possibly through various institutional arrangements. This is the key message to take from Sraffa's surplus theory in which it is distribution that determines the methods of production. It is also the key message to take from the Keynesian theory of effective demand, and the way in which it was developed into a theory of growth, where distribution is a cause of demand and growth. As Cohen and Harcourt (2003) argue, in line with Walsh and Gram (1980):

> While neoclassical economics envisions the lifetime utility-maximizing consumption decisions of individuals as the driving force of economic activity, with the allocation of given, scarce resources as the fundamental economic problem, the "English" Cantabrigians argue for a return to a classical political economy vision. There, profit-making decisions of capitalist firms are the driving force, with the fundamental economic problem being the allocation of surplus output to ensure reproduction and growth. (Cohen and Harcourt, 2003: 208)

In fact, the Cambridge Keynesians have essentially been concerned with a return to the CPE framework, in which the differences between various branches of the Cambridge Keynesian tradition can be traced to the differences between classical political economists themselves (Dow 1992). A central element in this reasoning is that distribution is an exogenous variable, and not an inevitable consequence of the marginal productivity of factors of production.

Vulgar Scarcity Theory and Classical Surplus Theory

Remember that saying that distribution is an exogenous variable at the level of "pure theory" does not mean that it is an exogenous variable at the level of "institutional analysis." At the level of institutional analysis, we have a class structure that determines distribution, which in turn depends upon the mode of production. If we want to develop this issue further, we must now move to what Pasinetti (2005) called an "institutional analysis" and study how a given class appropriates the surplus.

It was not only Marx, but also Veblen (1908) who centered his analysis on the appropriation of a share of the economic surplus by a given social group. Veblen criticized John Bates Clark (1891), who resorted to marginalist theory in order to argue that distribution is determined by the marginal productivity of factors of production. In so doing, Veblen anticipated the Cambridge capital theory controversies between post-Keynesians and neoclassical economists (Cohen and Harcourt 2003).

In fact, the analysis of Veblen and many "old" institutionalists is complementary to the one undertaken by Sraffa and the Cambridge Keynesians. While Sraffa and the Cambridge Keynesians focused on the *economic* analysis of the reproduction and distribution of a surplus, institutionalists focused on the *social* analysis of the distribution of the surplus and its appropriation by a "leisure class" at a broader cultural level (Veblen 1899). In this sense, classical surplus theory provides a framework that can be fruitfully combined with heterodox traditions like Marxian political economy, "old" institutionalism, and post-Keynesianism, amongst others.

Veblen (1898) believed CPE to constitute essentially a pre-Darwinian framework, which was not suitable for an evolutionary economics. A major reason that leads Veblen to criticize CPE is that the writings of classical political economists have often been interpreted in teleological terms, assuming that society follows a given *natural law*. Interpreting society in such terms leads to the belief that society remains in, or tends to, a given natural state. Concerning the classical approach to natural laws, Pasinetti wrote:

> The classical economists of the end of the eighteenth century thought that, in the economic field, one could single out "natural" institutions. They were too simplistic, or perhaps too ambitious. Historically, this has been proved not to be so. Those that may be called the "natural" features of an economic system remain at a deeper and more fundamental level. The organizational devices (what we may call the "institutions") that may be able to lead to the actual realization of those natural features are indeed open to various solutions. (Pasinetti 1993: 118)

Thus, Pasinetti notes that the natural system only concerns what he called the "pure theory" of the reproduction and distribution of the surplus, but at the level of "institutional analysis" there are various solutions. Terms like "natural prices" refer only to the "pure theory" of value, not to "institutional analysis." Marx's use of the term "prices of production," instead of "natural prices," is thus a more fortunate one in this context, since it avoids the usual connection made between CPE and natural laws at the institutional level.

However, here Pasinetti is conceding too much in his defense of CPE when accepting that classical economists thought that we could single out "natural" institutions. In fact, here Pasinetti used the expression "classical political economists" in a sense that become common after Marshall, but is very misleading, as Marx and Sraffa had noted. Remember that while Marshall claimed to be in continuity with Smith, Ricardo, and Mill, considering all of them to be classical political economists, for Marx and Sraffa there was a difference between the *vulgar* movement and CPE.

Now, the idea of "natural" institutions was more typical of vulgar political economy than of CPE. Marx (1999: 493) criticized the tendency of vulgar political economy to assume "natural" institutions that cannot be changed, arguing that vulgar political economy "confines itself to systematising in a pedantic way, and proclaiming for everlasting truths, the trite ideas held by the self-complacent bourgeoisie with regard to their own world, to them the best of all possible worlds." This "vulgar" approach to institutions is continued today within neoclassical economics, in which market competition among self-interested individuals is seen as a natural and permanent institutional arrangement towards which society converges. It is not only the existing distribution (determined by marginal productivity) or market prices (which rather than converging to a "price of production," are seen as irreducible subjective entities) that are proclaimed to be "everlasting truths" in neoclassical economics, but also the institutional arrangement of market competition. In this regard, the contributions of "old" institutionalism, like the contributions of other heterodox traditions, by stressing how the human agent is socially conditioned, and how societies change, can help provide an alternative conception that goes beyond the "vulgar" approach.

By arguing that CPE is underpinned by "natural laws," and that Marshall's approach is neo*classical*, Veblen (1898, 1900) also seems to be juxtaposing CPE and vulgar political economy and using the term "classical" to designate what is, in reality, vulgar political economy, an approach that became wrongly identified with CPE. In fact, Veblen (1898) saw the contributions of John Stuart Mill and Cairnes as a continuation of Smith's classical approach to natural laws. Sraffa, however, distinguished Mill and Cairnes, as vulgar political economists, from Ricardo and Marx. Sraffa also argued that Smith (or at least what Marx called the "exoteric" part of Smith) did have some "vulgar" tendencies.

Another institutionalist, John Kenneth Galbraith (1958), also argued that CPE is inadequate for the analysis of contemporary economy and society, since for him, CPE presupposes the existence of scarcity, while the contemporary economy and society is characterised by affluence. Galbraith (1958: 22) referred to Smith, Malthus, and Ricardo as the "founding trinity of economics, at least as the subject is known in the English-speaking countries," leading to a theory systematized by Ricardo. Galbraith (1958: 27) also argued that John Stuart Mill "refined, developed and organized the ideas" of the Ricardian tradition.

Galbraith indistinctively pointed to Smith, Ricardo, Malthus, and Mill as being engaged in a similar project, and thus he did not distinguish CPE from vulgar political economy. Galbraith discussed CPE and Ricardian economics in order to designate what is actually *vulgar* political economy, as developed by those who claimed to be following Ricardo (and who developed a system often termed, misleadingly, even by Keynes, as "Ricardian economics"). It was vulgar political economy that developed the idea of a stationary state of society, in which natural laws would bring a permanent state of scarcity.

However, for classical political economists, including Ricardo, the focus was on the study of the reproduction and distribution of the surplus, rather than the study of scarcity. Ricardo (1821: 6) noted that "[t]here are some commodities, the value of which is determined by their scarcity alone," such as "rare statues and pictures, scarce books and coins, wines of a particular quality," but he quickly added that "[t]hese commodities, however, form a very small part of the mass of commodities daily exchanged in the market," since we can always produce more commodities if we are "disposed to bestow the labour necessary to obtain them." Ricardo (1821: 6) then explained that it is the latter commodities that he addresses in his analysis, the value of which depends upon labor, and not the (rare) commodities the value of which depends upon scarcity. Scarcity is the central notion in the marginalist theory (which follows vulgar political economy in this regard), but not in CPE.

Historical Time and the Theory of Agency

Another problem that is often pointed out about CPE is that it constitutes an analysis of an equilibrium situation. In this context, Sraffa's revival of CPE is also seen as an analysis of equilibrium somehow related to some sort of "natural law." This would seem to be in stark contrast with the dynamic analysis of heterodox traditions like Marxian political economy, "old" institutionalism, or post-Keynesianism, where equilibrium analysis in logical time is replaced by historical analysis in real time.

However, classical political economists did not analyze situations of equilibrium. In fact, they did not even consider that there could be equilibrium because they explained value *without* considering changes in quantities. And without considering changes in quantities, it is not possible to address the question of whether quantities converge towards equilibrium.

As Sraffa (1925) explained, it was with marginalism that the idea of value changing with quantity became common. Since marginalists considered value to consist of marginal utility, which decreases with quantity, the idea of change in quantities is essential to their theory of value. Thus, the idea that value changes with quantities became common after the marginalist revolution. And Marshall engaged in an analysis of how equilibrium is reached in this context. However, classical theory, like Sraffa's system, does not address the question of whether the economy is converging towards an equilibrium position. Hence Joan Robinson's comment about Sraffa's system:

> It does not represent a stationary state of a equilibrium position. It is simply the position that has been reached, "today", as a result of accumulation of stocks and of technical knowledge over the past history. (Robinson 1985: 164)

Thus, Sraffa's (1960) system does not represent an equilibrium position within the Marshallian framework. Rather, it is an attempt to recover the classical theory of value, following his (1925, 1926) rejection of Marshall's approach, which Sraffa considered to be not a continuation of the CPE surplus theory, but of the supply and demand analysis of vulgar political economy. Joan Robinson came to see Sraffa's system in terms of an instantaneous snapshot of the economy, taking into account what has been reached today, in a present that nevertheless reflects the effect of historical time. Thus, there is no incompatibility between Sraffa's system and the heterodox perspectives that reject the neoclassical notion of equilibrium pioneered by Marshall.

The role of historical time is, like the notion of a social agent situated in a social structure, central to heterodox economics (Davis 2009; Lawson 2006, 2009). In the various contributions to heterodox economics, we find that the idea that the human agent is an *isolated* self-interested individual is abandoned in favor of a conception of humans as *social* beings.

Lawson (2006) argues that the various heterodox traditions presuppose a similar social ontology. When developing his argument, Lawson in fact ends up elaborating a realist social ontology that systematizes the key ingredients of the heterodox theories of agency. In this social ontology, human agents continuously reproduce and transform an underlying social structure, and fit into the social positions within that social structure.

In fact, we could argue that while Sraffa had been concerned with a revival of the classical theory of value, the heterodox traditions have been characterized by a theory of agency that is very similar to that of the classical theory as developed to its more elaborate stage by Marx; a theory where social structures, including social classes, are presupposed in human agency, which permanently reproduces and transforms these social structures.

As Pasinetti (1993) explained, CPE focused on labor, not on subjective utility. While labor can be, and in fact often is, a social activity, subjective utility is always the utility of an individual. Thus, while the classical framework of reproduction and distribution of a surplus produced by labor can be combined with an "institutional analysis" that presupposes a social agent placed in a given social structure (as arguably Smith and certainly Marx did), the marginalist theory led to a framework that relied upon an irreducible methodological atomism, starting from the notion of an individual who engages in exchange in order to optimize her or his subjective utility.

In both heterodox economics as well as CPE, we have social(ized) agents rather than individual atoms as in mainstream economics, and we have social *structures* as well as human agents. The objective existence of social structures is explained in a very clear way by Lawson (2006).

Now, it is because we acknowledge the existence of social structures that we can have a historical theory, which explains history in terms of changes in social (including technological) structures. If human agency were reduced to the atomistic interaction of agents who pursue their subjective self-interest, then there would be no reason to expect change unless there is a change in the individuals. For if society is nothing more than a sum of individuals, then unless individuals change, there would be no social change. But since in neoclassical economics individuals are characterized by subjective preferences that are specific to each individual, there is no objective way to address history and change.

The Classical Theory of Well-Being

Another author who recovers many elements of the classical theory of agency is Amartya Sen. Vivian Walsh (2000, 2003, 2008) and Hilary Putnam (2002) argue that a revival of CPE in the 20th century occurred in two stages. The first stage was Sraffa's revival of the theory of value and the second stage was Sen's revival of the philosophical anthropology of CPE. Sen (1977) criticized the "rational fool" presupposed in neoclassical economics. He (2009: 245) argued that Karl Marx had the best explanation for the way in which the human agent is socially conditioned. Sen drew from the contribution of Antonio Gramsci, an author who had a significant influence on Sraffa, as Davis (2002) and Sen (2003) explain:

> as Antonio Gramsci, perhaps the most innovative Marxist philosopher of the twentieth century, put it, nearly eighty years ago, in his *Letters from Prision*, while incarcerated in a fascist jail in Turi: "in acquiring one's conception of the world one always belongs to a particular grouping which is that of all the social elements which share the same mode of thinking and acting. We are all conformists of some conformism or other, always man-in-the-mass or collective man" [Gramsci 1975: 324]. (Sen 2009: 119)

However, the classical theory of agency was not systematically developed by Sen, who had been essentially concerned with reviving the classical theory of well-being. Classical political economists like Smith and Marx saw human well-being in terms of the various achievements, or activities, performed by human beings. This is a multidimensional approach very different from the unidimensional approach that neoclassical economists adopted after Bentham, which has recently been revived by Sen (Martins 2011b). Sen (1987, 1999) argued that human well-being should be assessed not in terms of *subjective* preferences, but rather in terms of the *objective* functionings and capabilities achieved by human beings, where a functioning is what a human being is or does and a capability is a potential functioning, which is what a human being can be or can do.

As Putnam (2002: 57) explained, Walsh's (1961) notion of *achievements* anticipated many aspects of Sen's capability approach, but as Walsh (2003: 382) reminded us too, he never saw the possibility of applying such a perspective to the problems of development, or to interpersonal comparisons of welfare, like Sen did. In so doing, Sen engaged in a revival of the classical theory of well-being. He also engaged in a critique of the neoclassical theory of agency, and as a result he ended up rejecting neoclassical economics. Thus Sen writes:

> It was argued by development economists that neoclassical economics did not apply terribly well to underdeveloped countries. This need not have caused great astonishment, since neoclassical economics did not apply terribly well anywhere else. (Sen 1984: 487)

However, even though Sen did criticize neoclassical economics and the "rational fool" presupposed in its theory of agency, his main concern was with the theory of well-being. Therefore, Sen is often not perceived as a critic of neoclassical economics, since he limits his critique to specific issues, such as well-being or rationality. If we want to find a more thorough revival of the classical theory of agency in which the human agent is more explicitly acknowledged to be situated in a social structure, and if we wanted to find a more sustained critique of neoclassical economics, then we have to look into the heterodox economics traditions, where a notion of a structured and evolving agent in a structured and evolving society is developed (Lawson 2006; Dow 2008; Davis 2009; Lee 2009).

Equipped with Sraffa's revival of the classical theory of value, Sen's revival of the classical theory of well-being, and the heterodox approach to agency, we can then develop a more satisfactory economic theory that, like Marx, recovers the classical approach, and goes beyond the neoclassical model.

Concluding Remarks

The distinction between heterodox economics and neoclassical economics is closely related to an earlier distinction made by Marx between CPE and vulgar political economy. As noted above, we can see the differences between classical and vulgar theory in terms of their theory of value, theory of agency, and theory of well-being. When we do so, we find that while neoclassical economics is essentially a development of vulgar political economy, in the heterodox traditions we find a development of the classical approach.

Sen argued, following the classical perspective of Smith and Marx, that human well-being depends upon the achievement of multiple objective functionings. In such an objective analysis, we reach the conclusion that once a given functioning is achieved, the human agent is satisfied and does not need more resources to achieve such a functioning. However, if we see well-being in terms of subjective preferences that are never satisfied, if subjective preferences are taken as an exogenous data that cannot be questioned, and if human agents are optimizers who always want more, then scarcity is seen as an inevitable result, as is the case in neoclassical economics.

Sraffa (D3/12/11/36) suggested that we must substitute subjective concepts with objective elements in our theory, noting how "[u]tility is simply . . . the object of consumption of the surplus." For Sraffa, we should build our theory around the notion of the surplus, rather than the notion of subjective utility.

By focusing on the surplus, we can understand the causal impacts of distribution on output and growth, as the Cambridge Keynesians did, and also see that it is distribution that affects the methods of production, as Sraffa and Robinson argued, rather than being the inevitable result of marginal productivities, as in the case of neoclassical economics.

Of course, distribution itself depends on the social structure (or the class structure). The neoclassical theory of agency sees the interaction of self-interested individuals as the natural institutional arrangement. But if we look at the heterodox traditions, we find an alternative conception of a human agent situated in a geographically and historically conditioned social structure, which changes with time, rather than being subject to static natural laws, as in the case of vulgar political economy.

Furthermore, some heterodox traditions like Marxian political economy, "old" institutionalism, and post-Keynesianism already provide important heterodox contributions to the analysis of the reproduction and distribution of a surplus. Post-Keynesians focus on the "pure theory" of the reproduction and distribution of a surplus, institutionalists focus on the "institutional analysis" of the distribution of the surplus and its appropriation by a "leisure class" at a broader cultural level, and Marxian political economy focuses on both of these aspects. Therefore, there is scope for a broader interaction between the classical surplus approach and the heterodox traditions, as suggested by Lee and Jo (2011) and Lee (2011), in order to achieve a different theory of value, agency, and well-being.

References

Clark, J. B. (1891). "Distribution as Determined by the Law of Rent." *Quarterly Journal of Economics* 5(2): 289–318.

Cohen, A., and G. C. Harcourt. (2003). "Whatever Happened to the Cambridge Capital Theory Controversies?" *Journal of Economic Perspectives* 17(1): 199–214.

Davidson, P. (2007). *John Maynard Keynes*. London and New York: Palgrave/Macmillan.

Davis, J. (2002). "Gramsci, Sraffa, Wittgenstein: Philosophical Linkages." *European Journal of the History of Economic Thought* 9(3): 384–401.

——. (2009). "The Nature of Heterodox Economics." In *Ontology and Economics: Tony Lawson and His Critics*. Ed. E. Fullbrook, pp. 83–92. London: Routledge.

Dow, S. (1992). "Post Keynesian School." In *A Modern Guide to Economic Thought: An Introduction to Comparative Schools of Thought in Economics*. Eds. D. Mair and A. Miller, pp. 176–206. Aldershot: Edward Elgar.

——. (2008). "Plurality in Orthodox and Heterodox Economics." *Journal of Philosophical Economics* 1(2): 73–96.

Galbraith, J. K. (1958). *The Affluent Society*. Boston: Houghton Mifflin.
Garegnani, P. (1998). "Sraffa: The Theoretical World of the 'Old Classical Economists'." *European Journal of the History of Economic Thought* 5(3): 415–429.
——. (2005). "On a Turning Point in Sraffa's Theoretical and Interpretative Position in the Late 1920s." *European Journal of the History of Economic Thought* 12(3): 453–492.
Gramsci, A. (1975). *Letters from Prision*. Trans. and ed. Lynne Lawner. London: Jonathan Cape.
Harcourt, G. C. (2003). "The Cambridge Economic Tradition." In *The Elgar Companion to Post Keynesian Economics*. Ed. J. King, pp. 44–51. Cheltenham and Northampton: Elgar.
——. (2006). *The Structure of Post-Keynesian Economics: The Core Contributions of the Pioneers*. Cambridge: Cambridge University Press.
Harcourt, G. C., and P. Kerr. (2003). "Keynes and the Cambridge School." In *A Companion to the History of Economic Thought*. Eds. W. J. Samuels, J. E. Biddle, and J. B. Davis. Malden: Blackwell.
Kahn, R. F. (1931). "The Relation of Home Investment to Unemployment." *Economic Journal* 41(162): 173–198.
Kaldor, N. (1967). *Strategic Factors in Economic Development*. New York: Ithaca.
Kalecki, M. (1971). *Selected Essays on the Dynamics of the Capitalist Economy*. Cambridge: Cambridge University Press.
Keynes, J. M. (1936). *The General Theory of Employment, Interest and Money*. London: MacMillan.
Lawson, T. (2006). "The Nature of Heterodox Economics." *Cambridge Journal of Economics* 30(4): 483–505.
——. (2009). "Heterodox Economics and Pluralism: Reply to Davis." In *Ontology and Economics: Tony Lawson and His Critics*. Ed. E. Fullbrook, pp. 93–129. London: Routledge.
Lee, F. S. (2009). *A History of Heterodox Economics*. London: Routledge.
——. (2011). "Heterodox Surplus Approach: Production, Prices and Value Theory."
Lee, F. S., and T. H. Jo. (2011). "Social Surplus Approach and Heterodox Economics." *Journal of Economic Issues* 14(4): 857–875.
Marshall, A. ([1890] 1920). *Principles of Economics*. London: Macmillan.
Martins, N. (2011a). "Globalisation, Inequality and the Economic Crisis." *New Political Economy* 16(1): 1–18.
——. (2011b). "The Revival of Classical Political Economy and the Cambridge Tradition: From Scarcity Theory to Surplus Theory." *Review of Political Economy* 23(1): 111–131.
Marx, K. ([1867] 1999). *Capital*. Oxford: Oxford University Press.

Meek, R. (1961). "Mr. Sraffa's Rehabilitation of Classical Economics." *Scottish Journal of Political Economy* 8(2): 119–136.

Mill, J. S. (1848). *Principles of Political Economy.* London: J. P. Parker.

Pasinetti, L. L. (1993). *Structural Economic Dynamics. A Theory of the Economic Consequences of Human Learning.* Cambridge: Cambridge University Press.

——. (2005). "The Cambridge School of Keynesian Economics." *Cambridge Journal of Economics* 29(6): 837–848.

Putnam, H. (2002). *The Collapse of the Fact/Value Dichotomy and Other Essays.* Cambridge, MA: Harvard University Press.

Ricardo, D. ([1817] 1821). *On the Principles of Political Economy and Taxation.* London: John Murray.

Robinson, J. (1962). *Essays in the Theory of Economic Growth.* London: Macmillan.

Robinson, J. V. (1985). "The Theory of Normal Prices and the Reconstruction of Economic Theory." In *Issues in Contemporary Macroeconomics and Distribution.* Ed. G. Feiwel, pp. 157–165. London: Macmillan.

Sen, A. K. (1977). "Rational Fools: A Critique of the Behavioral Foundations of Economic Theory." *Philosophy and Public Affairs* 6(4): 317–344.

——. (1984). *Resources, Values and Development.* Cambridge, MA: Harvard University Press.

——. (1987). *On Ethics and Economics.* Oxford: Basil Blackwell.

——. (1999). *Development as Freedom.* Oxford: Oxford University Press.

——. (2003). "Sraffa, Wittgenstein, and Gramsci." *Journal of Economic Literature* 41(4): 1240–1255.

——. (2009). *The Idea of Justice.* London: Allen Lane.

Sidgwick, H. (1883). *The Principles of Political Economy.* London: Macmillan.

Sraffa, P. (1925). "Sulle relazioni fra costo e quantita prodotta." *Annali di economia* 2(1): 277–328.

——. (1926). "The Laws of Returns Under Competitive Conditions." *Economic Journal* 36(144): 535–550.

——. (1960). *Production of Commodities by Means of Commodities: Prelude to a Critique of Economic Theory.* Cambridge: Cambridge University Press.

Veblen, T. (1898). "Why is Economics Not an Evolutionary Science?" *Quarterly Journal of Economics* 12(4): 373–397.

——. (1899). *The Theory of the Leisure Class.* New York: Macmillan.

——. (1900). "The Preconceptions of Economic Science: III." *Quarterly Journal of Economics* 14(2): 240–269.

——. (1908). "Professor Clark's Economics." *Quarterly Journal of Economics* 22(1): 147–195.

Walsh, V. (1961). *Scarcity and Evil.* Englewood Cliffs, NJ: Prentice Hall.

——. (2000). "Smith After Sen." *Review of Political Economy* 12(1): 5–25.

——. (2003). "Sen After Putnam." *Review of Political Economy* 15(3): 315–394.
——. (2008). "Freedom, Values and Sen: Towards a Morally Enriched Classical Economic Theory." *Review of Political Economy* 20(2): 199–232.
Walsh, V., and H. Gram. (1980). *Classical and Neoclassical Theories of General Equilibrium.* Oxford and New York: Oxford University Press.

Schumpeter, Commons, and Veblen on Institutions*

By Theofanis Papageorgiou,[a] Ioannis Katselidis,[b] and Panayotis G. Michaelides[c]

Abstract. This article compares Schumpeter, Veblen, and Commons with regard to institutions setting up the paradigm of institutional evolutionary economics. Their theories are of a complex nature, and as such, it is very difficult to situate them in a clear-cut tradition. The main similarity is their opposition to the thesis that market economy is an independent and self-regulating system, in an attempt to integrate economic, sociological, and political perspectives with regard to the functioning of the system. Also, change *per se* is in contrast to the notion of equilibrium. Of course, despite the parallels, the existence of differences is undeniable.

Introduction

There is no doubt that Joseph Alois Schumpeter, John Rogers Commons, and Thorstein Bunde Veblen are probably among the greatest economists of all time and are considered among the founders of institutional and evolutionary thinking in the discipline. Unfortunately, so far, some aspects of their works remain less widely discussed or even unexplored. For instance, according to Elliot (1993), Schumpeter's analysis of capitalist development provides a Continental quasi analogue to the writings of Veblen and Commons. In fact, the parallels that can be drawn in the works of Schumpeter, Veblen, and Commons have been inadequately acknowledged with the exception

*We would like to thank the Editor-in-Chief and the three anonymous referees for their helpful comments.

[a]National Technical University of Athens, Athens, Greece.

[b]Athens University of Economics and Business, Athens, Greece.

[c]Contact author: Laboratory of Theoretical and Applied Economics, School of Applied Mathematics and Physics, National Technical University of Athens, Athens, Greece; Heroon Polytechneiou 9, 157.80, Zografou Campus, Tel: 302107721624; fax: +302107721618, email: pmichael@central.ntua.gr.

American Journal of Economics and Sociology, Vol. 72, No. 5 (November, 2013).
DOI: 10.1111/ajes.12042

of a few important contributions such as O'Donnell (1973), Zingler (1974), Cramer and Leathers (1977), Broda (1998), Ferrarotti (1999), McFarling (2000), and Gurkan (2005).

In this context, a principal similarity that all three of them share in common is that their work does not focus on the market economy as an independent and self-correcting mechanism; their writings rather opted for the integration of economic, sociological, and political perspectives with regard to the functioning of the economic system. Given the presence of central elements of their views in institutional and evolutionary thinking, it is surprising that so little attention has been paid to their theoretical interaction.

This article aims at bridging this gap in the literature, comparing Schumpeter, Veblen, and Commons with regard to institutions. In this context, the connections between the three great theoreticians are sometimes primarily *substantive* and sometimes primarily *methodological* in nature. The theories of Veblen, Commons, and Schumpeter are of a rather complex nature, and as such, it is very difficult to situate them in a clear-cut intellectual tradition. For instance, the theoretical threads that tie evolutionary and institutional thinking with Marxism are also of great interest.[1]

Defining Institutions

Veblen and Commons

Commons defined an institution as "collective action in control, liberation and expansion of individual action. Collective action ranges all the way from unorganized custom to the many organized going concerns, such as the family, the corporation, the trade association, the trade union, the reserve system, the state" (Commons 1931: 649). Collective action functions through "working rules," which are in turn formed through statute law, decision of courts and administrative bodies, customs, and the less formal behavior of going concerns. Commons asserted that economic analysis has to do with the "activity"; thus he emphasized the role of the "transactions" in the economic interaction and the function of going concerns. The transaction "was defined as the rights of future ownership of things acquired and alienated through collective social working rules" (Zingler 1974: 334). In the same context, "conflict, dependence and order become the field of institutional economics, built upon the principles of scarcity, efficiency and futurity . . . but correlated under the modern notions of working rules of collective action controlling, liberating and expanding individual action" (Commons 1931: 656).

Commons made the concept of transaction the central unit of economic analysis, since this concept includes all the three above-mentioned challenges (Commons 1934a). The transaction is a relationship between economic actors and does not refer to "exchange," that is, a physical transfer, but to a legal transfer of ownership. The institutional framework within which transactions occur is characterized by the so-called working rules, including customary rules as well as the common and statute law (Commons 1924, 1934a). As Commons stated:

> The term "working rules" is appropriate to indicate the universal principle of cause, effect or purpose, common to all collective action. Working rules are continually changing in the history of an institution, and they differ for different institutions; but, whatever their differences, they have this similarity that they indicate what individuals can, must or may, do or not do, enforced by collective sanctions. (Commons 1931: 650)

Veblen identifies institutions in his *Theory of Leisure Class* as follows:

> Products of the past process, are adapted to the past circumstances, and therefore never in full accord with the requirements of the present . . . At the same time, men's present habits of thought tend to persist indefinitely, except as circumstances enforce a change. These institutions which so have been handed down, these habits of thought, points of view, mental attitudes and aptitudes, or what not, are therefore a conservative factor. (Veblen [1919] 1990: 239–240)[2]

Also, institutions are seen as: principles of action that underlie the current "business-like scheme of economic life," and as such, they are not to be called in question without questioning the existing order. Alternatively, they take the form of "settled habits of thought common to the generality of men" (Veblen [1919] 1990: 239).

In Veblen's approach several interesting characteristics of institutions may be traced: first, they are part of the social milieu and thus their underlying framework is much wider than mere economic and social. The capitalist civilization is a key notion to understanding the way in which institutions work and evolution takes place. In fact, he argued that the material framework of modern civilization is the industrial system, and the directing force that animates this framework is business enterprise (Veblen 1904: 7).

Second, institutions have a causal role in the shaping of human behavior and in the evolution of capitalism given that they are part of the contradictory powers that shape instincts, behaviors, and habits of thought. This schema has a two-way causal power, meaning that it shapes and at the same time is being shaped by institutions (Veblen 1909: 629). Also, he argued that the response that goes to make up human conduct takes place under institutional norms and only under stimuli that have an institutional bearing (Veblen 1909: 629).[3]

Contracts and property are among the fundamental institutions for Commons; contracts are embedded in working rules. As far as property is concerned, Commons also treated it as a fundamental institution, "defining all the activities which individuals and the community are at liberty or required to do or not to do, with reference to the object claimed as property" (Commons 1934a: 74); "hence, ownership becomes the foundation of institutional economics" (Commons 1934a: 5).

Using a holistic methodological apparatus, Commons regarded social systems as closely connected and interrelated parts, where the meaning and significance of each part was shaped by the totality of its possible connections with other parts of the system and with the system as a whole (Biddle and Samuels 1998: 44). For instance, we may regard transactions as the parts and the going concern as the whole. Alternatively, a transaction may be "the whole (as an outcome) of which the parts (its 'causes') are the five principles of scarcity, efficiency, working rules and custom, sovereignty and futurity" (Ramstad 1986: 1084). Interaction and interrelations must be known in order to predict the effects of an institutional change (Ramstad 1987). Also, collective action involving conflict of interest and dependence on each other constitutes the second power that determines institutional change. The principles that are different for each institution and are changing in the history of every institution are the ones that shape institutional change.[4] "Collective human will" certainly determines institutional change but at the same time is influenced by the institutional context.

Commons contended that the evolution of the economic system and institutions is a process of purposeful, "artificial selection." Institutional change is the result of the interaction between individual actions and particular organizations. Individuals "meet each other, not as physiological bodies moved by glands, nor as 'globules of desire' moved by pain and pleasure similar to the forces of physical and animal nature, but as prepared more or less by habit, induced by the pressure of custom to engage in those highly artificial transactions created by the collective human will" (Commons 1934a: 74).[5] Commons, by rejecting the psychological background of neoclassicism, asserted that institutional change occurs as a result of individuals' decisions, actions, and attempts to overcome their problems, which are associated with the (institutional) situation of each individual in society (Rutherford 1983).

Collective human will and collective action have a logic that may be seen as the common well-being. Two critiques may be constructed on this issue: on the one hand, it infuses a teleological aspect when conceiving institutional change as a change towards a better end, with an inert logic that solves existing problems, based on a common welfare; thus institutional change in Commons has teleological aspects, constituting, in fact, a differential dimension compared to the work of Veblen. On the other hand, society is a homogeneous but unclear totality; collective action is a unity implying that social classes and the interaction between them simply do not exist. The well-being and welfare of the society is common to every one of the members, imposing a vague universality to these abstracted notions; in Commons's words "collective action is inclusive" (1950: 21) and "a universal principle" (1934a: 72).

In contrast to Commons, the role of institutions in social change is highlighted when turning to the concept of selection, where Veblen famously promoted the idea that in social evolution there was a "natural selection of institutions." In his own words: "The life of man in society, just like the life of other species, is a struggle for existence, and therefore it is a process of selective adaptation" (Veblen [1899] 1994: 188). In this context, he believed that the progress that has been in human institutions and in human character may be set down, broadly, to a natural selection of the fittest habits of thought and to a process of enforced adaptation of individuals to an environment that has progressively changed with the growth of community and with the changing institutions (Veblen [1899] 1994).

On the other hand, technological change linked with institutional change in the Veblenian system imposes a process of habituation and thus adaptation. Habituation does not take place in an established norm; habituation is unique for every historical period and thus a major difference with Commons arises. Even though both were influenced by historicism they came to different conclusions. Rutherford (1998: 463) stated: "at base, his theory was one of new technology changing economic conditions, and new economic conditions leading to new ways of thinking and to new institutions through a (non-intentional) process of' habituation."

Veblen held that property has a special role as an institution; it is a prerequisite for economic change and institutional change being in itself an institution. In Veblen's work, property is a by-product of technological change. Albeit, adaptation is not a straightforward process; institutions have a unique method of adaptation to technical change. Veblen defines technology as "a joint stock of knowledge derived from past experience, and is held and passes on as an invisible possession of the community at large" (Veblen [1921] 2001: 28). Technological advance according to Veblen ([1914] 1990: 103) is an affair of the community, not a creative achievement of individuals and proceeds on past technical experiences, and any new technical possibility is the result of "a series of great inventions" (Basalla 1988: 26; Gurkan 2005: 8). As will be discussed below, there are factors that resist technical change. In that sense technical change does not act in a predetermined way upon institutions.[6]

It may be argued that Commons departed from the (neo)classical notions of efficiency and scarcity to arrive in a more "social" schema where collective action and struggle play a key role. Commons's intention was to widen the scope of economics by giving "to collective action its due place in economic theory" (Commons 1934a: 8). In that sense he moved to a conception closer to Veblen. In Veblen's system the evolutionary process escapes the individual ("elimination of personality").[7] In Veblen's opinion this elimination of personality "is incident to the growing resort to an apprehension of phenomena in terms of process than in terms of outcome as was the habit in earlier schemes of knowledge" (Veblen 1900: 158).

Veblen argued that socioeconomic evolution must be regarded as an unfolding of life (Veblen 1897: 137). According to Liagouras (2009: 4) he "was the first thinker to introduce to social sciences the idea of human history as an evolving process of change with neither predetermined end, nor a specific pattern of development." Also, regarding the evolutionary nature of capitalism, he held that an evolutionary economics should be a theory of cumulative sequence of (economic) institutions stated in terms of the process itself (Veblen 1898a: 393).

There is a profound discrepancy in the work of Commons, mainly deriving from the eternal and self-correcting character of collective human will. Collective human will exists *per se* constituting a trend of humanity; thus it is infused to human beings from their very birth: "Collective action, as well as individual action, has always been there" (Commons 1934a: 5) and it is the "expansion of the will of the individual far beyond what he can do by his own puny acts" (Commons 1950: 35). It is the expanding nature that makes it independent of individual action; but individual action depends on the collective one. Collective action does not preexist in the time span but in the construction and sequence of notions; individual action is built upon collectiveness.

But how does collective action expand individual action? Is there any place for individual interests? Commons (1924: 6) argued that cooperation "does not arise from a presupposed harmony of interests . . . It arises from the necessity of creating a new harmony of interests . . . [H]armony is not presupposition of economics—it is a consequence of collective action designed to maintain rules that shall govern the conflicts." There is a clear-cut teleological aspect on human action. Also, there is a clear influence from neoclassical economics and individualism. The main difference is the reversion of causality. The opposite direction of causality implies individualism.

Schumpeter

For Schumpeter, things are less complex. Institutions as such are introduced in his mature *Socialism, Capitalism and Democracy* where they play a key role. Institutional and noninstitutional factors enter into complex forms of interaction (Swedberg 2002: 247). In Schumpeter's work, the capitalist civilization consists of institutions as well as of items such as "motivation," "lifestyle," "atmosphere," "rationalism," art, science and so on that are prerequisites for capitalism to exist (Swedberg 2002: 249). Institutions are responsible for the emergence of certain behaviors, so that they can partly be seen as the crystallization of individuals' behaviors (Festre and Garrouste 2008: 379). Swedberg (2002: 250) argued that for Schumpeter institutions are a necessary but not sufficient condition for a vigorous capitalism. The key should be found at the capitalist civilization "mentality," "ethos," "lifestyle," "economic ethic," whereas institutions are ineffective in the absence of entrepreneurial motivation.

Schumpeter in his *Theory of Economic Development* stated that "economic sociology deals with institutions," which is contrasted to economic theory dealing with purely economic phenomena and mechanisms (Schumpeter [1934] 1983: 60–61). Institutional development is intended to achieve the synthesis of theory and history (Shionoya 2008: 7). The concept of institutions is a means of generalizing historical events, but is limited because of its historical relativity in the early works of Schumpeter (Shionoya 2008: 8). In a similar vein, Festre and Garrouste (2008: 374) argued that it is not possible to deal with economic change in Schumpeter's work without considering institutions. Although Schumpeter used to refer to himself as the "arch-enemy of Institutionalism," Festre and Garrouste (2008: 372) held that the connection between conflicting ends and Schumpeter's contribution to economic sociology favors an "institutionalist" interpretation of Schumpeter's theory of economic evolution, in which conflicts between self-interest and class-interest play an important role.

Schumpeter argued that the most fundamental institutions—which are property and contract—are now getting weaker in capitalist strata, along with the "recent" emergence of the third key institution "the big enterprise." Schumpeter asserted that property is hollowed out: shareholders and managers have substituted the traditional owner of the business and the latter has disappeared. "The big enterprise" is transformed to the engine of capitalist development and social transformation takes the entrepreneurs' place. In the meantime, the big enterprise "constitutes the avant-garde in ushering socialism"

(Swedberg 2002: 247). Economic change and institutional change take place through the "routinazation" of innovation, which imposes the institution of big enterprise; thus Schumpeter moves to a thesis closer to institutionalism. The argument implies a clear-cut adaptation towards innovation; however, the routinization of innovation brings in itself institutional change. This nondeterministic influence of innovation on institutions and its self-transformation is an interesting similarity between Schumpeter and Veblen.

Schumpeter attributes the internal dynamic of capitalism to "a vision of the economic evolution as a distinct process generated by the economic system itself" (Schumpeter 1911: 166).[8] For Schumpeter, the idea of evolution is not only linked to economic development in isolation but to political, social and institutional changes as well: "the term evolution . . . comprises all the phenomena that make an evolutionary process non-stationary" (Schumpeter 1954: 965).

The "ultimate causes" of the evolution of social functions are economic ones; this kind of evolution of social classes is not fast and rapid changes are mainly due to the failure of upper classes to keep their social functions. Technological change and innovation may be defused to the society and influence individual's behavior in the future. According to Festre and Garrouste (2008: 380): "Economic and social evolution is co-determined by individual and collective forces."

Property dominates institutional debates of the years pushed by a historicist methodological influence on the institutional thought. For Schumpeter institutional change takes place through innovation and, as will be discussed below, drives the collapse of capitalism. Innovation is a social function and as such it presupposes society. So, common in the works of all the authors under examination is that society becomes the cornerstone on which institutions are built; in this sense, Schumpeter rejects methodological individualism in the neoclassical sense of the term.

Institutions and the Future of Capitalism

Veblen and Commons

The role of institutions and the way institutional change takes place has implications for the conception of the future of capitalism. The substance given to collective human action and the form of institutional change are the bases on which to build an analysis of the future of capitalism. Also, intellectuals of that time were influenced by the dominant pessimism regarding the future of capitalism but also by the socialist views dictating the decline and final collapse of the capitalist era.[9]

Commons's prediction and wish was not the overthrow of capitalism, since his main concern was to "save Capitalism by making it good" (Commons 1934b: 143). He did not regard capitalism as a natural but instead as an institutional-artificial creation; thus, by changing its basic institutions, we could move towards "reasonable capitalism" (Commons 1950: 25).

Also the notion of selection and adoption is of interest. Despite the fact that his work is not incompatible with the idea that technological change can play a crucial role, it does not conclude that technology is the only, or even the principal, source of change. On the contrary, he attached great significance to the influence of expanding markets:

> It is the historical extension of markets over this broad expanse, from colonial times to the present, that has changed the character of competition, intensified its pressure, separated manufactures from agriculture, introduced the middleman, produced new alignments of social classes, and obliterated the futile lines that distinguish the jurisdiction of States. (Commons et al. 1918: 6)

Veblen in his *The Theory of Business Enterprise* took an anticapitalistic stance concerning the future of capitalism and later in his *Imperial Germany and the Industrial Revolution* he wrote that the effectual mutilation or inhibition of the machine system would gradually push business principles to the wall; whereas with a free growth of the machine system business principles would fall into abeyance (Veblen [1904] 1975: 177).

So, the revolutionizing nature of the machine process that is capable of liberating humanity from the "imbecile institutions of the past" is highlighted.[10] Veblen argued that technical change and its associated institutional structure revolutionizes capitalism in favor of engineers and industrial workers and against the pecuniary motives of the business class. He argued: "In the modern culture, industry, industrial processes, and industrial products have progressively gained upon humanity, until these creations of man's ingenuity have latterly come to take the dominant place in the cultural scheme" (Veblen [1919] 1990: 17). And concluded that: "Economic change is always in the last resort a change in the habits of thought. This is true even of changes in the mechanical process of industry" (Veblen 1898b: 189).

The "probabilistic" conception of socialism that Veblen adopted is heavily dependent on the nonpredetermined character of adoption, which in fact may appear also as selection driven from its unique way of habituation. The difference springs from the absence of an inherent logic to collective will and action.

Schumpeter

Schumpeter famously asked himself: "Can capitalism survive? No, I do not think it can" ([1942] 1975: 61). He argued that there were three main reasons for this. First, the role of entrepreneurs was becoming obsolete. Trained specialists were increasingly responsible for technological innovation; the latter being rationalized into a routine procedure. As this occurred, entrepreneurs were reduced to wage earners and lost their incentive to innovate. Second, the core groups that defended capitalism were weakening. Small entrepreneurs were being swallowed by big business, thereby shifting ownership toward shareholders whose investment in the system was much less direct. Capitalism is "constitutionally" unable to produce "emotional attachment to the social order"; it produces "almost universal hostility" to itself (Schumpeter [1942] 1975: 143; 145). Third, Schumpeter held that the institutional framework of capitalism was crumbling. Schumpeter illustrated this by pointing to the post–World War II policies of European governments, highlighting the "adaptive" character of institutions. According to Schumpeter, this increasing dependence on government would lead to "guided capitalism" and finally to "state capitalism," which is closely related to socialism (Schumpeter [1946] 1951: 204).

The lost heroism and romance in the economic world would transform into talents and energies of the noneconomic world: "Other than economic pursuits would attract the brains and provide the adventure" (Schumpeter [1942] 1975: 131).[11] It may be argued that both Veblen and Schumpeter sought for a "vehicle" for the decline of capitalism and found it in technology.

Institutions and Individuals

Veblen and Commons

The relation between institutions and individual action is rather complex both in Commons and Veblen. For Commons individual action is firmly constrained by working rules and collective action. For Veblen individual action is influenced by the collective technological and institutional context. There are two basic points relevant to individual action in these intellectuals. Firstly, the ways by which individuals are affected by the collective will and the technological context, respectively. And secondly, the weight of individual interests contrasted to collective interests and their role in shaping the social context.

Both Commons and Veblen attached significance to the habits and customs that influence human life. In particular, Commons talked about "habitual assumptions," which is quite similar to Veblen's "habits of thought." On the other hand, they seem to adopt a different point of view regarding the conception of human behavior. Namely, Commons emphasized the volitional aspect based on human action, while Veblen's analysis relied upon the instinct-habit psychology framework. Furthermore, Commons regarded the individual as an "institutionalized mind" (1934a: 73; 697). Individuals have the freedom of choice and action, but, at the same time, human wills and individuals as economically principal actors are formed by institutions and customs. Hence, individual action is constrained not only by general social and cultural rules of conduct, but also by the rules of those specific organizations of which the individuals are members.

Commons, in the early stages of his work, conceived of the entrepreneur as an important factor for economic evolution and growth. Therefore, he pointed out that entrepreneurs, besides the profit incentive, are also motivated by their strong wish for creation, disregarding the difficulties and dangers of a highly uncertain and unstable environment (Kaufman 2007). The entrepreneur, always being part of the collective social will and action, has an internal drive similar to volition. The reference to the entrepreneur does not change substantially the apparatus of a firm collective will that affects individual action; however, the conception of roles in the schema is serving as a question to the unified collective character of action.

In Veblen's work, the evolutionary process takes place not through the individual, but through the habits of thought, conventions, and institutions. Habits both endure and adapt in line with "changes in material facts." The material means of life take the form of "prevalent habits of thought, and it is as such that they enter into the process of industrial development" (Veblen 1898a: 375).

Veblen identifies three basic drives or instincts that govern human behavior: the instinct of workmanship or the impulse to work in order to "turn things to human use" closely connected to the habits of thought (Veblen 1898b: 190), the instinct of idle curiosity, referring to the propensity to understand and explain the external world through the use of imagination; and the instinct of parental bent, stressing human interest in the welfare of others (Veblen 1898b, [1906] 1919, 1914). The instinct of workmanship is the "more generic, more abiding trait of human nature," guided by this "proclivity for turning the material means of life to account" (Veblen 1898b: 190).

This process of technological change lies behind institutional change and changes in the habits of thought streaming from these basic human propensities. It may be argued that Veblen elaborates a notion of an evolutionary capitalism "driving from within." Likewise, Commons's institutional economics has also an evolutionary perspective, since working rules, which organize the economy and form individual preferences and choices, are revised unceasingly.

Veblen's approach may be classified in what is often called "impersonal and non-animistic" evolution of capitalism. According to Veblen, human evolution is impersonal. In his system the evolutionary process escapes the individual, and takes place through the habits of thought, conventions, and institutions, and this is often called the "elimination of personality" that dominated the Veblenian thought going hand in hand with his anti-teleological spirit. Furthermore, for Veblen (1898a: 390) human activity is itself the substantial fact of the process, and the desires under whose guidance the action takes place are circumstances of temperament that determine the specific direction in which the activity will unfold in any given case. In fact, "[i]t is on individuals that the system of institutions imposes those conventional standards, ideals and cannons of conduct that make up the community's scheme of life" (Veblen 1909: 627).

Schumpeter

Even though Schumpeter's *oeuvre* could be conceived as a unity,[12] it is also argued that his works reflect internal contradictions and theoretical inconsistencies; the major shift in emphasis in his work could probably be highlighted in *Capitalism, Socialism and Democracy* where a theoretical shift towards theses closer to economic history and economic sociology is evident. There he stresses the importance of the social milieu on individual action: "we know that every individual is fashioned by the social influences in which he grows up. In this sense he is the product of the social entity or class and therefore not a free agent" (Schumpeter 1931: 286). The above bears strong resemblance to the Veblenian notion of evolution. In Schumpeter's words: "Bureau and committee work tends to replace individual action." In that way, he moves to theses closer to Veblen and his conception of capitalist change, even though it could be argued that his theoretical schema misses partly the "evolutionary" spirit.

According to Schumpeter, there is a correspondence, sometimes weak, between the economic and social functions and individuals' conflicting ends. This correspondence is effective as soon as the individuals reveal some aptitudes to perform their economic and social functions.

Institutional change embodied in economic change takes place only when individuals overcome previously existing collective routines. In the same spirit with Commons and Veblen, Schumpeter attributed individual action, at least partly, to the social context. Being closer to Veblen, he escaped teleological theorizing of a unified society with a consensus over its welfare. Individual action is the premise for an overcoming of the existing collective routines. Individuals are not firmly restricted in the collective action and may alter collective routines. As Festre and Garrouste put it (2008: 374–375) "the fact that individual behavior is determined by a bundle of individual as well as collective ends . . . may explain the heterogeneity of observed behaviors." As will be discussed below, innovation and thus entrepreneurial action driven from "irrational" motives alters collective routines. As a result a homogeneous society is absent from the Schumpeterian framework.

Of course, a question of great interest in the work of Schumpeter is the following: "Who is the bearer of change in the capitalist process?" On the one hand, Schumpeter's innovations are introduced by entrepreneurs, moved by the "dream and will to found a private kingdom," the "joy of creating," and the "will to conquer," giving to the argument an anthropomorphic character. Schumpeter focuses on the individual as "the bearer of innovation," reflecting his adherence to "the Schumpeterian version of" methodological individualism.[13] The essence of evolution and development lies not in technical changes *per se* but in energetic human activities carrying out innovation (Shionoya 2008: 3). The motives are both social and psychological, the "will to found a private kingdom," a "dynasty" inspired by the ideal of the medieval lordship, including "from spiritual ambition down to mere snobbery," the "will to conquer," the will to prove superior to others, to succeed for the sake of success itself, and finally the intrinsic motive of getting things done, "the joy of creativity." It is the "spiritual constitution" that differentiates entrepreneurs from common people (Schumpeter 1911: 142–143, 163).

In this context Schumpeter also considered it necessary to make a sharp distinction between political and methodological individualism:

> Both concepts have nothing in common. The first refers to general statements like the freedom of people to develop themselves and to take part in well-being and to follow practical rules. The second does not include any proposition and does not involve a specific starting point. It just means that one starts from the individual in order to describe certain economic relationships. (Schumpeter 1908: 90–91)

In this sense, it is impossible to conceive social classes in a solely holistic or individualistic context: "We cannot help those who are unable to see that the individual is a *social* fact, the psychological an *objective* fact, who cannot give up toying with the empty contrasts of the individual *vs.* the social, the subjective *vs.* the objective" (Schumpeter [1927] 1951: 211). The class interest ever-present in all members of this class thus constitutes an autonomous social determinant "originally quite independent of [their] will" (Schumpeter [1927] 1951: 143).

Conclusions

This article compared Schumpeter, Veblen, and Commons with regard to institutions. Of course, their theories are of a rather complex nature, and as such, it is very difficult to situate them in a clear-cut intellectual tradition. The main similarity that Commons, Veblen, and Schumpeter share in common is the special attention they all attributed to institutions, setting up the *paradigm* of institutional evolutionary economics. In the meantime, all three of them were opposed to the thesis that market economy is an independent and self-regulating system, in an attempt to integrate economic, sociological, and political perspectives with regard to the functioning of the economic system. Thus, the economic system is not a self-correcting mechanism. Also, change *per se* is in direct contrast to the notion of (static) equilibrium.

Schumpeter, Austrian in origin and maybe more profoundly influenced by the Austrian School, rejected the basic notion of the marginalist revolution, the notion of the general static equilibrium elaborated by Leon Walras, in favor of "development," a more unstable and evolving notion of the economic process. According to Schumpeter:

> Development is the distinct phenomenon entirely foreign to what may be observed in the circular flow or in the tendency towards equilibrium . . . It is spontaneous and discontinuous change in the channels of the flow, disturbance of equilibrium which forever alters and displaces the equilibrium previously existing. (Schumpeter [1934] 1983: 64)

On the self-correcting nature of the economy Schumpeter seems to argue *ex post* that there is not a self-correcting mechanism and thus the economic system moves towards greater bureaucratization and to "guided" capitalism. However, fluctuations should, in some way, incorporate the notion of self-correction. Schumpeter believed that the break of equilibriums was succeeded by the crediting of the entrepreneurs. Thus he argued that without credit the cycle would be small and self-correcting.

Veblen, in a similar vein, regarded capitalist development as a "cumulative causation" having "no trend," "no final term," "no consummation." In his own words, "in the Darwinian scheme of thought, the continuity sought in and imputed to the facts is a continuity of cause and effect. It is a scheme of blindly cumulative causation, in which there is no trend, no final term, no consummation" (Veblen 1907: 304). In other words, Veblen conceived of evolutionary sciences as being concerned with nonteleological processes of cumulative change and causation. Thus, he succeeded to study the competition of the units as a dynamic process and not as a stationary process (Liagouras 2009: 2).

As was the case with Veblen and Schumpeter, Commons came to question the validity of the classical and neoclassical *paradigms*. Following the tradition of the (Wisconsin) institutional economists, he adopted an adductive/empiricist approach to theorizing, namely, he first collects the data and the observations, involving himself in the facts (that is, Ely's "look and see" method), and then adduces from the facts and other grounded empirical work the major premises for theorizing, so as to draw conclusions about reality. This approach was opposed to the deductive, *a priori* method of mainstream economics. Just like Schumpeter, Commons rejected the natural general equilibrium thesis, proposing instead an "organized equilibrium of equality" that the economy and society could reach through collective bargaining (Commons 1934b). Thus, he turned against the mainstream view of an independent and self-regulating economic system not influenced by the legal, political, and other social subsystems. In contrast, he put "an emphasis on the economy as an ongoing socio-cultural process," contending that "economic order is a product of institutional adjustment" (Whalen 1989: 452).

Despite Commons's assertion that the economy was not an automatically self-directing mechanism but a social organization, he did not believe that institutional economics replaces neoclassical theory but rather that it serves as a supplement to it (Biddle and Samuels 1998). Indeed, instead of replacing traditional theory, Commons asserted that institutional economics should focus on those factors and variables left out or taken as given in conventional economics. According to Commons, institutional change is the result of the actions of individuals and going concerns, but these actions in turn are constrained by social and ethical norms as well as by the political and judicial institutions that influence decisively the changing process of other rules or institutions.

For Schumpeter and Veblen, technology is probably the most crucial driving force of capitalist evolution favoring a concept of habituation of institutional change. They were probably both influenced by the intellectual environment of the period, namely, the excessive financialization of the economy that set forth a vast wave of innovations throughout the global economy. The unique process of technological change is closely related to their theses on the revolutionizing nature of capitalism.

On the other hand, Commons did not attach great significance to the role of technological change as the only—or even the major—source of economic and industrial change being consistent with the notion of artificial selection that rules institutional change. On the contrary, he emphasized the influence of expanding markets. Furthermore, Commons was rather more optimistic compared to Veblen and Schumpeter, since his prediction was not the overthrow of capitalism.

Of course, despite the parallels, the differences are undeniable. Commons made the concept of transaction the basic unit of his analysis, stating that the subject of economics is "the transactions of human beings in producing, acquiring and rationing wealth by cooperation, conflict and the rules of the game" (Commons 1934a: 121). The institutional context within which transactions occur is characterized by the so-called working rules, including customs as well as the common and statute law, but also from the collective will. For Commons, collective will and action is homogeneous; unified; excluding the possibility of any divergence.

Both Commons and Veblen stressed the fact that human life is highly influenced by habits and customs. More precisely, Commons developed the idea of "habitual assumptions," which has similarities to Veblen's "habits of thought." However, they seem to reach different conclusions as regards the conception of human behavior. Namely, Commons emphasized the volitional aspect based on human action, while Veblen's analysis was based upon the instinct-habit psychology framework. Veblen's social context was not homogeneous, it consisted of different classes and class antagonism. Finally, Schumpeter separated individuals to entrepreneurs and nonentrepreneurs; to nonrational and rational; thus, social will is not comprehensive.

In this framework, better understanding the theories delivered by Schumpeter, Commons, and Veblen could be very useful for clarifying several issues in the evolutionary and institutional approaches and between different schools or even strands of economic thought and for understanding current issues. Clearly, further and more extended research on the subject would be of great interest.

Notes

1. On Veblen and Marx there has been a long-standing controversy on the relationship between their theories. For instance, Walling (1905) emphasized the Marxian character of Veblen's thought, even though the majority of writers may seem to conclude that "Veblen was not an American Marxist" (Corey 1937: 168). On the other hand, Schumpeter too was called a "bourgeois Marx" by his famous teacher Eugene von Boehm-Bawerk, while Commons was not Marxist since he was a proponent of "representative democracy" (Commons [1913] 1964).

2. Describing institutions he favored an acknowledgment commonly called the Veblenian Dichotomy, on the one hand "instrumental" technology and on the other "ceremonial" institutions.

3. Often, institutions are considered as habits probably because of the famous phrase: "Institutions are settled habits of thought common to the generality of men" (Veblen 1909: 626). Following Coats (1954: 533) "every institutional situation is a product of everything that has proceeded it."

4. As Biddle and Samuels (1998: 292) put it: "Commons was unequivocally historicist if by historicism is meant a focus on both the reality of change and the ongoing process of becoming."

5. It is collective action that forms the very basis of each institution and determines the future of its existence (or disappearance).

6. The pivotal role of the conflict of occupational habituation as factor of institutional change is highlighted "while the technological scheme creates the economic possibilities of ownership, the discipline which it exerts upon the industrial classes who are habitually employed in it conflicts with that exerted by the institution of private property" (Harris 1934: 49).

7. Habits of thought could easily be related to an evolutionary process passing through the human being. However, according to Liagouras (2009: 6), "in the continuous impersonal process of selection, human individuals were subject to natural selection as carriers of concrete habits of thought."

8. In fact, "[t]here must be a purely economic theory of economic change which does not merely rely on external factors propelling the economic system from one equilibrium to another. It is such theory that I have tried to build" (Schumpeter [1937] 1989). See also Michaelides and Milios (2009).

9. The views concerning the future of capitalism that dominated socialistic and Marxist circles of thought built on the gradual proletarian overthrow of capitalism closely related to the theories of imperialism (for example, Hilfreding, Bucharin, Lenin). Along with the strong influence that these circles had, a pessimistic approach towards the future of capitalism dominated the intellectual atmosphere of the period, commonly referred to as "capitalism on decline."

10. "The machine technology takes no cognizance of conventionally established rules of precedence . . . Its scheme of knowledge based on the laws of material causation, not on those of immemorial custom, authenticity, or authoritative enactment" (Veblen [1904] 1975: 148).

11. However, owing to his evolutionary and dialectical nature his prediction leaves space for the opposite outcome: "capitalism produces also psychological, moral and political changes which affect habits and attitudes and these have the effect of turning the situation in a socialist direction. Other ideas and programs could perhaps prevent socialism into being—the idea of cooperative regime is one example" (Schumpeter 1931b: 386–387).

12. Of course, Schumpeter's work is often portrayed as a coherent whole with no sharp breaks between its different phases (see, among others, Swedberg 2002). Langlois (1991) has challenged whatever tendency there is in the economics literature to distinguish between an "early Schumpeter" and a "later Schumpeter."

13. Schumpeter's methodological individualism is not *the* methodological individualism of the marginalists. By this term, Schumpeter considers methodological individualism to mean "just that one starts from the individual in order to describe certain economic relationships" (Schumpeter 1908).

References

Basalla, G. (1988). *The Evolution of Technology*. Cambridge: Cambridge University Press.

Biddle, J. E., and W. J. Samuels. (1998). "John R. Commons and the Compatibility of Neoclassical and Institutional Economics." In *Economics and its Discontents: Twentieth Century Dissenting Economists*. Eds. R. P. F. Holt and S. Pressman. Aldershot and Lyme, NH: Edward Elgar.

Broda, P. (1998). "Commons Versus Veblen on the Place of the Individual in the Social Process." In *The Economic Mind in America: Essays in the History of American Economics*. Ed. Malcolm H. Rutherford, pp. 210–230. London and New York: Routledge.

Coats, A. W. (1954). "The Influence of Veblen's Methodology." *Journal of Political Economy* 62: 529–537.

Commons, J. R. ([1913] 1964). *Labor and Administration.* New York: Augustus M. Kelley.

——. (1924). *The Legal Foundations of Capitalism.* New York: Macmillan.

——. (1931). "Institutional Economics." *American Economic Review* 21(4): 648–657.

——. (1934a). *Institutional Economics: Its Place in Political Economy.* New York: Macmillan.

——. (1934b). *Myself.* Madison: University of Wisconsin Press.

——. (1950). *The Economics of Collective Action.* Madison: University of Wisconsin Press.

Commons, J. R., D. J. Saposs, H. L. Sumner, E. B. Mittleman, H. E. Hoagland, J. B. Andrews, and S. Perlman. (1918). *History of Labor in the United States.* 2 Volumes. New York: Macmillan.

Corey, L. (1937). "Veblen and Marxism." *Marxist Quarterly* 1: 62–68.

Cramer, D. L., and C. G. Leathers. (1977). "Veblen and Schumpeter on Imperialism." *History of Political Economy* 9(2): 237–255.

Elliot, J. (1993). "Schumpeter's Theory of Economic Development and Social Change: Exposition and Assessment." *International Journal of Social Economics* 12(6/7): 6–33.

Ferrarotti, F. (1999). "The Businessman as Protagonist in Veblen and Schumpeter." *International Journal of Politics, Culture and Society* 13(2): 241–248.

Festre, A., and P. Garrouste. (2008). "Rationality, Behavior, Institutional, and Economic Change in Schumpeter." *Journal of Economic Methodology* 15(4): 365–390.

Gurkan, C. (2005). "A Comparison of Veblen and Schumpeter on Technology." STPS Working Papers no. 509 [http://www.stps.metu.edu.tr/stpswp/series05/0509.pdf].

Harris, A. (1934). "Economic Evolution: Dialectical and Darwinian." *Journal of Political Economy* 42(1): 34–79.

Kaufman, B. (2007). "The Institutional Economics of John R. Commons: Complement and Substitute for Neoclassical Economic Theory." *Socio-Economic Review* 5: 3–45.

Langlois, R. (1991). "Schumpeter and the Obsolescence of the Entrepreneur." Working Paper 91–1503, Department of Economics, University of Connecticut.

Liagouras, G. (2009). "Socio-Economic Evolution and Darwinism in Thorstein Veblen: A Critical Appraisal." *Cambridge Journal of Economics* 33(6): 1047–1064.

McFarling, B. (2000). "Schumpeter's Entrepreneurs and Commons's Sovereign Authority." *Journal of Economic Issues* 34(3): 707–723.

Michaelides, P. G., and J. G. Milios. (2009). "Joseph Schumpeter and the German Historical School." *Cambridge Journal of Economics* 33(3): 495–516.

O'Donnell, L. A. (1973). "Rationalism, Capitalism, and the Entrepreneur: The Views of Veblen and Schumpeter." *History of Political Economy* 5(1): 199–214.

Ramstad, Y. (1986). "A Pragmatist's Quest for Holistic Knowledge: The Scientific Methodology of John R. Commons." *Journal of Economic Issues* 20(4): 1067–1105.

——. (1987). "Institutional Existentialism: More on Why John R. Commons Has So Few Followers." *Journal of Economic Issues* 21(2): 661–671.

Rutherford, M. (1983). "J. R. Commons' Institutional Economics." *Journal of Economic Issues* 17(3): 721–744.

——. (1998). "Veblen's Evolutionary Programme: A Promise Unfulfilled." *Cambridge Journal of Economics* 22: 463–477.

Schumpeter, J. (1908). *Das Wesen und der Hauptinhalt der theoretischen Nationalökonomie.* Berlin: Duncker and Humblot.

——. (1911). *Theorie der wirtschaftlichen Entwicklung.* Leipzig: Dunker & Humbolt.

——. ([1927] 1951). "Die sozialen Klassen im ethnisch homogen Milieu." *Archiv für Sozialwissenschaft und Sozialpolitik* 57: 1–67. Translated into English as "Social Classes in an Ethnically Homogenous Environment," in J. A. Schumpeter (1951).

——. (1931). "The Present State of Economics OR On Systems, Schools and Methods." *Kokumin Keizai Zasshi—Journal of Economics and Business Administration* 50(5): 679–705, cited in: http://www.schumpeter.info/text2~1.htm (accessed on 21 May 2013).

——. (1931b). "Les possibilites actuelles du socialisme." *L'Annee politique francaise et etrangere* XXIV: 385–418.

——. ([1934] 1983). *The Theory of Economic Development.* Cambridge, MA: Harvard University Press.

——. ([1937] 1989). "Preface to the Japanese Edition of *Theorie der wirtschaftlichen Entwicklung.*" In *Essays*, pp. 165–168. New Brunswick, NJ: Transaction.

——. ([1942] 1975). *Capitalism, Socialism, and Democracy.* New York: Harper and Brothers.

——. (1946). "Capitalism." In R. V. Clemence.

——. ([1949] 1951). "Economic Theory and Entrepreneurial History." In *Essays: On Entrepreneurs, Innovations, Business Cycles and the Evolution of Capitalism.* Ed. R. V. Clemence, pp. 253–271. Cambridge, MA: Harvard University.

——. (1954). *History of Economic Analysis.* New York: Oxford University Press.

Shionoya, Y. (2008). "Schumpeter and Evolution: An Ontological Exploration." In *Marshall and Schumpeter on Evolution: Economic Sociology of*

Capitalist Development. Eds. Y. Shionoya and T. Nishizawa. Cheltenham: Edward Elgar.

Swedberg, R. (2002). "The Economic Sociology of Capitalism: Weber and Schumpeter." *Journal of Classical Sociology* 2(3): 227–255.

Veblen, T. (1897). "Review of Max Lorenz, Die Marxisasche Socialdemokraae." *Journal of Political Economy* 6(1): 136–137.

——. (1898a). "Why is Economics Not an Evolutionary Science?" *Quarterly Journal of Economics* 12(3): 373–397. Reprinted in Veblen (1919).

——. (1898b). "The Instinct of Workmanship and the Irksomeness of Labor." *American Journal of Sociology* 4: 187–201. Reprinted in Veblen (1934).

——. ([1899] 1994). *The Theory of the Leisure Class: An Economic Study in the Evolution of Institutions.* New York, Macmillan.

——. (1900). "The Preconceptions of Economic Science: HI." *Quarterly Journal of Economics* 14(1,2): 240–269. Reprinted in Veblen ([1919] 1994: 148–179).

——. (1904). *The Theory of Business Enterprise.* New York, Charles Scribners. Reprinted (1975), New York, Augustus Kelley.

——. (1906). "The Socialist Economics of Karl Marx and his Followers I: The Theories of Karl Marx." *Quarterly Journal of Economics* 20(3): 578–595. Reprinted in Veblen (1919).

——. (1907). "The Socialist Economics of Karl Marx and His Followers II: The Later Marxism." *Quarterly Journal of Economics* 21(1): 299–322. Reprinted in Veblen (1919).

——. (1909). "The Limitations of Marginal Utility." *Journal of Political Economy* 17(9): 620–636.

——. (1914). *The Instinct of Workmanship, and the State of the Industrial Arts.* New York: Augustus Kelley. Reprinted (1990) with a new introduction by M. G. Murphey and a 1964 introductory note by J. Dorfman. New Brunswick, NJ: Transaction Books.

——. ([1919] 1990). *The Place of Science in Modern Civilisation and Other Essays.* New York: Huebsch. Reprinted (1990) with a new introduction by Samuels, W. J., New Brunswick, NJ: Transaction Books.

——. ([1921] 2001). *The Engineers & the Price System.* Kitchener: Batoche Book.

Walling, W. (1905). "An American Socialism." *International Socialist Review* 5: 577–578.

Whalen, C. (1989). "John R. Commons's Institutional Economics: A Re-Examination." *Journal of Economic Issues* 23(2): 443–454.

Zingler, E. (1974). "Veblen vs Commons: A Comparative Evaluation." *Kyklos* 27(3): 322–344, reproduced with original page numbers in Samuels (ed.) (1988).

Lost in Translation: Why Generalized Darwinism is a Misleading Strategy for Studying Socioeconomic Evolution

By George Liagouras*

ABSTRACT. The article is based on Lewontin's distinction between transformational and variational evolution. Given that transformational evolution is dominant in the social realm while variational evolution reigns in the organic world, the question is if Hodgson and Knudsen's Generalized Darwinism bridges the ontological gap between the two types of evolution. It is argued that the three successive strategies of the authors—deconstruction of Lamarckism, appropriation of the Price equation, redefinition of the replication notion—are all based on controversial semantic innovations. Most importantly, it is shown that Generalized Darwinism, in its effort to address the transformational character of social evolution through the notion of generative replication, is compelled to radically restrict the importance of Darwinian natural selection.

Introduction

Throughout his well-known book, *More Heat than Light*, Philip Mirowski (1989) showed how economics of the previous centuries was dominated by a "physics envy." Nevertheless, over the last two or three decades a tendency towards "biology envy" has become more pronounced. This is part of a more comprehensive movement in other social sciences (anthropology, psychology, management, linguistics). In most of the above cases, biology is perceived as the Mecca of socioeconomic analysis with Darwinism as the fundamental source of inspiration. This implies a revolution regarding the ontological and methodological foundations of social inquiry. For more than a century, an important, albeit contradictory, literature concerning the specificities of social sciences has emerged in reaction to the intrusion of

*Department of Financial and Management Engineering, Business School of Chios, University of the Aegean, Greece, E-mail: g.liagouras@fme.aegean.gr.

American Journal of Economics and Sociology, Vol. 72, No. 5 (November, 2013).
DOI: 10.1111/ajes.12041

mechanical approaches. As of late, the further development of research in this domain has been seriously undermined by the mounting trend of biology-based approaches. Commonly the latter adopt the prevalent objections to the application of a mechanical approach in social research. But at the same time they hold biology to be the only viable model for social sciences. The present article adheres ideologically to interdisciplinary scholarship in its questioning of the increasingly greater interference of biological reason in the social sciences (for example, Dugger 1981; Gould 1997; Fracchia and Lewontin 1999; Lawson 2003; Liagouras 2009; Brown 2012).

Biology envy in social sciences takes either a formalist or a philosophical expression. The rationale of the formalist version of the Darwinian social science can be summarized in the following three points:

- Evolution is the critical issue that differentiates social and life sciences from classical physics.
- Biology succeeded precisely where the opponents of the physics legacy in social sciences failed, that is to say, the elaboration of formal sophisticated models for studying evolution.
- Therefore, if the belated social theory wants to call itself an evolutionary science, it must adopt the advanced models and methods of biological science.

Such a rationale implies that there are significant ontological affinities between societal and species evolution. Most formalist scholars agree that this is not the case, primarily because human evolution is more Lamarckian than Darwinian. Therefore, they attempt to steer around the problem via reductionist strategies. There are scholars who reduce social life to culture and by extension conceive of cultural evolution as an *epidemiology* of cultural variants. While others examine human instincts and basic preferences hypothetically, following the "what would happen if" methodology of evolutionary game theory, and then they cavalierly project them on to complex modern societies.[1]

In parallel with the formalist inspiration taken from the modeling achievements of the neo-Darwinian synthesis in modern biology, there have been philosophical attempts at generalizing Darwinism into an overarching conceptual framework covering both biological and social sciences. The founding fathers of this current, that I call here "Darwinian Fundamentalism," are philosophers of biology like R. Dawkins (1976, 1982), D. Hull (1982, 1988), and D. Dennett (1995). Contrary to formalist scholarship, the tenets of "Darwinian Fundamentalism" hold that important communalities exist between the biological and social realms. The pursuit of coherence in the project of a Darwinian social science is seriously impeded by a limited knowledge of the social world on the part of philosophers of biology. "Generalized Darwinism" (Hodgson 2002, 2004; Hodgson and Knudsen 2006a, 2006b, 2006c, 2008, 2010; Aldrich et al. 2008) can be viewed then as the latest and most sophisticated branch of Darwinian Fundamentalism. A factor in favor of "Generalized Darwinism" is that Geoffrey Hodgson and Thorbjørn Knudsen are both distinguished social scientists who display an impressive knowledge of the economics and management literature. This also explains the choice of "Generalized Darwinism" as the topic of this article. If someone chooses to criticize the biology envy trend in the social sciences, (s)he had better opt for the more systematic and sophisticated version.

The central argument of Generalized Darwinism can be summarized in four successive points:

1. There are (nontrivial) ontological communalities in the evolution of all complex population systems, "from amoebas to humans."
2. Although Darwinism is identified with biology, its three main tenets of variation, inheritance (replication), and selection, properly abstracted or generalized, can provide an overarching—albeit incomplete—framework for the evolution of socioeconomic systems.
3. The distinction between genotypes and phenotypes, which is characteristic of the modern synthesis between Mendelian genetics and Darwinian biology (the so-called neo-Darwinian synthesis), can be generalized in terms of replicators and interactors, with a paradigmatic value for social sciences.
4. Given that Generalized Darwinism corresponds to the ontological communalities of all complex evolving systems, it operates on a high level of abstraction and therefore does not suffice to explain either biological or social phenomena. Its general principles must

be reinforced by "auxiliary," "detailed," or "secondary" mechanisms depending on the subject to be explained.

Could Generalized Darwinism then provide an overarching explanatory framework for studying social evolution? The following citation from Richard Lewontin, a leading Darwinian biologist of our times, clearly demonstrates the originality, as well as the controversial ramifications, of adopting the Darwinian framework in the study of the evolution of social systems:

> There are two basic dynamic forms for evolving systems. One is *transformational,* in which the collection of objects evolves because every individual element in the collection undergoes a similar transformation. . . . Most physical systems and social institutions evolve transformationally, and it was characteristic of pre-Darwinian evolutionary theories that they, too, were transformational. Lamarck held that a species evolved because its individual members, through inner will and striving, changed to meet the demands of the environment.
>
> The alternative evolutionary dynamic, unique as far as we know to the organic world, and uniquely understood by Darwin, is *variational* evolution. In a variational scheme, there is variation of properties among individuals in the ensemble, variation that arises from causes independent of any effect it may have on the individual who possesses it. That is, the variation arises at random with respect to its effect. The collection of individuals evolves by a sorting process in which some variant types persist and reproduce, while others die out. Variational evolution occurs by the change of frequency of different variants, rather than by a set of developmental transformations of every individual. (Lewontin 2001: 53–54)

It should be remarked that even a fervent supporter of Darwin's variational evolution such as Lewontin maintains that "most physical systems and institutions evolve transformationally."[2] Thus what makes Generalized Darwinism so original and controversial is the concept according to which variational evolution applies not only to "the organic world" *but also* to socioeconomic systems.

Many evolutionary scholars have already criticized Generalized Darwinism by pointing out the fundamental differences between natural and social evolution (Witt 2004; Buenstorf 2006; Cordes 2006; Nelson 2007a, 2007b; Vromen 2007, 2010; Levit, Hossfeld, and Witt 2011). Still, Hodgson and Knudsen in company with their allies have downplayed the importance of these critiques by referring to the existence of "huge differences of detail" (Aldrich et al. 2008: 583) that can be addressed via the adjunction of "auxiliary explanations." This article adopts an alternative strategy of argumentation. Step by step, it follows the elaboration of Generalized Darwinism to explore how it deals with the transformational character of social evolution. The principal thesis defended here is that Generalized Darwinism bridges the gap between transformational and variational evolution through a complex set of semantic innovations. The logic of the new language game that ensues is analyzed and critically assessed. The final outcome of this exercise is quite surprising. At the end of the road, Generalized Darwinism, in its effort to cope with the transformational character of socioeconomic evolution, is constrained to restrict the scope of Darwinian natural selection.

The structure of the article reflects an effort to reconstruct the framework of Generalized Darwinism by moving from the general to the specific. The second section, which follows, examines the rationale for a general theory of complex evolving systems, without making any reference to Darwinism. The third section sums up the logic of Generalized Darwinism in three points and then furnishes a critical discussion for each point. The remaining sections address more specific issues. As such, the fourth section explains how Hodgson and Knudsen define Lamarckism and why they reject it. This is a critical step in the argumentation considering that Lamarckism is the archetype of transformational evolution in the history of biology. The fifth and sixth sections examine the constructive aspect of Generalized Darwinism: its appropriation of the Price equation and its radical redefinition of the replication (inheritance) concept. Finally, the seventh section provides concluding remarks and some circumspect words about the scope of the article.

Too Abstract to Be Nontrivial: Could a General Theory of Evolution Really be Useful?

Suppose that Hodgson and Knudsen did not call their meta-theory "Generalized Darwinism" but "General Theory of Evolution" or "Expanded Synthesis of Evolution" or something of that nature. What difference would it make? My answer is twofold. Certainly, it would help avoid all the semantic disputes that will be discussed in the next sections. Nevertheless, such a meta-theory would necessarily be too abstract to be nontrivial.

In the first place, the relevance problem can easily be illustrated by the consequences such a meta-theory would have for biology. The major question for contemporary biology is if and how the Darwinian paradigm could assimilate new approaches that have arisen in partial or total opposition to it. Given that social scientists cannot claim to know biology better than the biologists themselves, Hodgson and Knudsen, very judiciously, avoid participating in these debates. They claim (Hodgson and Knudsen 2010) instead that their meta-theory can be accommodated by any given challenger of Darwinism: Lamarckism (2010: 65), the neutralist theory of Kimura (2010: 90), the evo-devo dispute (2010: 56), punctuated equilibria (2010: 43), self-organization (2010: 53), and (even) artificial selection (2010: 50). The list is so extensive that one might ask if there is *any* debate in biology that Hodgson and Knudsen's meta-theory cannot accommodate. Still, "accommodate" does not mean "resolve." Therefore, the question is what will be the added value of such a meta-theory, or, more bluntly, how could biologists benefit from knowing of its existence. It is rather difficult to come up with any kind of positive answer to the above question.

But let us assume for the sake of argument that this meta-theory could not benefit biology, but could instead be of great help to social scientists. The only way that this scenario is realizable would be by elaborating a more specific theory of social evolution from the General Theory of Evolution. Note that this is not a very logical sequence since the elaboration of generalizing principles of evolution would presuppose already knowing what the specific principles proper to the social and biological domains were. But let us admit that things can also turn the other way around. Somehow an interesting conjecture issued and the task now at hand is to assess its application in social sciences.

This necessitates combining different levels of abstraction. Such a demand is not an externally imposed requirement. It results from Hodgson's initial project in his seminal book on *How Economics Forgot History* (Hodgson 2001a: 322–327). Here he argues that a historically and geographically sensitive social science must draw from the following five levels of abstraction:

a) Open complex evolving systems,
b) Human society in general,
c) Civilized and complex human societies,
d) Specific socioeconomic systems (classical antiquity, feudalism, capitalism),
e) Historical and geographical varieties of the above socio-economic systems.

Obviously, the General Theory of Evolution operates at the level "a." In order to assess its advantageousness for social sciences we need to qualify it on the next three levels *at the very least*: first social evolution in general (level "b"), then evolution in civilized and complex human societies (level "c"), and finally the social system we want to study. Without such specifications, no judgment can be made either in favor or against Hodgson and Knudsen's meta-theory.

Unfortunately though, such particulars cannot be found in the publications of Hodgson and/or Knudsen. At least, not for the time being. From a formal point of view, one cannot dismiss the possibility that the two authors will eventually fill that gap. There are, however, two indications that discourage the hope of such a future contribution. The first counterargument resides in the fact that the book by Hodgson and Knudsen (2010) presents itself as a relatively flat alternative to Hodgson's complex five-level epistemology of 2001. Their alternative collapses the levels of abstraction into two tiers. On top, a "grand theory" or a "general framework" operating at the highest level of abstraction (evolving population systems) and at the bottom myriads of "middle-range theories" using "auxiliary hypotheses" to study "detailed mechanisms" of social evolution. Such a two-level epistemology appears plausible for biology, where a tight bundle of concepts is applied, with the help of "secondary" hypotheses, to all the phenomena of evolution. The same applies *a fortiori* to physics: "When metal airplanes and feathered birds fly, some similar principles are at work. But the detailed mechanisms are very different" (Hodgson and Knudsen 2010: 224).[3]

But what makes common sense for physics and biology does not pertain to social science. Imagine that one succeeds in finding some general principles of organization or evolution in a) colonies of amoebas, b) Roman civilization, and c) modern information or finance-led capitalism. The general principles that amoebas and the global financial system have in common would be of very little help to explain the organization of the latter, or the course that led to the 2008 world economic crisis. Unavoidably, the burden of the explanation falls on specific principles-mechanisms-hypotheses about the organization of modern global capitalism and its financial system. Therefore, contrary to physics and biology, the specific or detailed mechanisms are far from being auxiliary or secondary. In fact, they are the relevant ones. General mechanisms are simply too abstract to be relevant. That is why it would be a pity for social sciences if the biological notions of time, space, and method were substituted for Hodgson's initial combination of five levels of abstraction.

Finally, there is an even sounder reason for the scepticism towards any future elaboration of a history-friendly theory of social evolution. As stated above, Hodgson and Knudsen maintain that their general evolutionary framework is Darwinian. Arguing in favor of such a controversial claim is a difficult undertaking. Consequently, the authors' energies are redirected to a complex game of semantic innovations mainly inspired by Darwinian Fundamentalists (Dawkins 1976, 1983; Hull 1982, 1988). In the continuation of the article, I will explain how the influence of Darwinian Fundamentalists on Hodgson and Knudsen has been counterproductive and therefore regrettable.

Generalized Darwinism as a New Language Game

From the point of view of Darwinian Fundamentalism, Hodgson and Knudsen's Generalized Darwinism constitutes a major contribution to the further development of the initial argumentation of Dawkins and Hull. The new language game that results can be summarized by the following three points:

1. The ultimate postulate of the new language game is contained in the formula "Generalized A = A + non-A." According to this unusual axiom, Generalized Darwinism includes Darwinism and

all the possible alternatives to it: "several purported rivals to Darwinism are not rivals at all" (Hodgson and Knudsen 2010: 59). Therefore, all the approaches that are usually perceived as alternatives in common scientific language are transformed into secondary components of a much larger system called "Generalized Darwinism."

2. One might logically ask why this wider system is called "Generalized Darwinism" and not "Generalized Lamarckism" or "Generalized Self-Organization" and so on. The answer is that all the other alternatives to Darwinism cannot perform without the *accompaniment* of Darwinian selection. In other words, whatever might be the importance of adaptation, learning, innovation, and self-organization in nature and in society, there exists no effective way of screening the alternatives generated by the above factors. Only the Darwinian principle of natural selection can introduce such a cogent screening mechanism.
3. Generalized Darwinism, in spite of its claim as a universal theory of evolution, retains the neo-Darwinian (Weismannian) distinction between genotypes and phenotypes as the most crucial instrument in its toolkit. With the project of generalizing Darwinism, the differentiation between genotypes and phenotypes is broadened into a distinction between replicators and interactors. For an initial approximation of the meaning of these concepts, we can refer to Hull's definitions (Hull 1988: 408). Replicator is "an entity that passes on its structure largely intact in successive replications." Interactor is "an entity that interacts as a cohesive whole with its environment in such a way that this interaction *causes* replication to be differential." The most classic example of the replicator-interactor distinction in social sciences offered by Hodgson and Knudsen comes from the microeconomics and management literature. Firms are the interactors while their routines constitute the replicators. The process of market competition phases out the less efficient routines either through the elimination of failing firms or the replication of the more productive routines by lagging firms.

Each of the above three points is controversial. The first one contradicts the very fundamentals of biology. As Gould (2002: 163–165) remarked, the main alternatives to Darwinism have remained unchanged since the outset of the 20th century. The debate has never been whether Lamarckism, orthogenesis, or saltationism are viable theoretical alternatives to Darwinism, but rather if they have any empirical validity. The service rendered by the formula "Generalized A = A + non-A" is precisely how it downplays the above widely-accepted fact[4] by transforming the tradeoff between two opposite theories into a complementary relationship. Certainly, if a phenomenon like evolutionary change results from two distinct causes, the latter can be viewed as complementary in the production of the final outcome. Nevertheless, what is really at stake here is the relative significance of each cause. If cause "A" is responsible for 10 percent of the total change, this implies that cause "B" must be attributed the remaining 90 percent. And in this case, simple logic would have us characterize cause "B" as primary and cause "A" as secondary or auxiliary.

The last remark brings us to the second point, which is intimately connected to the first one. From a logical point of view, it is not readily understandable why a mechanism "A," which serves as a complement to a mechanism "B," would be considered far more important than "B," and inclusive of "B"? The ultimate argument provided by Generalized Darwinism against all the alternatives that minimize the role of Darwinian selection by focusing on the internal development of novelties is that "without Darwinian selection there would be no way of removing useless novelties" (Aldrich et al. 2008: 581). Yet, the argument is not very convincing with regard to both social and natural science. Supporters of alternative approaches in social sciences could easily reply that, whatever the importance of Darwinian natural selection, humans without adaptive and innovative capacities would be like amoebas.[5]

But the argument is also problematic regarding biology. In the same way that Darwin accepted Lamarckism as a secondary cause vis-à-vis natural selection, the alternatives to Darwinism do not hesitate in assigning natural selection a complementary role. Taking up the example of the previous paragraph again, the issue is which mechanism accounts for the 90 percent of evolutionary change. As explained by Gould, recognizing natural selection as a "*negative force*" capable of eliminating useless variants or novelties is a common denominator in the quasi-totality of all *non-Darwinians* before and after Darwin:

> Non-Darwinian evolutionists do not deny the reality, or the operationality, of natural selection . . . They held, rather, that *natural selection, as a headsman or executioner*, could only eliminate the unfit, while some other cause must play the positive role of constructing the fit. (Gould 2002: 139, italics added)

Thus the probing question is whether or not "natural selection should be viewed as a *positive force*, and as such the primary cause of evolutionary change" (Gould 2002: 139).

Finally, the third point about the centrality of the replicator/interactor distinction appears to be controversial as well. Setting aside for the time being the debates over the various definitions of the two terms, it still stands that the mechanism of natural selection does not depend on the distinction between genotypes (replicators) and phenotypes (interactors). Lewontin (1970) demonstrated that all Darwinian natural selection requires for operating are the following three conditions:

1. Different individuals in a population have different morphologies, physiologies, and behaviors (phenotypic variation).
2. Different phenotypes have different rates of survival and reproduction in different environments (differential fitness).
3. There is a *correlation* between parents and offspring in the contribution of each to future generations (fitness is heritable). (Lewontin 1970: 1, italics added)

The word "correlation" in the third condition demands our close attention. It means that it does not matter how the correlation is arrived at. It can be realized by Mendelian genetics, by cultural inheritance, or other means. If (positive) correlation[6] *somehow* transpires, then Darwinian selection operates. This in turn implies that in principle Darwinian evolution can operate with very different "units of selection," ranging from molecules to communities. Lewontin's argument has been further elaborated and fine-tuned by other scholars, like Godfrey-Smith (2000, 2009). But Darwinian Fundamentalists still prefer to circumscribe the scope of Darwinian natural selection in order to preserve the paradigmatic force of the distinction between genotypes and phenotypes.

Redefining and then Deconstructing Lamarckism

Even though the new language game described above provides adequate support for the case of Generalized Darwinism, Hodgson and Knudsen are justified in their resolute rejection of Lamarckism. The latter, like Darwinism, equates evolutionary change with gradual adaptation.[7] But then, it explains gradual adaptation by the combination of two forces:

a. "the creative response of organisms" (Gould 2002: 157) to the alterations in their environment (what would later be termed *directed* or *guided* variation), and
b. the capacity of parents to transmit their "innovations," or creative responses, to their offspring (the "*inheritance of acquired characters*" principle).

Regarding point (a), the detailed causal sequence goes as follows: major environmental changes are felt as permanent needs ("*besoins*") by the organisms that create new "habits" of behavior through their constant efforts to adapt; then the new habits, through the "use and disuse" of organs, lead to evolutionary improvements or acquired characters. On the contrary, no detailed mechanism is offered by Lamarck in support of point (b). For him, the inheritance of acquired characters is a self-evident "law of nature."

Endowing animals with the double capacity to adapt to environmental challenges and to pass their successful adaptations on to subsequent generations gives Lamarckism an anthropomorphic accent. Therefore, it is not surprising that the majority of biology-inspired accounts in economics and management literature consider social evolution to be more Lamarckian than Darwinian. As Hayek (1988: 25) put it: "cultural evolution *simulates* Lamarckism" (emphasis in the original).[8]

Dawkins (1983) and Hull (1982) had already provided arguments for an *a priori* rejection of Lamarckism in nature and culture (memetics). Hodgson and Knudsen (2006a, 2010) took it further and elaborated a more sophisticated argument that unifies the rejection of Lamarckism in life and social sciences:

1. First it is suggested that Lamarckism makes sense only within the context of the neo-Darwinian distinction between genotypes and phenotypes (replicators and interactors).
2. Consequently, Lamarckism is defined as "the possibility of the (genotypic) inheritance of acquired (phenotypic) characters by individual organisms": parents encode acquired characters in their genes that are then transmitted to their offspring.

Given the above two postulates it can then be asserted that:

1. In biology, Lamarckism is *a priori* possible, but only by riding on the back of the Darwinian theory (this is the "natural selection as executioner" argument).
2. In social sciences, Lamarckism is *impossible* because "it depends on relatively direct genotype-to-genotype replication, which is lacking at the social level" (Hodgson and Knudsen 2010: 84). This is obvious: individuals, organizations, etc. replicate genotypes (routines, habits, . . .) but do so only *indirectly* through the replication of phenotypes (traits, characteristics).

As we find with mathematical models, the beauty and elegance of the proof is impeccable. But the devil is in the postulates . . . "*Postulate number one*" could render suspicious even the most innocent of minds. Resetting a theory into the mold of an adversary is the surest way to destroy it.

More substantially, the argument is problematic on two fronts. First, if you pose the question of the pertinence of Lamarckian inheritance for social sciences, there is no reason why it must first be defined through neo-Darwinian genetics. What needs to be determined is if it corresponds to the ontology of the social world. And that is all those scholars who argued in favor of Lamarckian inheritance in social sciences actually achieved. Second, putting the burden of the proof on the fact that habits are not directly replicated is a self-defeating strategy for the project of Generalized Darwinism. In fact, what Hodgson and Knudsen really prove is that the paradigm of neo-Darwinian inheritance, based on the replication of genotypes, is ontologically irrelevant to social sciences. Remember that Lamarckism is not about the *inheritance of genotypes* but the *adoption of new habits*. Through use and disuse, habits create new characters, whose transmission to the next generation was naively advanced by Lamarck. Consequently, if there is a theory that clearly prescribes the direct transmission of habits, this is neo-Darwinism, not Lamarckism. Further on, we will examine the redefinition of the replication (inheritance) concept that Hodgson and Knudsen pursue in their effort to make Darwinism amendable to the existing literature on habits and routines.

For the moment let us explain why "*postulate number one*" is not valid for biology either. The argument Dawkins and Hull furnished to support the above postulate is that without the genotype/phenotype distinction Lamarckian inheritance is subject to two destructive critiques: first, it could not be differentiated from an epidemiological contagion; second, it could not explain why acquired improvements would be favored over acquired impairments or injuries. The argument is so far-fetched that one wonders if Lamarck could have possibly been such a frivolous thinker, and if so, then how did he manage to secure such an important place in the history of biology? Indisputably, there are open questions in the interpretation of Lamarck's theories.[9] But, in reality one need not be a specialist of Lamarck's system to see that both critiques are flawed.

Injuries and impairments cannot be acquired in Lamarck's system because the latter presuppose *permanent* alterations in the environment forcing animals to adopt, through continued efforts, new habits: "if the needs become permanent, the animals then adopt new habits which last as long as the needs that evoked them" (Lamarck 1809: 107). The contagion of viruses is simply irrelevant to Lamarck's system, which presupposes an *adaptive* response (or, borrowing from biological jargon, *directed* variation) of organisms to the challenges of their environment. Besides, the relationship between virus contagion and Lamarckism has already been scrutinized in the literature. In an article published in *The Lancet*, the possibility of a virus passing from parents to offspring was interpreted as empirical evidence in favor of Lamarckism (Fine 1979). Gould's reply was immediate: Lamarckism is, fundamentally, a theory of *directed* variation. Consequently, discoveries of nondirected variations, like virus contagions, are implausible as proof of Lamarckism (Gould 1980: 79–80). Here we might append that what is not viable as evidence in favor of Lamarckism cannot be used as reproof either.

The importance of creative response or directed variation for Lamarckism leads the way to a far more important problem: "*postulate number two*," which defines Lamarckism only by the inheritance of acquired characters. The first pillar of Lamarckism—directed variation, or the capacity of organisms to avoid the consequences of natural selection by adapting to their environment—is thus dismissed. The history of the above dismissal is very instructive. In the beginning, there was Dawkins (1983). When he discussed the classical Lamarckian alternative to Darwinism, "use and disuse plus inheritance of acquired characters," he proposed that "[i]t is convenient to discuss this in two parts" (Dawkins 1983: 18). Attacking separately "use and disuse" and "inheritance of acquired characters" permitted him to contend that Lamarckism is impossible *a priori.* Although Dawkins's maneuvre conveniently destroyed the Lamarckian straw man, one of his followers (Wilkins 2001) took it much further. He simply faced off the two pillars of Lamarckism, "directed variation" and "inheritance of acquired characters," as two opposite interpretations. Then he argued that both are irrelevant to cultural evolution. Hodgson and Knudsen built on Wilkins's definitions. They even went one step beyond by claiming that the "inheritance of acquired characters" is the only viable definition of Lamarckism.

Thanks to this definition, what is really dismissed is the existence of a tradeoff between natural selection and the adaptive capacity of organisms in the evolutionary processes. In a nutshell, the higher the adaptive capacity of organisms in their environment, the less important is the role of natural selection. In a purely Lamarckian world, an increased adaptive (auto-transformative) capacity of organisms would permit them to avoid the workings of natural selection. In a purely Darwinian world, the incapacity of organisms to modify their habits would make natural selection the unique driving force behind evolution.

To better understand the utility of "postulate number two" we need to flash back to the important management literature dedicated to

Darwinism and Lamarckism. By the beginning of the 1980s a Darwinian paradigm had been established (McKelvey 1982; Hannan and Freeman 1984) based on the hypothesis that firms cannot change their deep-seated routines. Therefore , their structural inertia exposes them to the mechanisms of natural selection. Then the Lamarckian *antithesis* pointing to the adaptive capacity of organizations for avoiding natural selection has led to a Darwinian/Lamarckian *synthesis*. The latter has been extremely productive both at the theoretical and empirical level. Thus, Levinthal (1991) argued that Darwinian selection and Lamarckian adaptation are not merely competitive or complementary processes but fundamentally interrelated. McKelvey (1994) referred to the "punctuated equilibria" approach to suggest that Darwinian selection operates during paradigmatic changes when radical uncertainty prevails. Instead, Lamarckian adaptation dominates over normal periods in relatively stable environments. All this theoretical movement stimulated an important output of empirical literature that examined the interplay of Darwinian and Lamarckian processes in practice (for example, Usher and Evans 1996).[10]

It is not difficult to understand why the above scholarship is extremely hazardous for the project of Generalized Darwinism. But if Lamarckism is defined according to "postulate number two," then Hodgson and Knudsen (2010: 83) are right in declaring that all the aforementioned literature is based on a "conceptual confusion." The real issue, however, concerns why Lamarckism should be defined in such a strange way and if such a definition could possibly yield analogous productive contributions.

Redefining Variation and Selection Through the Price Equation

However, attacking Lamarckism by discarding its most important characteristic—the capacity of organisms to transform themselves in order to avoid natural selection—is still not enough. It remains to be proven that what was embezzled from Lamarckism can be found in Darwinism. Here Hodgson and Knudsen go beyond Dawkins and Hull's argumentation by mobilizing the famous Price equation. Price (1972, 1995) conceived of an equation that would provide a mathematical formula of selection common to all sciences (from archeology to genetics) and by extension to all notions of selection (from artificial to natural selection). His astute statistical formula separates the totality of evolutionary change into two components: the selection effect and the transmission effect. The selection effect represents the external cause of change, whereas the transmission effect corresponds to the internal one.

The Price equation can also find important applications in social sciences. Thus, the neo-Schumpeterian scholar E. S. Andersen (2004) suggested that the component of transmission amounts to what in economics and management is called innovation *sensu latu* (that is, including different forms of learning, diffusion, and replication). Consequently, the totality of evolutionary change in economics can be separated into the selection and the innovation effect.

The adoption of the Price equation allows Hodgson and Knudsen (2006, 2010) to introduce human creativity and novelty into Generalized Darwinism by redefining the notion of variation in the most abstract way: "New variation is generated because replication is imperfect or because it involves novel combinations of existing variants" (Hodgson and Knudsen 2010: 99). Still the adoption of the Price equation is not devoid of tensions for the project of Generalized Darwinism.

The syllogism of Hodgson and Knudsen seems to go as follows:

a. Generalized Darwinism provides a common ontology for the evolution of all the complex population systems.
b. The Price equation seeks to offer a quantitative formula as a common denominator in all sciences dealing with selection processes.
c. Consequently, the Price equation constitutes a major contribution to the project of generalizing Darwinism.

An initial concern arises in reaction to the fact that the Price equation is by definition no more Darwinian than it is Lamarckian, or neoclassical for that matter. For example, the biologist A. Grafen (2002) used the Price equation to establish formal links between population genetics and optimization theory. In his model the population of biological models is replaced by a neoclassical omniscient agent maximizing under uncertainty. From a conceptual point of view, the result is hardly surprising. As Price had already suggested, his mathematical formula should apply just as well to "Darwinian natural selection" as it does to "optimization calculation, and decision-making by an intelligent agent" (Price 1995: 390). After all, that is why Price called his formula a "general selection theory" or a "Mathematical Theory of Selection" (Price 1995: 389) and not a Generalized Darwinian Theory of Selection.

More importantly, the adoption of the Price equation seems to be a self-defeating strategy for the Dawkins and Hull arguments adopted by Generalized Darwinism. The reason is that the tradeoff between the selection and innovation effects makes clear that the notion of Generalized Darwinism is a *contradictio in termis*. Actually, the above tradeoff is very useful in localizing the gap between Darwinism and its major alternatives in biology. The condition of nondirected variation in Darwinism implies that the internal transformation of entities is not a response to external selection pressures. On the contrary, the alternatives to Darwinism minimize the impact of selection pressure by magnifying the importance of the transmission effect. This is done either by endowing all biological entities with the human capacity for creative response to external challenges (Lamarckian anthropomorphism), or by directly rendering selective pressures superfluous to the auto-transformative dynamics of evolving entities (orthogenesis, saltationism, self-organization).

Whatever the empirical validity of the above alternatives to Darwinism, the Price equation shows that they cannot be considered complementary to Darwinism. To make things worse, the quantitative character of the Price equation can be used to undermine the proposed supremacy of Darwinian selection. If only 10 percent of total evolutionary change is due to the selection effect and the other 90 percent to the transmission effect, who could seriously argue that the complementary 10 percent is more significant than the 90 percent?

Hodgson and Knudsen (2010: 98–99) confront the above challenge with a new semantic innovation. They define Darwinian evolution as repeated cycles of "successor selection"; the latter being "one cycle of replication, variation and environmental interaction" in which "environmental interaction causes replication to be differential." The condition of "differential replication" is so vast that it levels the tradeoff between the selection and transmission effects, as well as the gap between the Darwinian (variational) and transformational notions of evolution (Lewontin 2001). Therefore, the system evolves either because "some variant types persist and reproduce, while others die out 'or because'" every individual element in the collection undergoes a similar transformation. The first case concerns nature, where the phasing out of some evolving entities (interactors) and consequently some of their host genes (replicators) leads to a differential replication. The second case refers to human society where the frequency of replicators, like habits and routines, changes without necessarily eliminating their individual hosts.

An article by Hodgson and Knudsen (2008) can help to better grasp the crucial importance of the term "successor selection." The article addresses the following important puzzle in the economic history of the transition from feudalism to capitalism: How was the expansion of markets possible prior to the consolidation of a modern state that ensured the enforcement of property rights (and respect of contracts)? Hodgson and Knudsen elaborate a series of simulation models showing that the enforcement of property rights *could have been* enhanced contingent on "behavioural adaptation among multiple guilds rather than the concerted action of one large guild" and "exogenous factors" (Hodgson and Knudsen 2008: 49).

For modeling purposes the adaptive capacity of the agents is even exaggerated (maximum expected incomes and sophisticated correlations). Thanks to the above advanced adaptive capacities of agents, the system moves gradually from lower to higher levels of property enforcement. Therefore, on the whole, the (endogenous) explanation of property rights enforcement is transformational rather than Darwinian. In the words of Lewontin (2001), the system evolves because "every individual element in the collection undergoes a similar transformation" and not because "some variant types persist and reproduce, while others die out." In the terms of the Price equation, evolutionary change is mainly due to the transmission effect and only marginally to the selection effect. This seems very compromising for the project of Generalized Darwinism. But if, by using the formula "Generalized A = A + non-A," we rebaptize Darwinian selection as "successor selection" then the problem automatically solves itself![11]

Redefining the Notion of Replication

There remains one last but extremely protuberant obstacle. As argued above, in the discussion about a definition of Lamarckism, neo-Darwinian inheritance is irrelevant to social evolution. Even if habits and routines are acknowledged as apt replicators, they do not replicate directly. Furthermore, in the process of social replication, the causality does not run from parents to offspring. Even in the cases where there is a well-established hierarchy to facilitate this (unfortunately for all of us who are parents and educators), the replicating entity plays an active role.

There are many conflicting and overlapping definitions of the replication concept in the respective literature. But no one by itself can adequately facilitate the project of Generalized Darwinism. Hodgson and Knudsen needed to innovate a good deal on this critical point. And indeed they did. The transformation of the replication concept by Hodgson and Knudsen follows a double movement. Their starting point is grounded in the literature that defines the replication concept in the broadest possible way. This relaxing process was initiated by Hull (1988: 408), who defined the replicator as "an entity that passes on its structure largely intact in successive replications." Hull's expression "largely intact" replaced the word "directly" from his earlier 1980 definition (Hull 1980: 318). Other authors have substituted the qualifier "similar" for "largely intact." Dan Sperber (2000) played a critical role in the discussion because he refined the concept by distinguishing between three *sine qua non* conditions: causality, similarity, and information transfer:

For B to be a replication of A,

(1) B must be caused by A (together with background conditions),
(2) B must be similar in relevant respects to A, and
(3) The process that generates B must obtain the information that makes B similar to A from A. (Sperber 2000: 169)

Hodgson and Knudsen (2010: 123) pertinently insist that the notion of causality implied by the broad interpretation of replication should be understood in the largest possible way. It simply requires that "without the source, the particular copy would not be created."

Practically speaking, this equates causality with preexistence: without the precondition of the source, the copying operation could not have been possible. The above equivocation between causality and preexistence is extremely important to the application of the replicator concept in the social domain where the imitator usually has the more active role. This becomes clear when the two authors comment on the literature concerning the diffusion of routines and, more importantly, replication as a strategy consciously implemented by the copying firm (Winter and Szulanski 2001). In this case, the success of the copying process depends on the capabilities of the copying firm. Furthermore, the firm that is copied will normally try to raise obstacles to prevent the competitor from copying its routines. The copying mechanism is substantially different from an offspring inheriting directly and passively its parents' genes. However, it remains true in both cases that "without the source, the particular copy would not be created."

Therefore, the transformation of the causality condition into a preexistence one appears adequate for bridging the gap between the biological and social domains, at least as regards the role of interactors in the replicating process. One may ask, however, what is the common denominator in a) inheritance in genetics b) spinoffs or consulting in management, c) interiorization of norms or values in sociology, d) relationships between parents and their children in psychoanalysis, and so on. Put differently, by so radically abstracting the notion of replication do we not run the risk of transforming it into an empty box that holds everything but informs us of nothing?

It must be noted, however, that the most salient feature of Hodgson and Knudsen's redefinition of replication can be found in their effort to limit its scope by adding a fourth condition: replication must generate increased complexity (Hodgson and Knudsen 2010: 122). Replicators must be generative in the sense of providing their host interactor with increasingly more information regarding the challenges existing in the environment. Consequently, programs or mechanisms that are not able to provide the required instructions for the ontogenetic development of the corresponding evolving entity do not qualify as generative replicators. To be more precise, Hodgson and Knudsen (2010: 112) clarify that generative replicators constitute a "special class of replicators," but they add that it is this special class that "is important in both social and biological evolution."

The inspiration for generative replication comes from the work of John von Neumann (1966) on "self-reproducing automata." In this work von Neumann "considered conditions under which automata would be capable of producing copies of themselves and of generating novelty and additional complexity" (Hodgson and Knudsen 2010: 121). Still, the anthropomorphic concept of self-reproducing automata clearly contradicts the Darwinian paradigm. Darwin's objective was to elucidate the complexity of our organic world by the inexorable force of natural selection. If living organisms were capable of generating substantial novelty and complexity in response to the environment, then the role of natural selection would be secondary, if not to say superfluous. This would be a Lamarckian world where directed variation (creative response of organisms) assumes the primary role.

Hodgson and Knudsen's focus on this special class of generative replicators puzzled even the most adept readers (Vromen 2010: 14). Still, such a focus is crucial for their project to bridge the gap between the social and biological domains, or between the transformational and the variational evolution. More precisely, they need to totally restructure the notion of replicator to make it compatible with the existing literature on habits and routines; material they know very well, and towards which they have made substantial contributions. Had there been any doubts about the Lamarckian character of replicators in the above redefinitions they are dispelled by the definition of habits as social replicators: "Habits are formed through the repetition of behaviour or thought. They are influenced by prior activity . . ." (Hodgson and Knudsen 2010: 137). Therefore, habits are continually in the process of reformulating according to the experiences of a subject facing its environment.

But then the problematic position of natural selection—*even as executioner or negative force*—also becomes manifest:

> With caveats concerning its haphazardness, selection may act as a check to weed out disadvantageous variation and promote effective traits. With diffusion, there are less effective mechanisms to verify that new component replicators are capable of creating advantageous development in the

> interactor. The interactor was already developed when it acquired the new replicators through diffusion. Of course, the newly acquired replicators will affect the further development of the interactor, but, because of the delay, the verification process is inferior. (Hodgson and Knudsen 2010: 145)

In addition, if the diffusion of best practices succeeds, this even further limits the role of Darwinian selection. It is here that we encounter the tradeoff between selection and adaptation in the management literature. Hodgson and Knudsen, after having denounced the "conceptual confusion" on which reposes the above literature, feel compelled to admit that given the possibility of the diffusion-replication of routines, the role of Darwinian selection diminishes considerably. Significantly enough, this is accompanied by a major conceptual shift. In their previous papers on the Price equation (Hodgson and Knudsen 2006c) they referred to Darwinian evolution as "generative selection." Now they call it "successor selection," reserving the predicate "*generative*" exclusively for replication. This implies that the locus of the *dominant* force producing increasing complexity was displaced from selection to replication.

In conclusion, the catchall strategy of Generalized Darwinism ends in a negation of the Darwinian revolution![12] This is hardly surprising if we recall from the introduction Lewontin's remark that Darwinian evolution is "unique as far as we know to the organic world." Consequently, Generalized Darwinism was left with two options: either remain faithful to the Darwinian model of natural selection and reduce the social to the organic world, or be mutated into an essentially transformational approach to address the transformational characteristics of human action. Fortunately enough, in the end it was the second option that prevailed. Perhaps the previous critiques that emphasized the reductionist slant of a biology-based meta-theory in social sciences (Witt 2004; Buenstorf 2006; Cordes 2006; Nelson 2007a, 2007b; Vromen 2007) played an important role in the final outcome.

Conclusion

It is time now to take stock of the previous discussion. The project of Generalized Darwinism was based on the astute formula "Generalized A = A + Non A." The development of the argument followed in two directions. The first one was to abolish the premise common to the majority of social scientists that social evolution is mainly, or by analogy, Lamarckian—in any case far more Lamarckian than Darwinian. This mission was accomplished by defining Lamarckism through the possibility of the inheritance of acquired characters, and therefore by omitting its second and most important pillar: the capacity of organisms to avoid the workings of natural selection by successively adjusting to the permanent and major changes in their environment.

The second line of argumentation was constructive. The objective was to redefine the biological notions of variation-replication-selection in such a way that Generalized Darwinism would be able to deal with the fundamental characteristics of social evolution commonly attributed to Lamarckism. The main inspiration came first from the distinction between the selection and innovation effect in the Price equation and then from the idea of a replication that generates increasing complexity (von Neumann's self-reproducing automata). Fortunately, the final outcome entailed the sacrifice of Darwinian natural selection on the altar of innovation and generative replication rather than the other way around.

Nevertheless, this happy end raises three major concerns about the project of Generalized Darwinism. First, the complex set of semantic innovations analyzed throughout this article showed that the final outcome, particularly the connection established between Darwinism and the respective literature on habits and routines, was artificial. Instead, it was demonstrated that the successive and sophisticated redefinitions Hodgson and Knudsen were compelled to elaborate are symptomatic of the gap between biological (mainly variational) and social (mainly transformational) evolution. Second, since Generalized Darwinism is ultimately forced to radically restrict the notion of natural selection, one might ask why call it Darwinism at all. Third, however we choose to phrase it, the essential question is what Generalized Darwinism could teach social scientists about habits, routines, and so forth that they do not already know. This third and final criticism is also found in other assessments of Generalized Darwinism (Vromen 2010: notes 11 and 18; Levit, Hossfeld, and Witt 2011: 559).[13] However, we must consider it a conjecture in the strict Popperian sense of the term. If the criticism is accurate, then Generalized Darwinism will continue to generate new semantic innovations rather than new findings about socioeconomic evolution.

Finally, it should be mentioned that the argument of this article poses two important limits at least. First, the critique of Generalized Darwinism here operates on a very abstract level. The objective was to analyze the tensions that issued from Generalized Darwinism's project to accommodate the ontological discrepancies between the social and the biological domain by reconstructing the evolution of its conceptual apparatus. Therefore, the whole argument makes abstraction from more concrete questions like the following:

- Is Generalized Darwinism capable of avoiding the reduction of social, political, and legal evolution to the cultural change?
- Are explanations regarding the origins of a system the same as explanations about its inner logic?
- Is Darwinian "struggle for survival" capable of analyzing the rules of the game and not just the strategies of the players?

Providing an argument for the above questions would have been more interesting and constructive, but it would have also necessitated another, much longer article.

A second limitation of the present article is that it abstracts from new tendencies in the philosophy of biology. Very schematically, over the last decade the neo-Darwinian synthesis (for example, Mayr 1982) has clearly been challenged by new theoretical frameworks, and especially by "developmental biology," which reasserts the importance of the dialectics between the organisms and their environment. The waning of the neo-Darwinian synthesis has proven fatal to the project of "Darwinian Fundamentalism" initiated by Dawkins. For that matter, the new trend in the philosophy of biology draws increasingly more on the findings of evo-devo debates. Should we infer the possibility of a new synthesis between social and biological approaches that could surmount the limitations facing Generalized Darwinism? It was not possible to address this question within the parameters of the present article. However, I would like to briefly signal two formal considerations.

Firstly, it is very hard to understand why social scientists should follow the latest fashion in the philosophy of biology literature. Is it not the moment to rethink the specificities of the social domain vis-à-vis the physical and biological world? Second, it's my hope that the tensions of Generalized Darwinism elucidated in this article could be of some general value as to the impasses created by the "biology envy" tendency in social sciences. It should be repeated that Generalized Darwinism was chosen as the object of criticism not for its deficiencies but rather for its strengths: it was judged to be the *most sophisticated* argument from the "biology envy" perspective. And in all likelihood, it will remain so in the foreseeable future.

Notes

1. The above judgment does not concern local and circumspect applications of biological tools, as it is the case with the study of the market competition process. The evolutionary microeconomics initiated by Nelson and Winter (1982) is a success story integrating Darwinian selectionist models as heuristics within a broader set of socioeconomic mechanisms. However, further examination of the aforementioned research program is beyond the scope of the present article.

2. It must be noted that the idea of transformational evolution can be subject to two different interpretations. In the social sciences of the 18th and 19th century the dominant version of transformational evolution was the teleological one. This was mainly due to the influence of Enlightenment philosophy, which viewed human history as a process of progress aimed towards a perfect society. Even Karl Marx, who considered himself a severe critic of the "bourgeois" thinkers, was captivated by the Enlightenment's view of progress. Today it is extremely rare to find scholars who believe in an Enlightenment-type ideology of progress. So the real question for contemporary social theory is if variational evolution could be a serious alternative to the existing post-teleological versions of transformational evolution.

3. See also the following example borrowed from biology: "Mice and elephants are both mammals, but they differ greatly in size, behaviour and life span" (Hodgson and Knudsen 2010: 38). The problem with such examples is that they are based on a category fallacy. The issue is if there are nontrivial communalities *between* life and social sciences rather than *within* physics, biology, or social sciences.

4. Beside Gould (2002), see also Mayr (1982, 1991), Bowler (1983), and Levit, Meister, and Hossfeld (2008). Note also that the argument I present here was already developed in Levit, Hossfeld, and Witt (2011).

5. Note also that the usual argument that human capacities are the result of natural selection is irrelevant to the analysis of complex societies. Whatever the origin (from natural selection to God) of human capacities, the latter are

a given for *Homo Sapiens*. And as the evolutionary psychologist Henry Plotkin (2004: 152) phrases it: "[d]eclaring a present trait an adaptation to the past is an odd way to do science."

6. Negative correlation is a rare exception in biology (Godfrey-Smith 2009: 65). But it is very common in human affairs, especially in subjects that involve psychoanalysis and sociology. Similar major differences between the biological and the social realm apply to dialectics that have been considered fundamental to human verbal exchanges since Plato.

7. There is a crucial difference between Lamarck's initial system and what is called Lamarckism. The latter reduces the former to its secondary mechanism, gradual adaptation (Gould 2002: 179–189). Nevertheless, the above difference has no bearing on our discussion of Lamarckism.

8. Hodgson became perplexed in the early 1990s by the discrepancies between Darwinian and social evolution (Hodgson 1993: 134–135). He tried to overcome the problem by reproducing Veblen's agnostic position (Veblen 1899: 190) between Darwinism and Lamarckism: "These differences [between Darwinism and Lamarckism] are important, but secondary to the two ontological principles of novelty and persistence discussed above, and there is no doctrinal requirement by institutional economists in favour of one particular type of evolutionary mechanism" (Hodgson 1999: 279). However, Lamarckism has been dead to biology for many decades now, thus completely incapable of fulfilling his request for a meta-theory of complex evolving systems.

9. Lamarck's causal sequence (environmental alterations—felt needs—new habits—use and disuse—acquired characters) presupposes an interaction between organisms and environment. Many of his followers and/or critics split his middle-ground theory into two polarized camps of interpretation: the subjectivist-mentalist one that endows organisms with intentional or volitional capacities and the objectivist-materialist one that sees environment impressing its commands on passive organisms. The above differences are beyond the reach of this article. Regardless of the version we retain, the importance for us here is that it led to a directed variation that would in turn allow organisms to adapt. Note, however, that Hodgson and Knudsen disqualify directed variation by equating it with individualist or intentional models of human action.

10. Scholars espousing the Austrian-Schumpeterian notion of entrepreneurship or novelty could reasonably argue that even Lamarckism is not an appropriate method to study microeconomic processes. "Real" entrepreneurs are not contending to adapt to the market environment, but instead try to transform it to their benefit. From a diametrically opposite point of view, Marxian-Keynesian scholars, but also long-wave Schumpeterians (Freeman 1991), could argue that both Lamarckism and Darwinism cannot adequately address macro-social evolution. See also, in a more philosophical register,

Lawson (2003: 123–133) and Brown (2012). However, for the economy of this discussion, the above external critiques shall not be pursued any further.

11. It seems that the most convenient way to interpret transformational processes in Darwinian terms entails making cultural variants (such as habits, routines, beliefs, strategies) the selection material. In this case, individuals are transformed from interactors acting for their survival into the environment that selects the *existing* cultural variants. Given that individuals are the selectors, instead of those being selected, there is no longer any need to be eliminated. Note, however, that the above alternative resolves the question of the transformational action of humans by removing it from the sphere of *explanandum*: new cultural variants are produced exogenously. Whatever the possible advantages or disadvantages of the above alternative, Hodgson and Knudsen are unwilling to adopt it because it destroys the paradigmatic distinction they make between the selection *of* (interactors) and the selection *for* (replicators).

12. The only solution for Hodgson and Knudsen is to limit generative replication to the social domain. However, their answer (Hodgson and Knudsen 2011) to Gers (2011) shows that they are hesitant about carrying this out. Certainly, if they did, it would be like avowing that there was an important *discontinuity* between social and biological evolution. But there is no other way to go about it. Arguing in favor of generative replication for generalizing Darwinism, when biologists and philosophers of biology have shown that Darwinian natural selection can operate without replicators, is not a sustainable position.

13. Kronfeldner (2010: 193) arrives at similar conclusions regarding the idea, launched by Donald Campbell, that creative hypothesis formation simulates Darwinian "blind" variation. After arguing as to why the above idea is problematic, she concludes that "the debate is not about factual issues, but about the interpretation of these factual issues in Darwinian terms."

References

Aldrich, H. E., G. M. Hodgson, D. L. Hull, J. Mokyr, T. Knudsen, and V. J. Vanberg. (2008). "In Defence of Generalised Darwinism." *Journal of Evolutionary Economics* 18(5): 577–596.

Andersen, E. S. (2004). "Population Thinking, Price's Equation and the Analysis of Economic Evolution." *Evolutionary and Institutional Economics Review* 1(1): 127–148.

Bowler, P. J. (1983). *The Eclipse of Darwinism: Anti-Darwinian Evolution Theories in the Decades Around 1900.* Baltimore: John Hopkins University Press.

Brown, C. (2012). "Transmutability, Generalised Darwinism and the Limits to Conceptual Integration." *Cambridge Journal of Economics*, published on line: doi:10.1093/cje/bes016.

Buenstorf, G. (2006). "How Useful is Generalized Darwinism as a Framework to Study Competition and Industrial Evolution?" *Journal of Evolutionary Economics* 16(5): 529–541.

Cordes, C. (2006). "Darwinism in Economics: From Analogy to Continuity." *Journal of Evolutionary Economics* 16(5): 511–527.

Dawkins, R. (1976). *The Selfish Gene.* Oxford University Press: Oxford.

——. (1982). *The Extended Phenotype: The Gene as the Unit of Selection.* Oxford: Oxford University Press.

——. (1983). "Universal Darwinism." In *Evolution from Molecules to Men.* Ed. D. S. Bendall. Cambridge University Press: Cambridge. Reprinted in *The Philosophy of Biology.* Eds. D. L. Hull and M. Ruse (1998), pp. 15–37. Oxford: Oxford University Press.

Dennett, D. C. (1995). *Darwin's Dangerous Idea: Evolution and the Meaning of Life.* London: Allen Lane.

Dugger, W. M. (1981). "Sociobiology: A Critical Investigation to E.O. Wilson's Evolutionary Paradigm." *Social Science Quarterly* 62(2): 221–233.

Fine, P. E. M. (1979). "Lamarckian Ironies in Contemporary Biology." *Lancet* 313: 1181–1182.

Fracchia, J., and R. C. Lewontin. (1999). "Does Culture Evolve?" *History and Theory* 38(4): 52–78.

Freeman, C. (1991). "Innovation, Changes of Techno-Economic Paradigm and Biological Analogies in Economics." *Revue Economique* 42(2): 211–231.

Gers, M. (2011). "Overqualified: Generative Replicators as Darwinian Reproducers." *Biology and Philosophy*, published on line: doi 10.1007/s10539-011-9281-3.

Godfrey-Smith, P. (2000). "The Replicator in Retrospect." *Biology and Philosophy* 15(3): 403–423.

——. (2009). *Darwinian Populations and Natural Selection.* Oxford: Oxford University Press.

Gould, S. J. (1980). *The Panda's Thumb: More Reflections in Natural History.* New York: Norton.

——. (1997). "Evolution: The Pleasures of Pluralism." *New York Review of Books* 26(June): 47–52.

——. (2002). *The Structure of Evolutionary Theory.* Cambridge, MA: Harvard University Press.

Grafen, A. (2002). "A First Formal Link Between the Price Equation and an Optimization Program." *Journal of Theoretical Biology* 217(1): 75–91.

Hayek, F. A. (1988). *The Fatal Conceit: The Errors of Socialism.* London: Routledge.

Hannan, M. T., and J. Freeman. (1984). "Structural Inertia and Organizational Change." *American Sociological Review* 49(2): 149–164.

Hodgson, G. M. (1993). *Economics and Evolution: Bringing Life Back to Economics.* Cambridge: Polity Press.

——. (1999). *Evolution and Institutions: On Evolutionary Economics and the Evolution of Economics.* Cheltenham (UK) and Northampton (MA, USA): Edward Elgar.

——. (2001). *How Economics Forgot History: The Problem of Historical Specificity in Social Science.* London and New York: Routledge.

——. (2002). "Darwinism in Economics: From Analogy to Ontology." *Journal of Evolutionary Economics* 12(2): 259–281.

——. (2004). *The Evolution of Institutional Economics: Agency, Structure and Darwinism in American Institutionalism.* London and New York: Routledge.

Hodgson, G. M., and T. Knudsen. (2006a). "Dismantling Lamarckism: Why Descriptions of Socio-Economic Evolution as Lamarckian are Misleading." *Journal of Evolutionary Economics* 16(4): 343–366.

——. (2006b). "Why We Need a Generalized Darwinism, and Why Generalized Darwinism is Not Enough." *Journal of Economic Behavior & Organization* 61(1): 1–19.

——. (2006c). "The Nature and Units of Social Selection." *Journal of Evolutionary Economics* 16(5): 477–489.

——. (2008). "The Emergence of Property Rights Enforcement in Early Trade: A Behavioral Model Without Reputational Effects." *Journal of Economic Behavior and Organization* 68(1): 48–62.

——. (2010). *Darwin's Conjecture: The Search for General Principles of Social and Economic Evolution.* Chicago: University of Chicago Press.

——. (2011). Underqualified—Maximal Generality in Darwinian Explanation: A Response to Matt Gers. *Biology and Philosophy*, published on line: doi 10.1007/s10539-011-9293-z.

Hull, D. L. (1980). "Individuality and Selection." *Annual Review of Ecology and Systematics* 11: 311–332.

——. (1982). "The Naked Meme." In *Learning, Development and Culture: Essays in Evolutionary Epistemology.* Ed. H. Plotkin, pp. 273–327. Wiley: New York.

——. (1988). *Science as a Process: An Evolutionary Account of the Social and Conceptual Development of Science.* Chicago: University of Chicago Press.

Kronfeldner, M. E. (2010). "Darwinian 'Blind' Hypothesis Formation Revisited." *Synthèse* 175(2): 193–218.

Lamarck, J. B. ([1809] 2011). *Philosophie Zoologique.* Cambridge: Cambridge University Press.

Lawson, T. (2003). *Reorienting Economics.* London and New York: Routledge.

Levinthal, D. A. (1991). "Organizational Adaptation and Environmental Selection-Interrelated Processes of Change." *Organization Science* 2(1): 140–145.

Levit, G. S., U. Hossfeld, and U. Witt. (2011). "Can Darwinism Be 'Generalized' and of What Use Would This Be?" *Journal of Evolutionary Economics* 21(4): 545–562.

Levit, G. S., K. Meister, and U. Hossfeld. (2008). "Alternative Evolutionary Theories: A Historical Survey." *Journal of Bioeconomics* 10(1): 71–96.

Lewontin, R. C. (1970). "The Units of Selection." *Annual Review of Ecology and Systematics* 1: 1–18.

——. (2001). *It Ain't Necessarily So.* London: Granta Books.

Liagouras, G. (2009). "Socio-Economic Evolution and Darwinism in Thorstein Veblen: A Critical Appraisal." *Cambridge Journal of Economics* 33(6): 1047–1064.

Mayr, E. (1982). *The Growth of Biological Thought: Diversity, Evolution and Inheritance.* Cambridge, MA: Harvard University Press.

——. (1991). *One Long Argument: Charles Darwin and the Genesis of Modern Evolutionary Thought.* Cambridge, MA: Harvard University Press.

McKelvey, B. (1982). *Organizational Systematics.* Berkeley: University of California Press.

——. (1994). "Evolution and Organizational Science." In *Evolutionary Dynamics of Organizations.* Eds. J. A. C. Baum and J. V. Singh, pp. 314–326. Oxford: Oxford University Press.

Mirowski, P. (1989). *More Heat than Light: Economics as Social Physics, Physics as Nature's Economics.* Cambridge: Cambridge University Press.

Nelson, R. R. (2007a). "Universal Darwinism and Evolutionary Social Science." *Biology and Philosophy* 22(1): 73–94.

——. (2007b). "Comment on: Dismantling Lamarckism: Why Descriptions of Socio-Economic Evolution as Lamarckian Are Misleading, by Hodgson and Knudsen." *Journal of Evolutionary Economics* 17(3): 349–352.

Nelson, R. R., and S. W. Winter. (1982). *An Evolutionary Theory of Economic Change.* Cambridge MA: Belknap Press of Harvard University Press.

Plotkin, H. (2004). *Evolutionary Thought in Psychology: A Brief History.* Oxford: Blackwell.

Price, G.R. (1972). "Extension of Covariance Selection Mathematics." *Annals of Human Genetics* 35(4): 485–490.

——. (1995). "The Nature of Selection." *Journal of Theoretical Biology* 175(3): 389–396.

Sperber, D. (2000). "An Objection to the Memetic Approach to Culture." In *Darwinizing Culture: The Status of Memetics as a Science.* Ed. R. Aunger, pp. 162–173. Oxford and New York: Oxford University Press.

Usher, J. M., and M. G. Evans. (1996). "Life and Death Along Gasoline Alley: Darwinian and Lamarckian Processes in a Differentiating Population." *Academy of Management Journal* 39(5): 1428–1466.

Veblen, T. ([1899] 1994). *The Theory of the Leisure Class: An Economic Study in the Evolution of Institutions.* London: Routledge/Thoemmes Press.

Von Neumann, J. (1966). *Theory of Self-Reproducing Automata.* Urbana: University of Illinois Press.

Vromen, J. J. (2007). "Generalized Darwinism in Evolutionary Economics: The Devil Is in the Details." Presented at the 2007 EAEPE (European Association for Evolutionary Political Economy) Conference in Porto.

——. (2010). "Heterogeneous Economic Evolution: A Different View on Darwinizing Evolutionary Economics." Jena, Max Planck Institute of Economics: Papers on Economics and Evolution.

Wilkins, J. S. (2001). "The Appearance of Lamarckism in the Evolution of Culture." In *Darwinism and Evolutionary Economics.* Eds. J. Laurent and J. Nightingale. Cheltenham (UK) and Northampton (MA, USA): Edward Elgar.

Winter, S. G., and G. Szulanski. (2001). "Replication as Strategy." *Organization Science* 12(6): 730–743.

Witt, U. (2004). "On the Proper Interpretation of 'Evolution' in Economics and its Implications for Production Theory." *Journal of Economic Methodology* 11(2): 125–146.

When Heterodoxy Becomes Orthodoxy: Ecological Economics in *The New Palgrave Dictionary of Economics*

By Óscar Carpintero*

Abstract. Modern ecological economics emerged in opposition to mainstream economics as a scientific approach with many key heterodox features. Among these are an open systems perspective, transdisciplinarity, and radical criticism of the conventional representation of economic process. The term "ecological economics" was included internationally in the second edition (2008) of *The New Palgrave Dictionary of Economics*, the most prestigious and widely used dictionary of economics. In our view, however, the entry does little to facilitate understanding of the heterodox features, and theoretical and methodological controversies that have developed in ecological economics over the last two decades.

Introduction

Is ecological economics terribly heterodox?
—Yes, I hope so.

Interview with Richard B. Norgaard (2004: 224).

The history of economics is replete with intellectual controversies regarding both theoretical approaches and economic policy analysis. The controversial nature of economics is, however, often blurred due to the academic hegemony and force of neoclassical economics throughout the 20th century. Other, less dominant contributions in recent years from post-Keynesian economics, old institutionalism, socioeconomics, Marxist and radical economics, feminist economics, or ecological economics have revealed the extent to which this apparent uniformity of economic discourse is rather problematic.

*Department of Applied Economics, University of Valladolid (Spain), Avda. Valle Esgueva 6, E-47011 Valladolid, Spain, Tel. ++ 34-983423346; fax: ++34-983423299, carpin@eco.uva.es

American Journal of Economics and Sociology, Vol. 72, No. 5 (November, 2013).
DOI: 10.1111/ajes.12043

Along with criticism of mainstream economics, the last 15 years have witnessed the formation of the Association for Heterodox Economics (AHE) and the International Confederation of Associations for Pluralism in Economics (ICAPE), ongoing discussion about the nature of heterodox economics (Coats 2000; Dow 2000; Backhouse 2000; Colander, Holt, and Rosser 2004; Lawson 2003, 2006; Lee 2008), a search for common ground between different critical approaches to enhance the theoretical and academic position of heterodox economics (Lawson 2003, 2006; Lavoie 2006; O'Hara 2007; Holt, Pressman, and Spash 2009) and, finally, progress in reconstructing the social and institutional history of some current heterodox traditions (Lee 2009; Mata 2005; Mata and Lee 2007; Cronin 2010; Røpke 2004, 2005). In the words of T. Lawson (2006: 483), "heterodox economics is alive and flourishing."

The mainstream response to heterodoxy is generally directly proportional to the degree of criticism of the conventional economic approach. Lee (2009) identifies two possible response categories used by conventional economics when referring to heterodoxy: heresy and blasphemy. In the former, the degree of disagreement with orthodoxy is partial. Ideas are only considered wrong or peculiar and can be tolerated without punishment or even be accepted in the future. Blasphemy, however, involves a heterodox rejection of the body of orthodox neoclassical economic ideas. When this occurs, the reaction is very different. If blasphemy is committed by economists who adopt alternative approaches (for example, Marxist economics, radical, post-Keynesian, Sraffian), mainstream economics seeks to silence, persecute, and exclude both the ideas and the economists who defend them.[1]

Heterodox ideas sometimes come from outside economics through the interaction of dissenting economists with teachings from other natural or social sciences (such as psychology, political science, ecology, thermodynamics). In these cases, the mainstream approach tends to give little attention to their contributions, or dismisses them as oddities that pose no threat to the hegemony of neoclassical economics. This also occurs when heterodox approaches raise obvious issues that are difficult to solve by orthodoxy, such as psychological assumptions regarding economic behavior, or the ecological dimensions of economic processes. Neoclassical economics attempts to incorporate these ideas while neutralizing their heterodox origins. This is partially the case for modern behavioral or psychological economics[2] and for ecological economics, as we will see in this article.

The methods for achieving this goal are varied. One tactic is to redefine the heterodox theory in a more conventional way. This can be done by developing textbooks with a clearly heterodox title but conventional content. Another tactic involves using a reference work in economics (for example, a well-known economics dictionary) to redefine the critical approach. In a rigorous dictionary, the basic concepts of various fields (macroeconomics, microeconomics, statistics, econometrics, history of economic thought) are collected, and the basic tools, biographies of leading economists, or features of different theoretical approaches are explained. *The New Palgrave Dictionary of Economics* is perhaps the work that best encompasses all of these features. It is a widely recognized, primary reference source for economic information and likely the most traditional, thorough, and complete dictionary of economics currently available.

Given the scientific quality of the authors who write the entries, this dictionary often serves as an introduction to economic concepts for students or scholars unfamiliar with a specific topic. Therefore, the terms should be defined very carefully. One of the purposes of this article is to highlight how the *Palgrave's* entry for "ecological economics" changes its essence by omitting the heterodoxy that has defined it since its origins, making it rather conventional. This distances ecological economics as a theoretical framework from its real objective. As a result, this entry does little to facilitate understanding of the theoretical and methodological issues that have developed in ecological economics over the last two decades.

So, in the following pages we discuss how ecological economics has been described in the *New Palgrave*, identifying the most important flaws of this attempt. In the next section, we will briefly recall and characterize the heterodox foundations of ecological economics (especially regarding its open systems perspective). Finally, we conclude with some constructive suggestions for improving the treatment of aspects of ecological economics within *The New Palgrave*.

The *New Palgrave* Definition of Ecological Economics: Historical, Theoretical, and Methodological Flaws

First published in four thick volumes in 1987 (Eatwell, Milgate, and Newman 1987), the 2008 edition of *The New Palgrave Dictionary of Economics* (Durlauf and Blume 2008) offers several formal and substantive improvements over prior editions.[3] Among them is a major overhaul of the subject matter and an online version accompanying the paper edition, for updating the contents and quickly incorporating advances in economic research.[4] The publishers note that:

> While some classic articles from the 1987 were retained, around 80% of the text was either entirely new or substantially rewritten to reflect the depth of change within the discipline between the editions. This new edition retains the inspiring tradition of bringing together the world's most influential economists writing in their own voice on their areas of expertise, but in its online incarnation it has married this tradition with the benefits of a dynamic, updated resource serving the information needs of a new generation of economists.[5]

Along with the new developments in mainstream economics, the 2008 edition has made an effort to incorporate two additional issues. First, it acknowledges the interconnectedness of economics with other social (psychology, sociology) and natural (physics, biology, ecology) sciences, which explains the inclusion of terms such as "economic sociology" (Swedberg 2008), "econophysics" (Rosser 2008), "evolutionary economics" (Witt 2008), "ecological economics" (Xepapadeas 2008), "economic epidemiology" (Philipson 2008), "economics of climate change" (Goulder and Pizer 2008), and "behavioural economics" (Simon 1987).[6] Secondly, the importance of methodological and philosophical discussion in economics and the plurality of the different approaches that develop within it is recognized and maintained. New entries such as "philosophy and economics" (Hands 2008), "methodology of economics" (Backhouse 2008), "heterodox economics" (Lee 2008), "feminist economics" (Nelson 2008), "pluralism in economics" (Dow 2008), and "post-Keynesian economics" (King 2008) are among the main examples in this regard.

Since the 1987 edition there have indeed been major changes in economic sciences. One of them was precisely the emergence and institutional strengthening of ecological economics as a theoretical approach. That same year, Joan Martínez Alier's *Ecological Economics* (1987) was published and a meeting took place in Barcelona that laid the groundwork for the International Society for Ecological Economics (ISEE) and the journal *Ecological Economics.* The academic, scientific, and institutional soundness of ecological economics has since provided reason enough to include this approach in the 2008 edition.

Inclusion of the term in effect implies scientific acknowledgment. However, the content of the publishers' note quoted earlier does not seem to have been maintained in this case. The entry devoted to ecological economics does not appear to "retain the inspiring tradition of bringing together the world's most influential economists writing in their own voice on their areas of expertise."[7] In this case, the reader does not find renowned ecological economists as authors of this entry. Given the long list of potential contributors,[8] *The New Palgrave* editors cannot adduce a lack of experts on the subject matter or an inadequate academic approach. Potential authors have frequently and recently contributed to the writing and editing of an abundant and systematic body of knowledge concerning ecological economics (for example, Common and Stagl 2005; Costanza 1991; Costanza, Perrings, and Cleveland 1997; Daly 1999; Faber, Manstetten, and Proops 1996; Martínez-Alier and Røpke 2008; Proops 1989; Røpke 2004, 2005; Söderbaum 2000; Spash 1999, 2009; van den Bergh 1996, 2001). Some of them have even written entries in other dictionaries and encyclopedias, displaying full knowledge of ecological economics' subject matter (Costanza 2008a, 2008b; Martínez-Alier 2004).[9]

Given such ample resources, it was surprising that the author finally selected to write the ecological economics entry was Anastasios Xepapadeas. It is not our intent to criticize here the high scientific and academic merits of Professor Xepapadeas, but this choice is curiously paradoxical. In 2008, he was president of EAERE (European Association of Environmental and Resource Economics), and had long been co-editor of the *Journal of Environmental Economics and Management.* Both the EAERE and the *Journal of Environmental Economics and Management* are the vehicles of expression of environmental and natural resource economics, and hence both of them represent conventional approaches with different emphases from those prominent in ecological economics (Spash 1999; van den Bergh 2001; Gowdy and Erickson 2005).[10] This circumstance undoubtedly explains the nature of his entry (Xepapadeas 2008). Anastasios Xepapadeas is undeniably *qualified to represent natural resource economics, but less so for ecological economics.*

Let us briefly review some basic elements of the *Palgrave's* entry. Xepapadeas's (2008) is divided into three sections: an introductory first paragraph, a second paragraph devoted to "ecological models," and a third section that deals with "ecological-economic modeling." The author begins by highlighting the interdisciplinary nature of ecological economics and providing a reasonable definition: "the study of the interactions and co-evolution in time and space of human economies and the ecosystems in which human economies are embedded." He stresses that the main task for ecological economics should be: "to bridge the gap between economy and ecology by uncovering the links and the feedbacks between human economies and ecosystems, and by using these links and feedbacks to provide a unified picture of ecology and economy and their interactions and co-evolution . . . In a sense, ecological economics aims at linking ecological models and economic models in order to provide insights into complex and interrelated phenomena stemming from and affecting both ecosystems and human economies" (Xepapadeas 2008). Generally speaking, there is no objection to this approach. The problem arises with Xepapadeas's narrow perspective on modeling and the scientific work he attributes to ecological economics.

The section devoted to "ecological models" shows successive models of population dynamics and evolutionary biology: the traditional bioeconomic model of Clark (1990); the predator-prey models supported by Lotka-Volterra equations; meta-population models to describe the competition between different species for scarce resources; or co-evolutionary patterns between parasites and hosts (Red Queen dynamics), with different scenarios that determine the "equilibrium." According to Xepapadeas (2008), these ecological models would constitute "the cornerstones of the development of meaningful ecological-economic models."

The interest of this type of analysis is undeniable, especially for natural resource economics, mathematical biology, or evolutionary economics. However, we maintain that these special concerns are hardly representative of the general issues, debates, and models related to ecological economics, which have been published in the journal *Ecological Economics* for more than 20 years. A regular reader of this journal would easily discover that research in this field can be classified into at least four main areas: a) conceptual and methodological analysis; b) empirical studies; c) analysis of environmental policies and institutional dimensions; and d) modeling to represent ecological-economic relationships (Proops and Safonov 2004). The Xepapadeas contribution to *Palgrave's* displays a notable weakness by dealing with only *one subset* of the last area mentioned.

The *Palgrave's* dictionary entry also fails to make any reference to the historical context from which ecological economics emerged. It gives no reference to the pioneering contributions of authors such as S. Podolinsky, F. Soddy, or P. Geddes (covered by Martínez Alier 1987); nor does it cite well-known contributions from more modern pioneers such as N. Georgescu-Roegen (1971), Herman E. Daly (1968), K. W. Kapp (1950), S. V. Ciriacy-Wantrup (1952), R. U. Ayres (Ayres and Kneese 1969), or R. B. Norgaard (1984).[11] In addition to leaving out the contemporary classics of ecological economics, Xepapadeas's review makes *almost no reference to articles published in the field of ecological economics since 1989.*[12] Such a lack of references to authors, topics, and works (many of them expressing the nature and significance of ecological economics) exposes the underlying deficiency of Xepapadeas's entry.

To continue, the Xepapadeas entry (2008) seems to reflect either unawareness or deliberate concealment of the heterogeneity of ecological economics with regard to the major theoretical issues, tools, and models that have been debated and developed within this approach over the past two decades (Proops and Safonov 2004; Røpke 2005; Spash 2009). He offers no analysis of ecological economics as a powerful criticism of conventional environmental and resource economics based on neoclassical theory and its attempts to develop and implement alternative tools and frameworks. Furthermore, he fails to address some of the theoretical and practical issues currently confronting ecological economics, such as: the bridges that must be built between economics and thermodynamics in order to study the biophysical foundations of economic growth and production-consumption processes (for example, Ayres and Kneese 1969; Georgescu-Roegen 1971; Faber, Niemes, and Stephan 1987; Baumgärtner 2000; Baumgärtner, Faber, and Schiller 2007; Mayumi 2001; Ruth 1993; Ayres, Ayres, and Warr 2002; Ayres and Warr 2009[13]); conceptual debates on sustainability measurements and indicators (Neumayer 1999; Lawn 2006); the importance of co-evolution for understanding broad and complex socioecological systems (Norgaard 1984, 1994; Gowdy 1994); the social metabolism and industrial ecology approach (Adriaanse et al. 1997; Ayres and Simonis 1994; Fischer-Kowalski and Hütler 1999; Ayres and Ayres 2002); the institutional dimension of natural resource management (Bromley 1989, 1991; Ostrom 1990, 2005); the problematic relationship between growth and environmental degradation (Daly 1996);[14] or the role of environmental policy and environmental ethics in achieving a sustainable society (Spash 1997, 2000).

Regarding ecological-economic modeling *sensu stricto*, we believe Xepapadeas adopts a very narrow perspective and avoids mentioning many contributions from ecological economics on the representation and explanation of ecological-economic processes. Examples include environmental input-output models, thermodynamic models, multi-criteria evaluation, agent-based models, and models of social metabolism and industrial ecology (for example, Proops and Safonov 2004).[15]

Finally, the "mathematical-biological" orientation of this entry, which emphasizes optimality conditions in behavior, allows it to be linked to sociobiology and the bioeconomic approach advocated by neoclassical authors such as G. Becker (1976), J. Hirshleifer (1977), or G. Tullock (1979). However, some heterogeneity exists here too and this is not the only meaning of bioeconomics. Georgescu-Roegen (1977a, 1977b) pointed this out more than three decades ago,[16] followed by several other authors close to ecological economics (for example, Passet 1979; Gowdy 1987b, 1991, 1994; Mayumi and Gowdy 1999; Mayumi 2001; Carpintero 2006).

Thus, it is easy to appreciate the extent to which these historical, methodological, and theoretical flaws in the *Palgrave* entry blur the heterodox hallmarks associated with ecological economics since its origins. In the next section, therefore, we will examine some of the reasons why ecological economics can be defined as a heterodox economic approach.

Why Ecological Economics is Heterodox

As a starting point, it should be noted that the requirements relating to heterodox economics recently suggested by F. Lee are particularly well met by ecological economics:

> heterodox economics refers to specific economic theories and community of economists that are in various ways an alternative to neoclassical economics. Consequently, it is a multi-level term that refers to a group of economic theories—specifically Post Keynesian-Sraffian, Marxist-radical, Institutional-evolutionary, social, feminist, Austrian and ecological economics—that hold to various degrees blasphemous positions vis-à-vis mainstream economics; to a community of *heterodox economists* who engage with and are associated with one or more of the heterodox approaches and embrace a pluralistic attitude towards them without rejecting contestability and incommensurability among theories; and finally to the development of a coherent *heterodox economic theory*. (Lee 2009: 6–7)[17]

Several of these features can be indeed observed in the emergence of ecological economics. From its very beginning in the early 1980s, this approach was institutionalized as a meeting place for two types of transdisciplinary scientists who were dissatisfied with their respective disciplines. On the one hand, economists were dissatisfied with how mainstream economics (environmental economics included) represented production and consumption processes without consideration of thermodynamics and ecology. On the other hand, ecologists and physicists were unhappy with the way their respective disciplines left human and socioeconomic dimensions aside. This combination has led to different characterizations of ecological economics and a "reasonably peaceful" coexistence among approaches, although not always conflict free (Røpke 2004, 2005; Spash 2010). In the early years, special efforts were made at building a pluralistic and transdisciplinary approach concerned with the border issues between nature and economy, with a methodology capable of overcoming disciplinary limitations.

A good starting point for calibrating the heterodox challenge posed by ecological economics might be to compare its vision of the economic process with what is commonly found in mainstream economics. In the latter, economic production processes are treated as an isolated system, separate from social and environmental processes. It only deals with objects of established monetary value moving mechanically round on a carousel of production and consumption. Here, production factors are appropriately valued, and "without loss or friction" turned into goods and services (Schumpeter 1934: 10), supplied by a circular flow of income from corporations to households and back again.

Such a definition of the economic process automatically generates an external environment where many issues are not considered. Many natural substances and ecosystem functions (photosynthesis, natural purification, biodegradation, solar energy) constitute *preexisting* elements that are not assigned market value, or are not producible. Waste and pollution generated by production processes are also *excluded* from this definition and given the general title of "externalities." In mainstream economics, the notion of a system of economic production as the mere "creation of added monetary value" is *independent from the environmental foundations upon which it is based.* In any text on standard economic analysis, whether introductory or advanced, the production of goods is described as depending *only* on two production factors: labor and capital.[18] Natural resources are not considered a constraint. When the biophysical links have been broken, we can believe that economic growth is measured in monetary terms and based upon the virtues of compound interest, which has almost nothing to do with the functioning of the physical world. The conventional approach addresses economic growth as the simple expansion of monetary aggregates (at constant prices) such as national income or gross domestic product (GDP), which, by definition, present serious environmental shortcomings. So, if natural resources no longer represent a restriction to the production of goods, and wealth can be increased limitlessly by means of economic growth, there is no point in worrying about the equality in their distribution. As the pie increases in size, everyone can have a slice without cutting into the slices of others, nobody loses out, and the Pareto criterion is satisfied.

Once environmental issues reached such a magnitude that they could not be hidden from public concern, mainstream economics tried a new twist on an old idea. Unfortunately, instead of incorporating forms of reasoning and management that went beyond the monetary value of things, the conventional economic approach has spent much of its intellectual energy searching for ways to extend "the measuring rod of money" to areas that had in the past been banished from the field of economics. This is precisely because the absence of markets makes it difficult to impute a monetary value. Here we find a paradoxical choice: orthodoxy seeks to solve the problem of monetary valuation by maintaining a conception of the economic system as a *closed* system and by enforcing a monetary valuation of areas previously excluded. In the relationship between economy and nature, mainstream economics has generally come to accept the idea that the environment should be treated as another variable in the economic system, along with labor or capital, for example. Then, the standard toolbox can be applied to it in a conventional manner. Thus nature and ecosystems are seen as subsystems of the economy, rather than seeing the economy as embedded within the larger systems of society and the biosphere.

Ecological economics takes the more realistic latter view: the economic system is a subsystem embedded in a larger system, the biosphere, and therefore its dynamics are restricted to, and should be compatible with, the laws governing the functioning of the biosphere itself (the laws of thermodynamics and ecology). Unlike the conventional approach, the production of goods and services is here considered an *open* system, co-evolving in close collaboration with other social and natural systems (Norgaard 1984, 1994; Gowdy 1994).[19]

Thinking in terms of open systems involves first rethinking the representation of the economic process; going beyond the traditional circular flow of income between households and firms to incorporate natural resources before they are assigned monetary value, and waste once they have lost their value. From this perspective the economic process can be described in terms of social metabolism: just as any organism takes energy and food from nature to live, grow, and reproduce, the economy extracts raw materials, energy, and work and transforms them into consumer goods, infrastructures, and waste (for example, Adriaanse et al. 1997; Ayres and Simonis 1994; Fischer-Kowlaski and Hütler 1999; Ayres and Ayres 2002). Gowdy and Erickson (2005: 208) suggest that ecological economics may therefore offer a "structuralist approach that categorises consumption and production as a unified social and biophysical process."

Second, from a methodological point of view and given the scope of "the relationships between ecosystems and economic systems in the broadest sense" (Costanza 1989: 1), the economist must be willing to adopt a *transdisciplinary* approach with other fields. Transdisciplinarity[20] is essential because problems, difficulties, and theoretical or political challenges often arise *at the boundaries* of the established disciplines. This entails building bridges between economics and other social (psychology, sociology) and natural (thermodynamics and ecology) sciences. From an ecological economics perspective, it is no longer methodologically or theoretically reasonable for research on production and consumption processes to not rigorously incorporate socioenvironmental aspects and data from the disciplines that analyze them.

We should take into account, for example, lessons from psychology on shortcomings associated with the "canonical model of economic behaviour" (homo economicus);[21] or the teachings of thermodynamics regarding the limitations of energy, materials, and wastes (for example, Georgescu-Roegen 1971; Faber, Niemes, and Stephan 1987; Baumgärtner, Faber, and Schiller 2007) as they affect economic management, and the proper measurement units (biophysical or land) for analyzing these issues. Conventional monetary and financial measurements that focus on a single (monetary) unit should be complemented with a broader spectrum of possibilities. In practical terms, this implies overcoming evaluation and decision-making tools such as the cost-benefit analysis (CBA), which are based on a single monetary criterion of accounting and choice, and introducing broader, social multicriteria approaches that are more rigorous and span more dimensions (Munda 2008).[22]

Third, and precisely for that reason, ecological economics is skeptical of mainstream strategies for analyzing environmental sustainability in a closed system, using single unit measurements or "ecologically reformed" monetary indicators such as Green GDP or genuine savings to assess the environmental sustainability of a country or region (the "weak sustainability" approach; Pearce and Atkinson 1993; World Bank). Ecological economics insists that the economy must be seen as a subsystem of the environment, thus sustainability should be analyzed as a "scale issue." It refers to the size of the economic system within the biosphere, which raises an important question: How can this size be measured? Ecological economists proposed at least two alternatives: (1) a "resource flows approach" based on accounting for energy and materials that flow through the economy (socioeconomic metabolism); and (2) a "land use approach" based on estimating how much territory is needed for the production and consumption of a country (for example, ecological footprint, land use-land cover approach). Both alternatives allow us to obtain information about the capacity of ecosystems to supply resources and to absorb waste and emissions. Ecological economics is therefore concerned with highlighting the limitations of energy and material consumption as constraints on any situation of unrestricted growth in the production of goods and services.

A fourth issue emphasized in the open system approach of ecological economics has to do with analyzing the *rules of the game* for economic activity. The market is an economic institution that cannot exist or work without rules to regulate its functioning, which are usually established by the public sector. These rules of the game determine and guarantee property rights, define costs, penalties, incentives, labor conditions, and the requirements for the development of production processes. Thus "efficiency" (which relates production and costs), "profitability," or "optimum" results are not parameters that have fallen from the sky, but that depend on both the institutional framework that regulates and defines the market itself, and the distribution of income and wealth (economic power). From this viewpoint, a bridge has been built between ecological economics and the teachings of old institutional economics applied to natural resources. This was largely the work of pioneers in the mid-20th century, such as S. Ciriacy-Wantrup (1952) or K. W. Kapp (1950), who understood the relevance of some of the findings of the old institutionalism—namely, Veblen and Commons—for the analysis of the relationships between the economy and nature. Ciriacy-Wantrup and Kapp have been recovered as a link by the modern ecological version of the "old" institutionalism (Bromley 1989, 1991, 2006; Vatn 2005; Ostrom 1990; Berger 2008; Berger and Forstater 2007; Aguilera and Sánchez 2002, 2005).[23]

Along these lines are three long-standing, foundational questions at the base of any institutional reflection on management and use of natural resources, which have been skillfully addressed (Bromley 1982: 842–843): a) Who controls the rules of management (institutions) that determine the rate of use of natural resources? b) Who is in a position to receive the benefits of a certain criterion of use?, and c) Who must pay the costs associated with the use of natural resources? Answering these questions requires looking beyond the usual mechanisms of mercantile exchange and focusing on economic and social power processes and their distribution, which develop independently and condition these mechanisms. We have long known that every economic decision is preceded by a distributive conflict and the development of any activity has implications for distribution. From this perspective, environmental problems are largely associated with unequal appropriation of environmental space and decision making.[24] Without a critical analysis of the rules of the game and power structures linked to economic performance it will be difficult to reverse the process of ecological degradation.

Many of these heterodox traits and the open system framework were already apparent in the pioneering and transdisciplinary works of Georgescu-Roegen (1971), Boulding (1966), Daly (1968, 1977), Kapp (1950), Ciriacy-Wantrup (1952), and Ayres and Kneese (1969).[25] These and other contributions laid the groundwork for ecological economists to build their own approach (for example, Martínez Alier 1987; Costanza 1991; Faber, Manstetten, and Proops 1996; van den Bergh 1996, 2001; Spash 1999; Gowdy 1994; Norgaard 1994). The contrast between the current synthesis of the features of ecological economics and those of mainstream economics (even those applied to the environment such as environmental and resource economics) shown in Table 1 could not be more pronounced. More than a decade ago, Clive Spash (1999: 413) wrote: "There is clearly a divergence between the conformity to neo-classical economics favored by resource and environmental economists and the acceptance of more

Table 1

Differences between ecological economics and mainstream (neoclassical) economics

Conceptual issue	Mainstream (neoclassical) economics	Ecological economics
Basic World View	Mechanistic, static, atomistic	Dynamic, systems, evolutionary
Representation of Economic Process	Closed system; theory of allocation of fixed resources; production function	Open system Production as a biophysical process, thermodynamics; extended input-output approach, joint production of goods and polluting wastes
Rationality Hypothesis	Unbounded rationality Individual consumers and firms at the center of analysis	Bounded rationality Analyze humans as social actors, consumers versus citizens
Value Criteria	Mono-criteria assessment Reduce value to commensurable monetary units; utility function	Value pluralism Multicriteria assessment Separate value into incommensurable categories
Decision Criteria	Efficiency as the sole criterion, usually based on potential Pareto improvements	Needs fulfilled and inter- and intergenerational equitable distribution, stability, and resilience of environmental and social systems
Academic Stance	Disciplinary	Transdisciplinary/interdisciplinary
Assumptions About Technological Progress	Very optimistic	Prudently skeptical
Uncertainty	Reduce uncertainty to risk Market outcome focus to decision making	Precautionary principle to deal with pure uncertainty and ignorance; process-oriented, co-evolutionary focus to decision making
Evolutionary Change	Evolution as constrained optimization, survival of the fittest view of market outcomes, individual-based selection	Importance of contingency, historical accidents, path dependency, conflicts, circular, and cumulative causation Considers altruism and group selection as well as selfishness
Primary Macro Goal	Growth of GDP	Ecological economic sustainability

Source: Adapted from Gowdy and Erickson (2005: 213), Costanza, Daly, and Bartolomew (1991: 5), and van den Bergh (2001: 16).

radical critiques apparent in ecological economics. Thus, the progressive elements of ecological economics are increasingly incompatible with those practicing neo-classical economics who try to reduce all concepts to fit within the confines of their models."

Although intermediate approaches are possible, as is a specific emphasis on some of these traits, the differences listed provide a framework for discussions about key issues for economic analysis and the design and implementation of public policies. Examples include the relationship between growth and environment and its connection with the improvement or decline in welfare and quality of life, the impact of trade on the conservation of ecosystems, or the role of technological progress in solving the ecological crisis. In the controversy over these theoretical differences and practical issues, heterodox and blasphemous proposals and those with a less critical emphasis have coexisted within ecological economics. This may be interpreted as recognition of the plurality existing in the heterodox currents themselves and also in ecological economics (Norgaard 1989). However, over the past decade there have been several attempts to minimize the heterodox features of ecological economics and draw it closer to conventional economics. Among these are the increasing interest in monetary environmental valuation (a hallmark of environmental economics) without taking into account its severe shortcomings; confidence in monetary environmental valuation mechanisms for achieving sustainability, to the detriment of multicriteria social evaluation methods, biophysical indicators, and nonmarket regulation instruments; or the identification of rigorous reasoning with the widespread and indiscriminate use of mathematics and optimization tools, to the detriment of other forms of social scientific argumentation (Spash 2010).

Conclusion

In this article, we sought to remember and emphasize the heterodox features of ecological economics, and bring to light a recent attempt, involving *The New Palgrave Dictionary of Economics*, to neutralize the challenge this approach poses to mainstream economics. Such tactics might be deemed as similar to certain strategies of mainstream economics intended to reduce the academic capacity of other heterodox schools of economic thought.[26]

Certainly, a dictionary like *The New Palgrave*, which seeks to strike a difficult balance between selectivity and comprehensiveness, cannot cover every term. This may be due to the terms themselves lacking the necessary theoretical or historical background, or derive from editorial selection criteria. To conclude this article, we suggest some issues worth reconsidering in order to improve the treatment of certain aspects of ecological economics in *The New Palgrave*.

First, given the current importance of environmental problems associated with the use of natural resources and waste generation, it is strange that the entry devoted to "entropy"—written by Nicholas Georgescu-Roegen for the 1987 edition—was not reprinted in the 2008 edition (as was done with other older entries) or replaced with a new entry written by another author. Second, several ecological-economic terms already have sufficient strength and academic dissemination to merit recognition and definition in the dictionary. Examples would include economic metabolism, industrial ecology, ecological footprint, thermodynamics and economics, transdisciplinarity, sustainable development,[27] bioeconomics, multicriteria evaluation, biodiversity economics, and ecologically unequal exchange. Adding these terms into the electronic version would improve the dictionary as a whole. Third, selecting biographies of renowned economists for a dictionary with the caliber of *The New Palgrave* is undoubtedly a difficult task. However, it would be appropriate to include at least a few economists who have done a great deal of work towards increasing our understanding of nature-economy relationships. The list of candidates would be long and include many of the authors quoted in this article, but for the sake of brevity and garnering sufficient consensus, we propose at least this short list: K. Boulding,[28] K. W. Kapp, S. V. Ciriacy-Wantrup, and H. E. Daly. The first three are no longer living but have earned a sufficient reputation in ecological economics as well as institutional economics and evolutionary economics. Their inclusion would fill a biographical gap in three different and complementary theoretical approaches. The fourth is perhaps the most famous ecological economist alive, and his work well deserves at least this recognition.

Based on the arguments put forward here, and as the updated online version allows, we would suggest that the editors might find it desirable to commission a new "ecological economics" entry written by one of the living ecological economists cited in this article; an entry that, at the very least, might incorporate the plurality and heterodoxy that have characterized ecological economics since its beginning.

Acknowledgments

The author would like to thank Joan Martínez Alier, three anonymous reviewers, and the Editor for their helpful comments. Financial support from the Spanish Ministry of Science and Innovation (Project CSO2010-21979, Project HAR2010-18544, and Project ENE2010-19834) is also acknowledged.

Notes

1. Lee (2009:9) describes in detail the methods used by mainstream economists throughout the 20th century, which include ostracism, use of academic influence to prevent the hiring of blasphemous economists, dismissals for teaching "inappropriate" economic theories, denial of tenure, and exclusion from public research funds.

2. There is a certain discrepancy among the supporters of psychological economics with respect to the implications of their contributions to orthodoxy. While some of the pioneers (Herbert Simon or Peter Earl) show dissatisfaction with the neoclassical approach and consider that their results clearly question orthodoxy and lay the foundations for an alternative theory, other modern authors (Camerer, Loewenstein, or Rabin) do not consider the findings of behavioral economics to be inconsistent with neoclassical economics or alternative to the main school of thought. Apparently, the latter authors have attempted to maintain the *status quo* and adapt the canonical "rational choice" model. They use mathematical tools to modify and transform anomalies into explainable concepts within the general framework. This attitude has greatly assisted neoclassical economics in digesting the results. Unfortunately, some of the sharp criticism has been lost in the process of formalizing results to make them acceptable to orthodoxy. Categories and hypotheses have been incorporated that improve mathematical treatment but reduce the capacity for explanation. Here also, the difference between both approaches partly justifies the distinction between "old" and "new" behavioral economics (Sent 2004).

3. The 2008 edition has grown to eight volumes. The 1987 edition updated and reformatted the original *Dictionary of Political Economy*

published between 1894 and 1896 by Obert H. I. Palgrave. Between 1923 and 1926, Henry Higgs published an edition titled *Palgrave's Dictionary of Political Economy.*

4. The online version added new articles and updates in 2009, 2010, and 2011.

5. See "About the New Palgrave Dictionary of Economics" (http://www.dictionaryofeconomics.com).

6. Thanks to an entry written by H. Simon, *behavioural economics* appeared in the 1987 edition (Simon 1987). Fortunately, this entry was also reprinted in the 2008 edition. The editors have also added numerous entries related to this approach (*behavioural public economics, behavioural genetics, behavioural finances, behavioural economics, and game theory*).

7. See "About the New Palgrave Dictionary of Economics" (http://www.dictionaryofeconomics.com).

8. Solely by way of example, and by no means exhaustive, the list may include any one of the numerous present or former members of the Editorial Board of the journal *Ecological Economics.*

9. For the purpose of this article, only a few key and well-known references are listed.

10. The dictionary also contains an entry for "environmental economics" written by Robert N. Stavins (Stavins 2008). This, along with the incorporation of some mainstream concerns into the entry devoted to ecological economics, implies a dual bias in favor of the mainstream economic approach.

11. Xepapadeas's scant mention of Kenneth Boulding's classical article on "spaceship Earth" seems insufficient to fill this void. Also, the non-English language works of at least R. Hueting ([1974] 1980), R. Passet (1979), M. Faber et al. ([1983] 1987), or J. M. Naredo (Naredo and P. Campos; Naredo 1987) should be cited.

12. Only *one* article of the 21 references listed was published in *Ecological Economics.*

13. The book by Ayres and Warr (2009), though published a year after Xepapadeas's entry, compiles works on the material and energetic basis of economic growth in the USA and Japan during the 20th century.

14. De-growth movement contributions (Martínez Alier et al. 2010; Kallis 2011) did appear after Xepapadeas's entry and have benefited the discussion about the problematic relationship between growth and environment.

15. Proops and Safonov (2004) offer a more rigorous and complete sample of these contributions to ecological economics modeling than that of Xepapadeas (2008).

16. As Georgescu-Roegen (1977a: 105) claims: "I propose to show that the economic process is only an extension of biological evolution and, hence, the most important economic issues must be considered from this entirely new view point. One significant consequence of this evolutionary extension is the

dependence of our species on some very scarce resources . . . A second important and wholly surprising consequence is the perennial inequalities between social classes within one and the same society as well as between different societies. The same evolutionary extension, not the causes generally assumed by standard economics, is mainly responsible for these inequalities."

17. Due to the author's particular interests and background, the outstanding book by Lee is only focused on community studies of two different heterodox approaches (post-Keynesian and Marxian-radical). For ecological economics, Røpke (2004, 2005) is perhaps the most complete study on the emergence of this approach and the development of the ecological economist community.

18. Classical influence is seen in the tendency to include nominally "land" as a third factor of production in economic textbooks. However, we should not be misled on this point. It is easily observable that these textbooks and all subsequent developments related to production functions in micro- and macroeconomics generally avoid actually referring to land as a production factor and focus only on labor and capital, turning land into a merely nominal factor.

19. Ecological economics serves as a unifying thread within heterodox schools. According to Gowdy and Erickson (2005: 219): "It is the school of thought that explicitly recognises the interconnections and interdependencies of the economic, biophysical and social worlds."

20. A reviewer has pointed out that the "transdisciplinary term is notoriously hard to specify and in many definitions does not exclude interdisciplinary or is even identical to it." We agree. It is not our intention to raise a sharp methodological distinction between both terms. They could both be used inclusively from an ecological economics viewpoint. K. W. Kapp (1977: 528) wisely stressed many years ago: "In fact, in dealing with problems of environmental disruption and protective policies we are inevitably concerned with the manifold interdependencies between socioeconomic and ecological-physical systems. However, nothing seems to be less explored and more difficult than to deal systematically with the interaction of different systems either by *trans*disciplinary studies conducted by individual scholars from one discipline or by *inter*disciplinary research undertaken jointly by groups of experts from different disciplines, each bringing his own specific language, concepts, and theories to bear upon the common problem." The recent history of modern ecological economics seems to agree with Kapp's suggestion, with individual examples such as N. Georgescu-Roegen, K. Boulding, K. W. Kapp, M. Faber, and R. U. Ayres or group research such as that which has been developed at the Wuppertal Institute and the Institute for Social Ecology in Vienna.

21. Although pioneers of ecological economics (Georgescu-Rogen, Daly, and Boulding) have a tradition of criticizing the canonical model of *Homo economicus*, subsequent authors have also been enthusiastic about the results of psychological and experimental economics. This is evident in the research

of Spash and Hanley (1995), Spash (1997, 2000, 2002), and Gowdy and Mayumi (2001) on the transcendence of lexicographic preferences in the theory of choice and in environmental valuation, which places methods of monetary valuation of environmental quality in quarantine. Also promising is research on the relevance of the results of psychological and evolutionary economics in explaining the economic behavior of individuals in relation to the success of public and environmental policies (Gowdy 1993, 2004, 2008; Gowdy and Seidl 2004; van den Bergh, Ferrer i Carbonell, and Munda 2000; van den Bergh and Gowdy 2009).

22. Individual and collective decisions involve multiple dimensions that are almost always incommensurate with evaluation. However, incommensurability does not mean that it is impossible to compare and establish an ordinal preference after subjecting them to a process of multicriteria evaluation. This kind of evaluation helps with decision making in a situation of conflict, by acknowledging that a decision cannot be based on optimum technical criteria, but rather on well-informed deliberation and democratic participation (Martínez Alier, Munda, and O'Neill 1998). An example of this can be found in regard to allocation of public funds for different transportation proposals (public, private, pedestrian) by assessing their environmental or social costs (such as pollution or traffic deaths) with different units of measure. Other real-world applications of multicriteria approaches would include risk management, power plant siting, waste management, and economic policies.

23. However, institutional economists were given to different views on environmental issues. In the mid-1980s, DeGregori (1985, 1987) noted the confidence of traditional institutional economics in technological progress as the solution to environmental problems and resource shortages. A criticism of this work, based on arguments from ecological economics, can be found in Gowdy (1987a).

24. One of the reviewers of this article pointed out that the moral dimension is also relevant: even equal distribution does not necessarily eradicate irresponsible behavior without improved ethics.

25. Røpke (2004: 301) claims that: "The contributions from Boulding, Georgescu-Roegen, Daly, Ayres and Kneese had much in common with the ideas brought forward in relation to systems ecology. It was probably not accidental that these authors had broad scientific backgrounds: Boulding and Georgescu-Roegen were the very unusual kind of Renaissance men, cutting across several disciplines, including meta-theories such as systems theory, Daly had studied ecology, and Ayres and Kneese combined physics and economics (also others who later became important contributors of ecological economics had broad disciplinary backgrounds)."

26. For example, a detailed analysis for the post-Keynesian and Marxist-radical cases can be found in Lee (2009).

27. The "sustainability" entry, rightly written by Bromley (2008), could be complemented in this way.

28. Kenneth Boulding's biography was included in the 1987 edition but was removed from the 2008 edition. Although the online version allows access to the 1987 edition, this would be a good opportunity to update the content of Boulding's entry.

References

Adriaanse, A., S. Bringezu, A. Hammond, Y. Moriguchi, E. Rodenburg, D. Rogich, and H. Schütz. (1997). *Resource Flows: The Material Basis of Industrial Economies.* New York: World Resources Institute, Wuppertal Institute, Netherland Ministry of Housing Spatial Planning and Environment, National Institute of Environmental Studies.

Aguilera F., and J. Sánchez. (2002). "Social Participation, Institutional Change and Land Property in Building up Sustainability. A case study of land use conflict in Tenerife (Canary Islands)." *Environment and Planning C* 20: 593–612.

——. (2005). "Water Markets in Tenerife: The Conflict Between Instrumental and Ceremonial Functions of the Institutions." *International Journal of Water* 3(2): 166–185.

Ayres, R. U., and L. W. Ayres, eds. (2002). *Handbook of Industrial Ecology.* Cheltenham: Edward Elgar.

Ayres, R. U., L. W. Ayres, and B. Warr. (2002). "Energy, Power and Work in the US Economy, 1900–1998." *Energy* 28(3): 219–273.

Ayres, R. U., and A. V. Kneese. (1969). "Production, Consumption and Externalities." *American Economic Review* 59: 282–297.

Ayres, R. U., and U. Simonis, eds. (1994). *Industrial Metabolism: Reestructuring for Sustainable Development.* New York: United Nations University Press.

Ayres, R. U., and B. Warr. (2009). *The Economic Growth Engine. How Energy and Work Drive Material Prosperity.* Cheltenham: Edward Elgar.

Backhouse, R. (2000). "Progress in Heterodox Economics." *Journal of the History of Economic Thought* 22(2): 149–155.

——. (2008). "Methodology of Economics." In *The New Palgrave Dictionary of Economics. Second Edition.* Eds. Steven N. Durlauf and Lawrence E. Blume.

Baumgärtner, S. (2000). *Ambivalent Joint Production and the Natural Environment. An Economic and Thermodynamic Analysis.* Heidelberg and New York: Physica-Verlag.

Baumgärtner, S., M. Faber, and J. Schiller. (2007). *Joint Production and Responsibility in Ecological Economics. On the Foundations of Environmental Policy.* Cheltenham: Edward Elgar.

Becker, G. S. (1976). "Altruism, Egoism and Genetic Fitness: Economics and Socio-Biology." *Journal of Economic Literature* September: 817–826.

Berger, S. (2008). "K. William Kapp's Theory of Social Costs and Environmental Policy: Towards Political Ecological Economics." *Ecological Economics* 67(2): 244–252.

Berger, S., and Forstater, M. (2007). "Towards Political Institutionalist Economics. Kapp's Social Costs, Lowe's Instrumental Analysis, and the European Institutionalist Approach to Environmental Policy." *Journal of Economic Issues* 41(2): 539–546.

Boulding, K. (1966). "The Economics of the Coming Spaceship Earth." In *Toward a Steady-State Economy.* Ed. H. E. Daly, pp. 121–132. San Francisco: W.H. Freeman.

Bromley, D. W. (1982). "Land and Water Problems: An institutional Perspective." *Journal of American Agricultural Economics* 64(5): 834–844.

——. (1989). *Economic Interests and Institutions.* Oxford: Basil Blackwell.

——. (1991). *Environment and Economy.* Oxford: Basil Blackwell.

——. (2006). *Sufficient Reason: Volitional Pragmatism and the Meaning of Economic Institutions.* Princeton, NJ: Princeton University Press.

——. (2008). "Sustainability." In *The New Palgrave Dictionary of Economics. Second Edition.* Eds. Steven N. Durlauf and Lawrence E. Blume. http://www.dictionaryofeconomics.com/

Carpintero, O. (2006). *La bioeconomía de Georgescu-Roegen.* Barcelona: Montesinos.

Ciriacy-Wantrup, S. V. (1952). *Resource Conservation: Economics and Policies.* Berkeley: University of California Press.

Clark, C. (1990). *Mathematical Bioeconomics: The Optimal Management of Renewable Resources*, 2nd edition. New York: Willey Interscience.

Coats, A. W. (2000). "The Progress of Heterodox Economics." In *Evolution and Path-Dependence in Economic Ideas: Past and Present.* Eds. P. Garrouste and S. Ioannides. Aldershot: Edward Elgar.

Colander D., R. P. F. Holt, and J. B. Rosser, Jr. eds. (2004). *The Changing Face of Economics.* Ann Arbor: University of Michigan Press.

Common, M., and S. Stagl. (2005). *Ecological Economics: An Introduction.* Cambridge: Cambridge University Press.

Costanza, R. (1989). "What is Ecological Economics." *Ecological Economics* 1: 1–7.

——. (1991). *Ecological Economics: The Science and Management of Sustainability.* New York: Columbia University Press.

——. (2008a). "Ecological Economics I." In *Encyclopaedia of Ecology* (online version): 999–1006.

——. (2008b). "Ecological Economics II." In *Encyclopaedia of Ecology* (online version): 1006–1011.

Costanza, R., H. E. Daly, and J. Bartholomew. (1991). "Goals, Agenda and Policy Recomendations for Ecological Economics." In *Ecological Econo-*

mics: The Science and Managment of Sustainibility. Ed. R. Costanza. pp. 1–20. New York: Columbia University Press.

Costanza, R., Ch. Perrings, C. Cleveland, eds. (1997). *The Development of Ecological Economics.* Cheltenham: Edward Elgar.

Cronin, B. (2010). "The Diffusion of Heterodox Economics." *American Journal of Economics and Sociology* 69(5): 1475–1494.

Daly, H. E. (1968). "On Economics as a Life Science." *Journal of Political Economy* 76: 392–406.

——. (1977). *Steady-State Economics.* San Francisco: W.H. Freeman.

——. (1996). *Beyond Growth: The Economics of Sustainable Development.* Boston: Beacon Press.

——. (1999). *Ecological Economics and the Ecology of Economics.* Cheltenham: Edward Elgar.

DeGregori, T. R. (1985). *A Theory of Technology: Continuity and Changes in Human Development.* Ames: Iowa State University Press.

——. (1987)."Resources Are Not: They Become; An Institutional Theory." *Journal of Economic Issues* 21(3): 1241–1263

Dow, S. (2000). "Prospects for the Progress of Heterodox Economics." *Journal of the History of Economic Thought* 22(2): 157–170.

——. (2008). "Pluralism in Economics." In *The New Palgrave Dictionary of Economics. Second Edition.* Eds. Steven N. Durlauf and Lawrence E. Blume. http://www.dictionaryofeconomics.com/

Durlauf, S. N., and L. E. Blume, eds. (2008). *The New Palgrave Dictionary of Economics Online.* London: Palgrave Macmillan. http://www.dictionaryofeconomics.com/

Eatwell, J., M. Mulgate, and P. Newman, eds. (1987). *The New Palgrave Dictionary of Economics.* London: Macmillan.

Faber, M., R. Manstetten, and J. Proops. (1996). *Ecological Economics: Concepts and Methods.* Cheltenham: Edward Elgar.

Faber, M., H. Niemes, and G. Stephan. ([1983] 1987). *Entropy, Environment and Resources.* Heidelberg: Springer Verlag (German edition, 1983).

Fischer-Kowalski, M., and W. Hütler. (1999). "Society's Metabolism. The Intellectual History of Materials Flow Analysis, Part II, 1970–1998." *Journal of Industrial Ecology* 2(4): 107–136.

Georgescu-Roegen, N. (1971). *The Entropy Law and the Economic Process.* Cambridge, MA: Harvard University Press.

——. (1977a). "Bioeconomics: A New Look at the Nature of Economic Activity." In *The Political Economy of Food and Energy.* Ed. L. Junker, pp. 105–134. Ann Arbor: University of Michigan Press.

——. (1977b). "Inequality, Limits and Growth from a Bioeconomic View Point." *Review of Social Economy* XXXV(3): 361–375.

Goulder, L. H., and W. A. Pizer. (2008). "Economics of Climate Change." In *The New Palgrave Dictionary of Economics. Second Edition.* Eds. Steven

N. Durlauf and Lawrence E. Blume. http://www.dictionaryofeconomics.com/

Gowdy, J. M. (1987a). "GAIA and Technological Utopianism: A Comment on De Gregory." *Journal of Economic Perspectives* 21(1): 473–476.

——. (1987b). "Bio-Economics: Social Economy Versus Chicago School." *International Journal of Social Economics* 14: 32–42.

——. (1991). "Bioeconomics and Post Keynesian Economics." *Ecological Economics* 3(1): 77–87.

——. (1993). "Georgescu-Roegen's Utility Theory Applied to Environmental Economics." In *Entropy and Bioeconomics.* Eds. J. C. Dragan, E. K. Seifert, and M.C. Demetrescu, pp. 230–240. Milan: Nagard.

——. (1994). *Coevolutionary Economics: The Economy, Society and the Environment.* Dordrecht: Kluwer Academic Publishers.

——. (2008). "Behavioral Economics and Climate Change Policy." *Journal of Economic Behavior and Organization* 68(3–4): 632–644.

Gowdy, J., and J. Erickson. (2005). "The Approach of Ecological Economics." *Cambridge Journal of Economics* 29: 207–222.

Gowdy, J. M., and K. Mayumi. (2001). "Reformulating the Foundation of Consumer Choice Theory and Environmental Valuation." *Ecological Economics* 39(2): 223–237.

Gowdy, J., and I. Seidl. (2004). "Economic Man and Selfish Genes: The Implications of Group Selection for Economic Valuation and Policy." *Journal of Socio-Economics* 33: 343–358.

Hands, D. W. (2008). "Philosophy and Economics." In *The New Palgrave Dictionary of Economics. Second Edition.* Eds. Steven N. Durlauf and Lawrence E. Blume. http://www.dictionaryofeconomics.com/

Hirshleifert, J. (1977). "Economics from a Biological Viewpoint." *Journal of Law and Economics* XX: 1–52.

Holt, R. F., S. Pressman, and C. L. Spash, eds. (2009). *Post Keynesian and Ecological Economics.* Cheltenham, Edward Elgar.

Hueting, R. ([1974] 1980). *New Scarcity and Economic Growth: More Welfare Through Less Production?* Amsterdam: North-Holland (Dutch edition, 1974).

Kallis, G. (2011). "In Defence of Degrowth." *Ecological Economics* 70: 873–880.

Kapp, K. W. (1950). *The Social Costs of Private Enterprise.* Cambridge, MA: Harvard University Press.

——. (1977). "Environment and Technology: New Frontiers for the Social and Natural Sciences." *Journal of Economic Issues* XI(3): 527–540.

King, J. E. (2008). "Post Keynesian Economics." In *The New Palgrave Dictionary of Economics. Second Edition.* Eds. Steven N. Durlauf and Lawrence E. Blume. http://www.dictionaryofeconomics.com/

Lavoie, M. (2006). "Do Heterodox Theories Have Anything in Common? A Post-Keynesian Point of View." *Intervention. Journal of Economics* 3(1): 87–112.

Lawn, P. A., ed. (2006). *Sustainable Development Indicators in Ecological Economics.* Cheltenham: Edward Elgar.

Lawson, T. (2003). *Reorienting Economics.* London and New York, Routledge.

——. (2006). "The Nature of Heterodox Economics." *Cambridge Journal of Economics* 30: 483–505.

Lee, F. (2008). "Heterodox Economics." In *The New Palgrave Dictionary of Economics. Second Edition.* Eds. Steven N. Durlauf and Lawrence E. Blume. http://www.dictionaryofeconomics.com/

——. (2009). *A History of Heterodox Economics.* New York: Routledge.

Martínez Alier, J. (1987). *Ecological Economics: Energy, Environment and Society.* Oxford: Basil Blackwell.

——. (2004). "Ecological Economics." In *International Encyclopaedia of the Social and Behavioural Sciences* (online version): 4016–4023.

Martínez Alier, J., G. Munda, and J. O'Neill (1998). "Weak Comparability of Values as a Foundation for Ecological Economics." *Ecological Economics* 26(3): 277–286.

Martínez-Alier, J., U. Pascual, F. D. Vivien, and E. Zaccai. (2010). "Sustainable De-Growth: Mapping the Context, Criticisms and Future Prospects of an Emergent Paradigm." *Ecological Economics* 69: 1741–1747.

Martínez Alier, J., and I. Røpke, eds. (2008). *New Developments in Ecological Economics.* Cheltenham: Edward Elgar.

Mata, T. (2005). "Dissent in Economics: Making Radical Political Economics and Post Keynesian Economics, 1960–1980." Ph.D. thesis. London School of Economics and Political Science.

Mata, T., and F. Lee. (2007). "The Role of Oral History in the Historiography of Heterodox Economics." *History of Political Economy* 39(annual supplement): 154–171.

Mayumi, K. (2001). *The Origins of Ecological Economics.* London: Routledge.

Mayumi, K., and J. M. Gowdy, eds. (1999). *Bioeconomics and Sustainability.* Cheltenham: Edward Elgar.

Munda, G. (2008). *Social Multi-Criteria Evaluation for Sustainable Development.* Heidelberg: Springer Verlag.

Naredo, J. M. (1987). *La economía en evolución.* Madrid: Siglo XXI.

Naredo, J. M., and P. Campos. (1980). "Los balances energéticos de la economía española." *Agricultura y Sociedad* 15: 163–256.

Nelson, J. (2008). "Feminist Economics." In *The New Palgrave Dictionary of Economics. Second Edition.* Eds. Steven N. Durlauf and Lawrence E. Blume. http://www.dictionaryofeconomics.com/

Neumayer, E. (1999). *Weak Versus Strong Sustainability: Exploring the Limits of Two Opposing Paradigms.* Cheltenham: Edward Elgar.

Norgaard, R. B. (1989). "The Case for Methodological Pluralism." *Ecological Economics* 1: 37–57.

——. (1984). "Coevolutionary Development Potential." *Land Economics* 60: 160–173.

——. (1994). *Development Betrayed: The End of Progress and a Coevolutionary Revisioning of the Future.* London and New York: Routledge.

——. (2004). "Interview." In *The Changing Face of Economics.* Eds. Colander D. R. P. F. Holt and J. B. Rosser, Jr., pp. 215–250. Ann Arbor: University of Michigan Press.

O'Hara, P. A. (2007). "Heterodox Political Economy Specialization and Interconnection—Concepts of Contradiction, Heterogeneous Agents, Uneven Development." *Intervention. Journal of Economics* 4(1): 99–120.

Ostrom, E. (1990). *Governing the Commons: The Evolution of Institutions for Collective Actio*n. New York: Cambridge University Press.

——. (2005). *Understanding Institutional Diversity.* Princeton, NJ: Princeton University Press.

Passet, R. (1979). *L'Economique et le vivant.* Paris: Payot.

Pearce, D., and G. Atkinson. (1993). "Capital Theory and Measurement of Sustainable Development. An Indicator of Weak Sustainability." *Ecological Economics* 8: 103–108.

Philipson, T. (2008). "Economic Epidemiology." In *The New Palgrave Dictionary of Economics. Second Edition.* Eds. Steven N. Durlauf and Lawrence E. Blume. http://www.dictionaryofeconomics.com/

Proops, J. (1989). "Ecological Economics: Rationale and Problem Areas." *Ecological Economics* 1(1): 59–76.

Proops, J., and P. Safonov, eds. (2004). *Modelling in Ecological Economics.* Cheltenham: Edward Elgar.

Røpke, I. (2004). "The Early History of Modern Ecological Economics." *Ecological Economics* 50: 293–314.

——. (2005). "Trends in the Development of Ecological Economics from the Late 1980s to the Early 2000s." *Ecological Economics* 55: 262–290.

Rosser, J. B. (2008). "Econophysics." In *The New Palgrave Dictionary of Economics. Second Edition.* Eds. Steven N. Durlauf and Lawrence E. Blume. http://www.dictionaryofeconomics.com/

Ruth, M. (1993). *Integrating Economics, Ecology and Thermodynamics.* Dortrecht: Kluwer Academic Publishers.

Schumpeter, J. (1934). *The Theory of Economic Development.* Cambridge, MA: Harvard University Press.

Sent, E. (2004). "Behavioral Economics: How Psycology Made Its (limited) Way back into Economics." *History of Political Economy* 36(4): 735–760.

Simon, H. A. (1987). "Behavioral Economics." In *The New Palgrave Dictionary of Economics.* Eds. Eatwell, J., M. Mulgate, and P. Newman, Vol. 1. pp. 221–224. London: Macmillan.

Söderbaum, P. (2000). *Ecological Economics. A Political Economics Approach to Environment and Development.* London: Earthscan Publications.

Spash, C. L. (1997). "Ethics and Environmental Attitudes with Implications for Economic Valuation." *Journal of Environmental Management* 50: 403–416.

——. (1999). "The Development of Environmental Thinking in Economics." *Environmental Values* 8: 413–435.

——. (2000). "Ecosystems, Contingent Valuation and Ethics: The Case of Wetland Recreation." *Ecological Economics* 34: 195–215.

——. (2002). "Informing and Forming Preferences in Environmental Valuation: Coral Reef Biodiversity." *Journal of Economic Psychology* 23(5): 665–687.

——. (2009). *Ecological Economics: Critical Concepts in the Environment.* 4 Volumes. London: Routledge.

——. (2010). "Socio Ecological Economics: Understanding the Past to See the Future." *American Journal of Economics and Sociolgy* 70: 341–375.

Spash, C. L., and N. Hanley. (1995). "Preferences, Information and Biodiversity Preservation." *Ecological Economics* 12(3): 191–208.

Stavins, R. N. (2008). "Environmental Economics." In *The New Palgrave Dictionary of Economics. Second Edition.* Eds. Steven N. Durlauf and Lawrence E. Blume. http://www.dictionaryofeconomics.com/

Swedberg, R. (2008). "Economics Sociology." In *The New Palgrave Dictionary of Economics. Second Edition.* Eds. Steven N. Durlauf and Lawrence E. Blume. http://www.dictionaryofeconomics.com/

Tullock, G. (1979). "Sociobiology and Economics." *Atlantic Economic Journal* 7: 1–10.

van den Bergh, J. C. J. M. (1996). *Ecological Economics and Sustainable Development: Theory, Methods and Applications.* Cheltenham: Edward Elgar.

——. (2001). "Ecological Economics: Themes, Approaches, and Differences with Environmental Economics." *Regional Environmental Change* 2: 13–23.

van den Bergh, J., A. Ferrer i Carbonell, and G. Munda. (2000). "Alternative Models of Individual Behaviour and Implications for Environmental Policy." *Ecological Economics* 32(1): 43–61.

van den Bergh, J., and J. Gowdy. (2009). "A Group Selection Perspective on Economic Behavior, Institutions and Organizations." *Journal of Economic Behavior and Organization* 72(1): 1–20.

Vatn, A. (2005). *Institutions and Environment.* Cheltenham: Edward Elgar.

Witt, U. (2008). "Evolutionary Economics." In *The New Palgrave Dictionary of Economics. Second Edition.* Eds. Steven N. Durlauf and Lawrence E. Blume. http://www.dictionaryofeconomics.com/

World Bank (2012) *World Development Indicators.* New York. http://data.worldbank.org/data-catalog/world-development-indicators

Xepapadeas, A. (2008). "Ecological Economics." In *The New Palgrave Dictionary of Economics. Second Edition.* Eds. Steven N. Durlauf and Lawrence E. Blume. http://www.dictionaryofeconomics.com/article?id=pde2008_E000221doi:10.1057/9780230226203.0423

Are Mainstream and Heterodox Economists Different? An Empirical Analysis

By Michele Di Maio*

Abstract. We explore the differences between mainstream and heterodox economists based on the responses to a questionnaire from a representative sample of Italian economists. Using different definitions for mainstream and heterodox economics, we compare the individual and academic characteristics of the economists belonging to these groups. We measure the within and between disagreement for each group and we test whether belonging to one or the other group predicts differences in economists' opinions on economic policy. Results show that: 1) mainstream and heterodox economists differ as to individual and academic characteristics and political views; 2) the disagreement within heterodox economics is lower than within mainstream economics; 3) some of commonly used ways of grouping heterodox and mainstream schools of thought have little explicative power in relation to individual opinions; 4) on critical economic policies, the opinions of heterodox and mainstream economists are significantly different even after controlling for a number of individual characteristics, including political opinions.

Introduction

Economists are used to disagreeing about almost everything, the definition of their own discipline included (Backhouse and Medema 2009; Lee 2011). Part of this persistent and irreducible disagreement among economists is without doubt related to their belonging to

*Michele Di Maio, Department of Economic Studies, University of Naples "Parthenope," Via Medina 40, 80133, Naples, Italy. E-mail: michele.dimaio@uniparthenope.it. I would like to thank the editor (Frederic S. Lee), two anonymous referees, Luca De Benedictis, and Chiara Toglia for their comments and suggestions. All remaining errors are obviously my own. All the supplementary material on the Survey of Italian Economists can be found at the webpage http://micdimaio.googlepages.com/surveyofitalianeconomists.

American Journal of Economics and Sociology, Vol. 72, No. 5 (November, 2013).
DOI: 10.1111/ajes.12044

different schools of thought.[1] Admittedly, in this, economics is not different from all other social sciences in which confrontation between different schools of thought is the norm.[2]

While there are several schools of thought in economics, they are often divided into two main groups: mainstream and heterodox.[3] The history of economic ideas alternates periods in which it seems that only one school of thought is about to prevail and a body of shared knowledge to emerge,[4] to others in which it clearly appears that alternative approaches and methodological differences are there to stay. Interestingly, these differences do not remain confined in the ivory tower of academic research but they have important implications for practical economic policy (Lee 2010a). Cases of confrontation between the two groups have been numerous, the last one being the recent economic crisis, its causes and possible remedies.[5]

The objective of this article is to empirically explore the differences between mainstream and heterodox economists. Using the responses to a questionnaire from a representative sample of Italian economists, we describe the differences between the members of the two groups in terms of individual and academic characteristics and political views. Next, we measure the disagreement within and between these two groups using as a test-bed a large set of propositions on the Italian economy. Finally, we analyze whether being heterodox rather than mainstream predicts differences in economists' opinions about economic policy.

To show that economists' disagreement about economic policy is related to differences in the economists' schools of thought is crucial for two main reasons. First, it would illuminate a not-yet explored source of variation in economists' opinions (Whaples 2006). Second, it could provide evidence that belonging to a school of thought may differentiate economists not only by their academic visions but also in relation to their judgment on very specific economic policies. Needless to say, this result has important policy implications.

Our task faces several difficulties. The first one is to define the object of analysis. How to define a school of thought and the mainstream and heterodox groups is not obvious. Our choice has been to just make the respondent self-identify with a school of thought.[6] The second difficulty concerns the fact that there are several possible confounding factors one should consider when evaluating the role of schools of thought in explaining economists' disagreement. To deal with this issue, we perform a regression analysis in which we include a set of control variables concerning individual and academic characteristics of the respondent and also her political views. This allows us to eliminate some of the possible confounding elements in evaluating if being a mainstream rather than a heterodox economist makes a differences to her opinion about the effectiveness of a set of economic policies.

The history of economics is characterized by the confrontation between different schools of thought. Nonetheless, the only paper we are aware of that presents an empirical analysis that takes into account the possibility that belonging to different schools of thought is one of the determinants of economists' disagreement is De Benedictis and Di Maio (2011). The present article uses responses to the same questionnaire used in that article but it extends the analysis and focuses on the differences between mainstream and heterodox economics.

Our analysis delivers a set of interesting results that are relevant in the debate on the characteristics, degree of internal homogeneity, and future perspectives of both mainstream and heterodox economics. First, mainstream and heterodox economists differ as to individual and academic characteristics and political views. Second, heterodox economists are not more fractious as a group than mainstream ones in terms of within-group disagreement. This is also true for all the single heterodox schools of thought (but for the evolutionary school) when compared to the mainstream one. Third, some of the commonly used ways of grouping heterodox and mainstream schools of thought have little explicative power in relation to individual economist's opinions. Finally, on critical economic policies, the opinions of heterodox and mainstream economists are significantly different even after controlling for a number of individual characteristics, including the political view.

The article proceeds as follows. The next section discusses the literature relevant for the present article. The third section describes the survey and its main variables. The fourth section presents the empirical analysis. The fifth section concludes the paper.

Related Literature

There are two strands of literature that are related to our article. The first is the literature concerning the causes of economists' disagreement and its measurement. The second is the vast and heterogeneous set of contributions that describe the differences between mainstream and heterodox schools of thought in terms of assumptions, methods, and conclusions, and that, analyzing the sociology of economic research, discusses the perspective for the existence of a plurality of approaches in economics.

There is now a growing literature on the measurement of the disagreement among economists. Kearl, Pope, Whiting, and Wimmer (1979) were the first to measure and compare economists' opinions. Using responses from U.S.-based economists, they argued that the apparently common perception of disagreement among economists was wrong. Most of the subsequent studies tend to confirm this result: consensus is high among economists. Yet disagreement is notably larger when one considers economic policy questions. The sources of economists' disagreement analyzed in the literature have been the most different. Several studies have focused on the role of the political view of the respondent, showing that it is an important source of variation with respect to an economist's judgment about policy prescriptions (Randall 1985; Fuchs, Krueger, and Poterba 1998; Klein and Stern 2006, 2007; De Benedictis and Di Maio 2011). Others have emphasized the role of the cultural and national identity of the respondents (Frey, Pommerehne, Schneider, and Gilbert 1984; Mueller 1995; Aiginger, McCabe, Mueller, and Weiss 2001). Actually, looking at the history of economic ideas, it is quite obvious to think that belonging to different schools of thought is a possible source of variation in economists' opinions (Dow 2007; Lee 2009). Yet, to the best of our knowledge, there are no previous studies that have empirically tested this statement. The only partial exception is De Benedictis and Di Maio (2011) where the school of thought of the respondent is shown to be an important confounder in the relation between the political values and the economists' opinions on the economy.

Strife between schools of thought has characterized economics since its beginning days (Gide and Rist 1909; Hutchinson 1953).[7] Yet schools of thought are still important today. Schools of thought not only guide the research activity of many economists but they also influence journals' quality perceptions and the evaluation of individual research (Axarloglou and Theoharakis 2003). Their persistent importance is confirmed by the impressive number of 23 schools of thought listed in Eatwell, Milgate, and Newman (1987) and by the large number of journals, associations, and conferences related to specific schools of thought (see Lee 2010a). This is true even if the importance the profession has given to the methodological approach differs across countries and in particular between Europe and the United States (Frey, Pommerehne, Schneider and Gilbert 1984; Aiginger, McCabe, Mueller and Weiss 2001).[8] Schools of thought have had a smaller role in U.S. academia because each school of thought tends to have self-defined criteria for evaluating quality. This makes it difficult to compare the performance of scholars across schools (Frey and Eichenberger 1993; Corsi, D'Ippoliti, and Lucidi 2010). Given the formally competition-based U.S. recruitment system, it can be argued that this has had the unintended consequence of making easier the marginalization of the heterodox approaches from academia.

Nonetheless there are numerous elements suggesting that the interest towards heterodox approaches to economics is increasing and that the role and importance of alternative schools of thought is somehow growing. Lee (2008) reports that the number of international associations of heterodox economics is steadily growing and has reached the number of 24. Dow (2000) emphasizes that the communities of heterodox economists are getting more numerous in the last decades. While several authors have argued that theoretical pluralism is a valuable asset per se and thus should be preserved (Maki 1997), the debate between schools is not limited to assumptions, principles, and theorems. For instance, heterodox economists often contest what they consider an unfair distribution of power in the discipline (George 2007) and they express concerns about the possible evolution of the discipline (Prychitko 1998; Lee, Cronin, McConnell, and Dean 2010). There is evidence that the Europeans are more open toward nonmainstream views (see, for instance, the papers in the 1995 *Kyklos* special issue (Frey and Frey 1995)). Yet the results from a recent survey reported in Frey, Humbert, and Schneider (2010) suggest that German-speaking economists favor the neoclassical school of thought by and large. Moreover, it emerges that respondents appreciate the contributions of Anglo-Saxon economists much more than their fellow compatriots' contributions. This is interesting because it shows that the influence of mainstream is increasing among young economists.

The Questionnaire, the Sample, and the Schools of Thought in the Italian Academia

On May 2007, an e-mail was sent to 1,511 Italian economists, inviting them to fill in an on-line questionnaire about their opinions concerning the Italian current economic situation.[9] Four hundred and ninety-six economists responded, a reply rate of 33 percent.[10] Since the focus of the present article is on Italian academic economists employed in Italian universities, we exclude from the sample Italian economists working abroad, PhD students, postdocs, and nonacademics.[11] The final sample includes 335 respondents. Data have been postweighted according to the three strata (gender, academic position, and region of work) that can be observed in the data on the population of Italian academic economists collected by the Italian Minister of Education, University and Scientific Research (MIUR) on Italian economists employed in Italian universities.[12] This procedure gives us a representative sample of Italian economists.

Distribution of Italian Economists Across Schools of Thought

Defining the distinctive characteristics of the different schools of thought is not easy. For instance, Lawson (2006) argues that there is no straightforward way of identifying the nature of any one of the several heterodox schools of thought. Indeed, there is a good deal of debate within most, if not all, the various schools about which are the characterizing elements of the school itself.

In our questionnaire, we adopted an agnostic approach and decided not to enter the discussion about what mainstream economics and heterodox economics are or, for instance, what distinguishes the neoclassical paradigm from the evolutionary one.[13] Instead, the respondent was self-reporting the school of thought she belongs to.[14]

Table 1

The Distribution of Italian Economists Across Schools of Thought

SCHOOL OF THOUGHT	Number of respondents	%
Eclectic	95	28
Neoclassical/Mainstream	59	18
I do not refer to any specific school of thought	56	17
Keynesian/Post-Keynesian	36	11
Keynesian/Neo-Keynesian	27	8
Institutionalist/Neo-Institutionalist	23	7
Evolutionary	17	5
Marxist/Sraffian/Neo-Marxist	13	4
Behavioral	5	1
Regulationist	3	1
Austrian/Neo-Austrian	1	0
Total	335	100

NOTE: The table includes the responses to the question: How would you define your methodological orientation? Schools of thought are ordered by number of members. Multiple answers were possible: respondents who indicated three or more options (seven cases out of 335) were defined as Eclectic; double responses (32 cases) were randomly assigned to one of the two options indicated; specific responses (15 cases) have been reclassified according to similarity (e.g., Marxist-Leninists have been classified as Marxist).

To minimize errors and possible misinterpretations, the respondent had to choose her school of thought from a given list. The list of schools of thought is reported in Table 1. Multiple choices were allowed. Each respondent was also given the possibility to add to the predefined list her own school of thought in the case it was not already included.

Our categorization of the different schools of thought is very similar to the one adopted by Axarloglou and Theoharakis (2003). The main difference with their list is that we also included the Eclectic category.[15] Our list includes all the schools of thought discussed in Colander, Holt, and Rosser (2004) but it also considers other approaches.[16]

Table 1 reports the distribution of Italian economists across schools of thought. Almost one-third of the economists in our sample defines themselves as Eclectic. The other two larger groups are the Neoclassical/Mainstream (18 percent) and the "I do not refer to any specific school of thought" group (hereafter No-school) (17 percent). If this latter group and Eclectic are summed, it results that almost half of the sample is not categorized in any of the traditional schools of thought. Among these, after Neoclassical/Mainstream, the largest are Post-Keynesian (11 percent) and Neo-Keynesian (7 percent). Even if much less relevant as a percentage, our sample also features Institutionalist/Neo-Institutionalist[17] (7 percent), Evolutionary (5 percent), Marxist/Sraffian (4 percent), and Behavioral economists (1 percent). These results indicate that numerous schools of thought are present in Italian academia, even if their relevance in terms of numerosity of members is very heterogeneous.

Respondents were allowed to declare more than one school of thought. Descriptive statistics (not reported) show that when respondents indicate to belong to more than one school of thought these were, in most of the cases, all but the mainstream one. This result confirms the view discussed in Lee (2010a) that heterodox economists are often engaged with more approaches, testifying to the pluralism of heterodox economists.

Comparing Mainstream and Heterodox Economists

Schools of thought are sometimes divided into two opposing fronts to define dichotomies such as mainstream vs. nonmainstream or orthodox vs. heterodox. While these are common ways of grouping economists, are they informative? For instance: Are members of these groups different concerning individual and academic characteristics? Or, how much does the dichotomy mainstream vs. heterodox account for differences in economists' opinions?

There are different views concerning the usefulness of such dichotomies. For instance, Colander, Holt, and Rosser (2004) argue that beyond the rejection of the orthodoxy there is no single unifying element that characterizes heterodox economics.[18] George (2007) notes that while modern economics has a tightly defined orthodoxy, the heterodoxy is highly fragmented. According to Lee (2010a), heterodox economics includes a number of different approaches because it is a multi-level term that refers to a group of broadly commensurable economic theories. Actually, two elements characterize heterodox economics: 1) the heterodox community is distinct from the community of mainstream economists; 2) heterodox economics is characterized by plurality of approaches. Dow (2007) argues that, even if the dualism of orthodoxy vs. heterodoxy is somehow too simplistic, it still may be useful.

There are different ways of grouping schools of thought to construct dichotomies such as mainstream vs. heterodox. The following analysis evaluates how much the different possible ways of grouping schools of thought into dichotomies really identifies subsets of economists that are different as to their individual and academic characteristics and political values. This would finally indicate which dichotomy would be better able to predict differences across economists' opinions.

Obviously, the way in which we group schools of thought under a common label like mainstream and heterodox is crucial to our analysis. Since there is no unique or agreed way to define each group, we will consider different alternatives.[19] The list of the groups and their composition is reported in Table 2 where the eight groups are paired so as to make up four dichotomies. The first group we define is mainstream. This group includes only the Neoclassical/Mainstream school of thought. We also consider an alternative definition of mainstream labeled MainstreamLarge: it includes both the Neoclassical/Mainstream and Neo-Keynesian school. The third group is nonmainstream: it includes all the schools of thought in our list but the Neoclassical/Mainstream one: Eclectic, Institutionalist, Post-Keynesian, Neo-Keynesian, Marxist, Austrian, Evolutionary, Regulationist, Behavioral. Then we consider two possible definitions for the heterodox group. The first one is derived from the JEL classification system where current heterodox approaches (JEL-B5) are said to be: Marxist, Institutionalist, Sraffian, Evolutionary, and Austrian. We call this group HeterodoxJEL. The second includes all the schools of thought in the HeterodoxJEL group plus Post-Keynesian, Regulationist, and Behavioral.[20] We call this group HeterodoxLarge. Finally, we define two groups following the discussion in Lee (2010b).

Table 2

Group Composition

Group definition		Schools of thought included in each group
1	Mainstream	Neoclassical/Mainstream
	Nonmainstream	Eclectic, Institutionalist, Post-Keynesian, Neo-Keynesian, Marxist, Sraffian, Austrian, Evolutionary, Regulationist, Behavioral
2	MainstreamLarge	Neoclassical/Mainstream, Neo-Keynesian
	HeterodoxJEL	Marxists, Institutionalist, Sraffian, Evolutionary, Austrian
3	MainstreamLarge	Neoclassical/Mainstream, Neo-Keynesian
	HeterodoxLarge	Marxists, Institutionalist, Sraffian, Evolutionary, Austrian, Post Keynesian, Regulationist, Behavioral
4	MainstreamExtra	Neoclassical/Mainstream, Neo-Keynesian, Behavioral
	HeterodoxAlt	Marxists, Institutionalist, Sraffian, Evolutionary, Post-Keynesian, Regulationist

The first group is called MainstreamExtra: with respect to MainstreamLarge, it additionally includes behavioral economists while it excludes Austrians.[21] The second is called HeterodoxAlt, which is the HeterodoxLarge group excluding the Behavioralists and the Institutionalist/Neo-Institutionalists.

Mainstream and Heterodox Economists: Are They Different?

We begin describing the differences in the individual characteristics of the groups' members. Table 3 reports the results from regressing a binary variable indicating the group the respondent belongs to on a number of variables describing the characteristics of the respondent (age, gender, academic position, type of research (empirical or theoretical), and political views). We run four separate probit regressions, one for each of the different possible categorizations of the respondents in dichotomies as for Table 2.

Table 3

Differences in Individual Characteristics Between Mainstream and Heterodox Economists

	Nonmainstream vs. Mainstream	HeterodoxJEL vs. MainstreamLarge	HeterodoxLarge vs. MainstreamLarge	Heterodox vs. MainstreamExtra
	(1)	(2)	(3)	(4)
AGE	0.512***	0.343**	0.375**	0.290**
	(0.132)	(0.158)	(0.134)	(0.132)
MALE	0.305	0.304	0.195	0.134
	(0.251)	(0.314)	(0.273)	(0.271)
ACADEMIC POSITION	−0.271**	−0.246*	−0.178	−0.151
	(0.123)	(0.132)	(0.115)	(0.115)
RESEARCH	−0.215**	−0.046	−0.073	−0.063
	(0.099)	(0.121)	(0.105)	(0.105)
MARKET	−0.650***	−0.284*	−0.301**	−0.384***
	(0.160)	(0.167)	(0.137)	(0.138)
SOCIAL MOBILITY	0.052	0.074	0.046	0.010
	(0.126)	(0.145)	(0.130)	(0.129)
RIGHT	−0.236*	−0.109	−0.269***	−0.205
	(0.131)	(0.152)	(0.138)	(0.136)
#	233	120	154	153
F-test	0.000	0.020	0.000	0.000
Pseudo R^2	0.27	0.11	0.14	0.13

NOTE: Results from probit regression. A constant is included in all regressions but it is not shown. Robust standard errors in parentheses. Dependent variables: (1) NoMAIN = 0 if school of thought (SoT) is Neoclassical/Mainstream. NoMAIN = 1 for all other SoT; (2) HetJEL = 1 if SoT is Marxian, Sraffian, Institutional, Evolutionary, or Austrian. HetJEL = 0 if SoT is Neoclassical/Mainstream or Neo-Keynesian; (3) HetLarge = 1 if SoT is Marxian, Sraffian, Institutional, Evolutionary, Austrian, Post-Keynesian, Regulationist, or Behavioral. HetLarge = 0 if SoT is Neoclassical/Mainstream or Neo–Keynesian; (4) Het = 1 if SoT is Marxian, Sraffian, Institutional, Evolutionary, Post-Keynesian, or Regulationist. Het = 0 if SoT is Neoclassical/Mainstream, Neo-Keynesian, or Behavioral.

Column (1) shows the difference between the economists belonging to the nonmainstream group with respect to the mainstream one. The two groups are significantly different. Nonmainstream economists are older, with a lower academic position, more empirically oriented, less market oriented, and more left-wing than mainstream ones. Columns (2) and (3) instead compare the characteristics of the economists belonging to the MainstreamLarge group and economists belonging to the heterodox group as defined by HeterodoxJEL or HeterodoxLarge. In both cases, heterodox economists are older and less market oriented than MainstreamLarge ones. Moreover, economists belonging to the HeterodoxLarge group are more left-wing than MainstreamLarge ones. Finally, Column (4) indicates that Heterodox-Alt economists when compared with MainstreamExtra are significantly older and less market oriented.

It is interesting to note that, whatever the dichotomy used, results about AGE suggest that is very likely that mainstream economists will dominate Italian academia in the next few years. This may indeed be a problem if a proper system of balance between schools of thought will not be put in place. If this does not happen, mainstream economists will continue to significantly increase their appointment power in Italy.

Field of Research

We now consider the differences between mainstream and heterodox economists as to the field of research. Each respondent was asked to indicated her fields of research as categorized by the JEL codes. We use these results to answer two questions. Are heterodox economists clustered around some specific fields? Are there fields in which the presence of mainstream and heterodox is significantly different? The answers depend on the definition used to group schools of thought.[22] Using the dichotomy mainstream/nonmainstream there are no significant differences as to the field of research. Instead, when using the other definitions of heterodox economists (HeterodoxJEL; HeterodoxLarge; Heterodox) heterodox economists turn out to be significantly more involved than mainstream ones in JEL B (Schools of Economic Thought and Methodology) and JEL O (Economic

Development, Tech. Change, and Growth). When using HeterodoxJEL, heterodox economists are also significantly less involved in JEL E (Macroeconomics and Monetary Economics) than mainstream ones. Using HeterodoxLarge, it turns out that heterodox economists are less present in the field of Labor and Demographic Economics (JEL J). Finally, according to HeterodoxAlt, heterodox economists turn out to be significantly less present in the Microeconomics field (JEL C) compared to mainstream economists.

Mainstream and Heterodox Economists: Are Their Opinions Different?

In the previous section, we have shown that mainstream and heterodox economists (or any definition used to group schools of thought) are different as to individual characteristics and political views. In this section, we analyze the differences concerning their opinions on the economy. We will answer a number of questions: Are the opinions of mainstream and heterodox economists different? In which group is the within disagreement about economic policy higher? Does the group a respondent belongs to, once controlled for individual characteristics, predict the respondent's opinion on a given economic policy?

As a test-bed we analyze the responses of our representative sample of Italian economists to a questionnaire containing a list of propositions about the Italian economy. The list included 58 propositions: 40 about the causes of the Italian economic slowdown (Causes hereafter) and 18 about policy proposals to be adopted to overcome the current economic difficulties in Italy (Policy Proposals hereafter). The lists of all propositions are reported in Table 6 (Causes) and Table 7 (Policy Proposals) in the Appendix.[23] For each of the 40 Causes, the respondent expressed her level of agreement with the fact that the content of that proposition was an important cause of the current difficulties of the Italian economy. The answer was expressed on a Likert scale with four ordered options, coded as follows: strongly disagree = 1; partially disagree = 2; partially agree = 3; strongly agree = 4. Respondents had also the option "No opinion." As for the Policy Proposals, the respondent was asked her opinion on the fact that the policy described in the proposition could be useful in making the Italian economy recover. The answer was given using the same Likert scale used for the Causes.

Disagreement Within Mainstream and Heterodox Economists

One of the main criticisms of heterodox economics is that its level of internal coherence is supposedly lower than in mainstream economics. For instance, Colander, Holt, and Rosser (2004) argue that heterodox economics is more fractious as a group than mainstream economics is. On the contrary, Lee (2010a) provides indirect evidence to support the conclusion that heterodox economics is more coherent than mainstream. Our survey is able to provide novel evidence to shed light on this important point.

How Much Disagreement is there Between and Within Schools of Thought?

We begin measuring the between and within school of thought disagreement. To measure the between schools of thought disagreement, we compute the correlation between the (mean) opinion by school of thought for each of the 58 propositions. As for causes, the results indicate that the correlations between the (mean) opinions are quite high (see Appendix Table 9). The only exception are Marxists: the correlation between the opinion of Marxist and other schools of thought (but for Post-Keynesian and Evolutionary) on which are the causes of the difficulties of the Italian economy is very low. Looking at the results for policy proposals, things are a bit different (see Appendix Table 10). First, the correlations between schools of thought opinions are in general lower than on causes. This suggests that schools of thought differ more on the evaluation of effectiveness of the different policy proposals than on the diagnosis of the causes of the difficulties of the Italian economy. This result is confirmed by the lower between variation of causes with respect to policy proposals.[24] Second, there is a substantial difference between the opinions on the one side of mainstream and on the other side of Marxists, Post-Keynesian, and Evolutionary economists. While the correlation between mainstream and Marxist is close to zero, for the latter two schools it results that the correlation with mainstream (even if positive) is not significant.

To measure the level of disagreement within schools of thought, we use the relative entropy index (Kearl, Pope, Whiting, and Wimmer 1979; Frey, Pommerehne, Schneider, and Gilbert 1984; Alston, Kearl, and Vaughan 1992; Fuchs, Krueger, and Poterba 1998; De Benedictis and Di Maio 2011).[25] The relative entropy index takes a maximum value (rel.entropy = 1) when economists' responses are equi-distributed along the Likert scale, and reach its minimum value (rel.entropy = 0) when all responses are fully concentrated in one category of the Likert scale. For each school of thought, we compute the average relative entropy index on the full set of causes and policy proposals. Results are reported in Table 4. The higher the average relative entropy by school of thought the higher the disagreement among economists belonging to the specific school of thought on the set of causes and policy proposals listed in the questionnaire. The results show that for all schools of thought the within disagreement is larger on causes than on policy proposals. Moreover for both causes and policy proposals, the school of thought that is characterized by

Table 4

Within School of Thought Disagreement

	Causes Rel.Entropy	Policy Proposals Rel.Entropy
Eclectic	0.81	0.76
No-school	0.77	0.75
Evolutionary	0.78	0.75
Neoclassical/Mainstream	0.76	0.74
Keynesian/Neo-Keynesian	0.77	0.72
Keynesian/Post-Keynesian	0.78	0.69
Institutionalist/Neo-Institutionalist	0.74	0.67
Marxist/Sraffian/Neo-Marxist	0.71	0.61

Note: Entropy is the average value of the relative entropy index computed for each cause and policy proposal considering the opinions of the economists belonging to the specific school of thought. Schools of thought ranked from high to low relative entropy index on policy proposals.

the highest within disagreement is the Eclectic while the lower dispersion is found within Marxists.

How Much Disagreement is there Within Mainstream and Heterodox Economists?

We now measure and compare the disagreement within the mainstream and heterodox groups as identified according to the definitions described in Table 2. As before, we measure the within disagreement for each group using the relative entropy index. Results are reported in Table 5. It turns out that the within disagreement among mainstream economists is lower than among nonmainstream ones. This result clearly depends on the inclusion of Eclectic economists in the latter group. Instead, mainstream economists show higher within disagreement with respect to heterodox economists independently from the definition used for the latter group for both causes and policy proposals. This is an interesting result since it suggests that the policy implications deriving from the theoretical premises of the mainstream approach are not univocal and they may be influenced by individual characteristics, for

Table 5

Within Group Disagreement

	Causes Rel.Entropy	Policy Proposals Rel.Entropy
Mainstream	0.76	0.74
MainstreamLarge	0.77	0.73
MainstreamExtra	0.76	0.73
Non-Mainstream	0.78	0.72
HeterodoxJEL	0.75	0.68
HeterodoxAlt	0.75	0.67
HeterodoxLarge	0.71	0.65

Note: The table reports the (weighted) relative entropy index for each group over the 40 causes and the 18 policy proposals. The weights are the share each school of thought represents with respect to the group considered. Groups ranked from high to low relative entropy index on policy proposals.

example the political view and individual values. In the following section, we will take also this element into consideration in our analysis. Finally, reading together the results in Tables 4 and 5 provides support to the view that heterodox economists are no more fractious than mainstream economists and perhaps a little less so.

Mainstream and Heterodox: Is Their View of the Economy Different?

We now move to verify whether the dichotomy mainstream vs. heterodox is able to predict differences in economists' opinions. Is being a mainstream or a heterodox, controlling for other individual characteristics, correlated with the way in which an economist looks at the economy?

Since the dichotomies we described in Table 2 are usually employed to describe the divisions inside the profession, it is interesting to assess the ability of these dichotomies to capture systematic differences in economists' opinions on the economy. For each dichotomy, we regress the respondent's opinion on the corresponding dummy variable (NoMAIN, Het-JEL, HetLarge, and Het).[26] In all regressions we include as controls the same set of individual variables: age, gender, region of birth, region of work, whether the respondent has moved from her birthplace, the field of research,[27] the academic position, the political view, and the degree of optimism. We also control for other possible confounding elements more specifically related to the content of the questionnaire, such as the worry (level and changes in the last five years) of the respondents with respect to the specific Italian economic situation, her knowledge of the Italian economy and of the debate on the Italian economic situation. Counting the number of propositions in which the dummy variable is significant gives an indication of how much each dichotomy is able to account for disagreement across economists. The results (not shown) indicate that the variable NoMAIN is significant for only three causes and three policy proposals, which suggests that the dichotomy mainstream/nonmainstream does not capture very well the differences in opinions across economists. The reason is that—as we showed in the previous section—the nonmainstream group is very heterogeneous. The other dichotomies seem to be more informative. The dummy HetLarge is significant for five causes and four policy proposals, Het is significant for seven causes and three policy proposals while HetJEL turns out to be significant for nine causes and six policy proposals. Interestingly, in each case HetJEL is significant and so are HetLarge and Het. Thus we choose to focus on the variable HetJEL and we discuss for which causes and policy proposals a significant difference emerges between mainstream and heterodox economists as grouped according to this variable.

Causes

Most of the causes on which heterodox and mainstream economists disagree are related to the international position of Italy. Heterodox are more likely to blame the European Commission economic policy for the difficulties of the Italian economy. On the contrary, mainstream economists are more likely to believe that the causes of the current situation are related to the type and quality of domestic export and the country's inability to attract foreign direct investments. A second set of causes is related to the structural characteristics of the economy. Differently from heterodox, mainstream economists consider the low quality of the intangible infrastructures (justice, regulation authorities, government agencies), the existence of barriers to entry to the domestic market and the low degree of domestic competition as main causes of the difficulties of the Italian economy. Differences emerge also with respect to the North-South economic divide: while heterodox economists consider it a cause of the current difficulties, the mainstream blame the lack of adequate infrastructures on the Mezzogiorno.[28] The two groups markedly differ in their opinions of the effects of the policies adopted to reduce public debt, with the heterodox considering them one of the causes of the current situation. Finally, differences are quite marked also as for the role of the labor market. Mainstream economists are much more likely than the heterodox to include the low labor market flexibility as one of the causes of the difficulties of the Italian economy.

Policy Proposals
There are a number of policy proposals on which mainstream and heterodox economists' opinions are significantly different. To begin with, heterodox economists consider to proceed with more liberalizations and to proceed with more privatization significantly less favorably than mainstream. They also disagree with mainstream as to the efficacy of making more flexible the labor market or reducing labor union power as effective instruments to make the economy recover. In both cases, heterodox are less in favor of these policies than mainstream. Heterodox economists are also more likely to support public investment in strategic sectors and funding public research. This confirms their lower trust in the possibility that the private initiative or the market would be able to make the economy recover. In accordance with their opinion on the causes, heterodox are less likely to believe that improving the quality of exported goods for unchanged specialization pattern may ameliorate the current situation.

Interestingly, taken together these results suggest that heterodox economics should be interpreted as a positive descriptive term: heterodox economics is not only about rejecting mainstream economics but about doing economics differently.

Additional Results

The previous analysis is based on a representative sample of Italian academic economists working in Italy. Yet we also received responses to our questionnaire from Italian economists working abroad and from PhD students and postdoc researchers working in Italy. Since it is not possible to determine the representativeness of these subsamples with respect to the corresponding populations, we decided not to include them in the main analysis. Nonetheless, we think that these are both important dimensions that are worth exploring. They indeed may give some indication as to the possible evolution of the profession.

Home or Abroad
We begin expanding our sample by including Italian economists who work abroad.[29] How different are Italian economists abroad

with respect to domestic ones in terms of the probability of being heterodox?

We run four different regressions: in each we regress a variable indicating whether the respondent is working abroad or in Italy on one of the four different dichotomous variables we have used to define the respondent being heterodox or mainstream (see Table 2) controlling for age, gender, place of birth, place of work, fields of research, and political views. The results show that Italian economists working abroad are significantly less likely to be heterodox than domestic ones for all the dichotomous definitions of heterodox vs. mainstream. They are also more likely to be younger, more right-wing, and, not surprisingly, less favorable to the intervention of the government in favoring social mobility. The positive effect of being mainstream on the probability of being employed abroad disappears when the group mainstream becomes larger: when Neo-Keynesian and/or Behavioral are also included, the difference in the probability to be employed abroad disappears. This can be interpreted as evidence that what makes a real difference in terms of the possibility to access international academia is only being neoclassical/mainstream.

Tenured or Not

As a second extension, we include in our sample current PhD students and postdocs working in Italy.[30] As before, we run four different regressions: in each we regress a variable indicating the respondent being tenured or not on one of the four different dichotomous variables we have used to define the respondent being heterodox or mainstream (see Table 2) controlling for age, gender, place of birth, place of work, fields of research, and political views. Results indicate that being heterodox rather than mainstream (whatever the definition used) is never significantly correlated with the probability of having tenure. Interestingly, the only significant variable in these regressions is AGE: this is not surprising given that the strong relation between tenure and age is a well-known characteristic of Italian academia. More research should verify this relation in other countries where the advancements in one's career are more competition based so as to see what effect being Heterodox has on the possibility to get tenure. The evidence that being heterodox does not affect the probability of tenure could also be interpreted as indicating that Italian academia has been relatively open to plurality of approaches in the past. In fact, this outcome is also due to the survival of some heterodox quarters in the Italian academia. In this sense, the Italian case seems more like an exception (or simply a case of organized reaction) to mainstream economics cleansing the discipline of heterodox economists and economics as it happens all around the world (Lee 2010a).

Conclusions

In the last decades, there has been a proliferation of heterodox economics associations, conferences, and journals. This suggests that differences in theoretical and methodological approaches in economics—far from disappearing—are likely to persist and strengthen.

In this article, using a representative sample of Italian economists, we explored the differences between mainstream and heterodox economists as to individual and academic characteristics, political views, and their opinions about economic policy. To the best of our knowledge, this is the first article that compares heterodox and mainstream economists using the responses to a common questionnaire, making possible to compare individual responses.

Our analysis delivers a set of interesting results that would be useful in the debate on the characteristics, degree of internal homogeneity, and future perspectives for both mainstream and heterodox economics. The results of our analysis can be summarized as follows.

First, we show that heterodox and mainstream economists are significantly different in terms of individual and academic characteristics and political views, whatever the definition used to construct the two groups. Second, as far as opinions on the economy are concerned, heterodox economists are not more fractionated than mainstream economists and perhaps a little less so. Our results show that the disagreement within the heterodox is lower than within the mainstream. This indeed suggests that heterodox economics is a positive descriptive term, in the sense that heterodox economists do not only disagree with the mainstream ones but they share a system of theoretical instruments of analysis from which they derive a common set of policy prescriptions. We also found that the disagreement within schools of thought belonging to the heterodox group is, in general, smaller than the within disagreement among the schools in the mainstream group. Finally, we showed that heterodox and mainstream economists have significantly different opinions about the effectiveness of economic policies even controlling for a number of individual characteristics including the political view. In this respect we showed that the way in which heterodox and mainstream groups are defined has important implications for the ability of such dichotomy to explain disagreement between economists. We find than not all definitions are useful. For instance, the mainstream vs. nonmainstream distinction turns out to be not significant. Instead, the mainstream vs. heterodox dichotomy identifies a number of significant differences between economists from the two groups in terms of opinions about economic policy. This suggests that a meaningful distinction should have some theoretical content in order to help predicting and understanding economists' disagreement.

Our results indicate some possible future difficulties for heterodox economics. Looking at the differences in age and academic position between heterodox and mainstream economists, one may easily conclude that mainstream economists currently and in the future will still dominate the Italian academia. The fact that mainstream economists de facto control the appointment power and will expand even more in the next few years raises some concerns about the persistence of plurality of approaches in the Italian academia.

This article contributed to increase our understanding of the differences between mainstream and heterodox economists. Still more research should be devoted to this important topic. This is not only in the interest of the academia. In fact, the dynamics and the outcomes of confrontations between mainstream and heterodox economists have a large—even if not alway visible—impact on the public economic policy debate. For instance, whether an economist belongs to the dominant school does affect the probability that her opinion would be asked and taken into account by the policymakers. It follows that heterodox economics losing importance in academia does also make more likely that alternative and critical views on economic policies will disappear from the public debate. Hopefully everybody would agree that this is something one should be worried about.

Notes

1. On the other hand, the existence of different schools of thought can be indeed interpreted as the result of the fact that there are different views about what economics should be.

2. This is true for anthropology (Borofsky 1994), psychology (Hayes 2000), sociology (Urry 1990), and also political sciences (Almond 1990).

3. This categorization is problematic given the different possible ways of defining the two groups. We throughly discuss this issue in the fourth section.

4. For instance, Niehans (1981) states that "[t]he economic doctrines taught in Nairobi, Sao Paulo, New Delhi, Tel Aviv, Geneva, Harvard, and Bowling Green State . . . have a large common core."

5. For an example, see the debate generated in Italy by a letter of a group of nonmainstream economists concerning the causes and the possible solutions to the recent crisis (http://www.letteradeglieconomisti.it/english.htm) or the criticism raised in the United States by a group of mainstream economists against the 2009 Obama's recovery plan (http://www.cato.org/special/stimulus09/cato%20stimulus.pdf).

6. One possible alternative to our choice would have been to define a school of thought by theory. The problem with it is that it would be difficult to clearly identify different schools of thought because most of them (especially in the mainstream group) share the same theoretical fundamental blocks.

7. Famous cases of confrontations between schools are the Methodenstreit between the German Historical School and the Austrian School at the end of the 19th century (Roncaglia 2005), the Capital Controversy between the two Cambridges at the end of the 1960s (Harcourt 1972), and the most recent debates on rational expectations (Pesaran 1987) and the behavior of economic agents (Kahneman and Tversky 1979).

8. Colander (2005) observes that, with respect to the results of his previous study carried out in the mid 1980s (Klamer and Colander 1990), there is a significant decrease in the interest of PhD students in the United States in the history of economic thought.

9. The mailing list included members of the Italian Economic Association (SIE), the International Association of Italian Economists (AIDEI), and participants at several economic conferences held in Italy between 2005 and 2006, and was completed with the information contained in the Minister of University and Research (MIUR) website on Italian academics active in economic fields. At the moment of the survey there were 1,845 academic economists employed in Italian universities. In the e-mail message it was clearly stated that no specific knowledge was required to answer the questionnaire, that no individual statement would be revealed, and that anonymity was guaranteed. The details concerning the survey design can be found in De Benedictis and

Di Maio (2011) and on the webpage http://sites.google.com/site/micdimaio/surveyofitalianeconomists.

10. In comparison, the response rates in previous economists surveys are: 34 percent in Alston, Kearl, and Vaughan (1992), 31 percent in Fuller and Geide-Stevenson (2003), 36 percent in Whaples and Heckelman (2005), 27 percent in Klein and Stern (2006), and 40 percent Waples (2006). Usually surveys of economists within subfields tend to yield higher response rates: for example, 41 percent of AEA labor economists in Whaples (1996).

11. See below for an analysis of the results concerning Italian economists working abroad and PhD students and postdoc researchers.

12. The procedure of poststratification weighting was based on the reciprocal of the probability of inclusion of each individual (Groves, Flowe, Couper, Lepkowski, Singer, and Tourangeau 2004).

13. On this debate, see Colander (2000), Colander, Holt, and Rosser (2004, 2007), Davis (2006, 2008), Dequech (2007), Koppl (2006), Lawson (2006), and Lee (2008).

14. Italy is a perfect case study for evaluating the role of schools of thought in determining economists' opinions. Traditionally, Italian academia has indeed been characterized by the presence of a variety of approaches and this plurality has always been tried to be preserved (Corsi, D'Ippoliti, and Lucidi 2010). Among the initiatives with this objective there are the four international PhD student conferences "Research in Economics" held in Siena, Pavia, Torino, and Pisa between 2003 and 2008, the conference organized by the SIE (Societa' Italiana degli Economisti) in 2007, and the activities of the group of researchers that maintains the website www.debating.it. There have been also other initiatives like the Bologna students' Manifesto that, inspired by the Post-Autistic movement, has stimulated and keeps alive the debate in Italy.

15. Note that in the questionnaire, a definition for Eclectic was not given.

16. While we are well aware of the distinction discussed in Colander, Holt, and Rosser (2004) between mainstream and neoclassical approaches (orthodoxy), we preferred to consider them together to minimize the confusion in the respondents who are not into this debate.

17. Institutionalist economists may be quite different from Neo-Institutionalist economists since the former rejects mainstream/neoclassical theory while the latter uses it. In any case, one should note that in our sample there are no cases in which—when the respondent indicates to belong to two different schools of thought—if she/he is Institutionalist/Neo-Institutionalist she/he also declares to be Mainstream. This suggests that in our sample the Institutionalist/Neo-Institutionalist category is very likely to include only Institutionalist economists.

18. For a discussion on the elements that define a heterodox school and for a brief historical account of heterodox schools, see Coats (2000), Backhouse (2000), and Lee (2009).

19. Since our aim is to group different schools of thought under a common label, in the following analysis we exclude economists who declared not to belong to any specific school of thought.

20. This group closely resembles the definition of heterodox(s) in Prychitko (1998). Dow (2000) defines as heterodox schools of thought the Post-Keynesian economics, Institutionalist economics, Neo-Austrian economics, Behavioral economics, Social economics, and Feminist economics. For a thoughtful discussion of the concept of heterodox economics, see also Lee (2008).

21. Austrian economics are indeed quite tricky to be classified. One may consider them mainstream economists because of the theory they use, but still their approach is quite peculiar. At the same time, looking at the responses to our questionnaire indicates that they are quite different for the average heterodox ones.

22. Table 8 in the Appendix reports the answers concering the field of research.

23. To minimize the possible selection bias as to the proportions to be included, the following strategy was adopted. We surveyed the literature on the Italian economy and we included in the questionnaire all the propositions mentioned in at least one paper or book on the performance of the Italian economy published during the last 15 years. De Benedictis and Di Maio (2011) describe the details of the methodology employed to select the contributions from which Causes and Policy Proposals have been extracted.

24. The between variation is the sum (over all propositions) of the variance of respondents' opinion with respect to the mean opinion of the school of thought they belong to.

25. The relative entropy index is defined as the ratio between the level of entropy associated with the actual distribution of opinions across the possible answers to a specific question and the maximum theoretical level of entropy for that question (given the number possible answers), where entropy is defined as

$$\text{Entropy} = \sum_{i=1}^{n} p_i \log_2 (1/p_i)$$

and maximum entropy occurs when the probability of the events is equi-proportional (that is, where opinions are equally distributed across the possible answers). It immediately follows the definition that relative entropy (rel.entropy) ranges from 0 to 1.

26. For variables definitions, see note to Table 3.

27. As for the FIELD of research (as categorized by JEL codes), results show that all fields are represented in our sample, even if the variance is very high. The largest group, with 17 percent of the respondents declaring it to be their primary field, is macroeconomic and monetary economics. The other

large groups are industrial organization (12 percent), economic development and growth (11 percent), international economics (10 percent), public economics (9 percent), and microeconomics (9 percent).

28. Mezzogiorno is the way in which in the literature on the Italian economy one refers to the Southern regions of the country.

29. There are 67 economists working abroad. Detailed results for the following analysis are available upon request from the author.

30. These are 39 respondents. Detailed results for the following analysis are available upon request from the Author.

References

Aiginger, K., M. McCabe, D. Mueller, and C. Weiss. (2001). "Do American and European Industrial Organization Economists Differ?" *Review of Industrial Organization* 14(4): 383–404.

Almond, G. (1990). *A Discipline Divided: Schools and Sects in Political Science.* London: Sage.

Alston, R., J. R. Kearl, and M. Vaughan. (1992). "Is There a Consensus Among Economists in the 1990s?" *American Economic Review* 82: 203–209.

Axarloglou, K., and V. Theoharakis. (2003). "Diversity in Economics: An Analysis of Journal Quality Perceptions." *Journal of the European Economic Association* 1(6): 1402–1423.

Backhouse, R. E. (2000). "Progress in Heterodox Economics." *Journal of the History of Economic Thought* 22(2): 149–155.

Backhouse, R. E., and S. G. Medema. (2009). "On the Definition of Economics." *Journal of Economic Perspectives* 23(1): 221–233.

Borofsky, R. (Ed.) (1994). *Assessing Cultural Anthropology.* Columbus: McGraw-Hill.

Coats, A. W. B. (2000). "Opening Remarks." *Journal of the History of Economic Thought* 22(2): 145–148.

Colander, D. (2000). "The Death of Neoclassical Economics." *Journal of the History of Economic Thought* 22(2): 127–143.

——. (2005). "The Making of an Economist Redux." *Journal of Economic Perspec-tives* 19(1): 173–198.

Colander, D., R. P. F. Holt, and J. B. Rosser. (2004). "The Changing Face of Mainstream Economics." *Review of Political Economy* 16(4) 485–499.

——. (2007). "Live and Dead Issues in the Methodology of Economics." *Journal of Post Keynesian Economics* 30(2): 303–312.

Corsi, M., C. D'Ippoliti, and F. Lucidi. (2010). "Pluralism at Risk? Heterodox Economic Approaches and the Evaluation of Economic Research in Italy." *American Journal of Economics and Sociology* 69(5): 1495–1529.

Davis, J. B. (2006). "The Turn in Economics: Neoclassical Dominance to Mainstream Pluralism?" *Journal of Institutional Economics* 2(1): 1–20.

——. (2008). "The Turn in Recent Economics and Return of Orthodoxy." *Cambridge Journal of Economics* 32(3): 349–366.

De Benedictis, L., and M. Di Maio. (2011). "Economists' View About the Economy: Evidence from a Survey of Italian Economists." *Rivista Italiana degli Economisti* XVI(1): 11–59.

Dequech, D. (2007). "Neoclassical, Orthodox, Mainstream, and Heterodox Economics." *Journal of Post Keynesian Economics* 30(2): 279–302.

Dow, S. C. (2000). "Prospects for the Progress of Heterodox Economics." *Journal of the History of Economic Thought* 22(2): 157–170.

——. (2007). "Variety of Methodological Approach in Economics." *Journal of Economic Surveys* 21(3): 447–465.

Eatwell, J., M. Milgate, and P. Newman. (1987). *The New Palgrave: A Dictionary of Economics.* New York: Palgrave Macmillan.

Frey, B., and R. Eichenberger. (1993). "American and European Economics and Economists." *Journal of Economic Perspectives* 7(4): 185–193

Frey, B. S., S. Humbert, and F. Schneider. (2010). "What is Economics? Attitudes and Views of German Economists." *Journal of Economic Methodology* 17(3): 317–332.

Frey, B., W. Pommerehne, F. Schneider, and G. Gilbert. (1984). "Consensus and Dissension Among Economists: An Empirical Inquiry." *American Economic Review* 74(5): 986–994.

Frey, R. L., and B. S. Frey. (Eds.) (1995). "Is There an European Economics?" *Kyklos, Special Issue* 48(2): 185–343.

Fuchs, V., A. Krueger, and J. Poterba. (1998). "Economists' Views About Parameters, Values, and Policies: Survey Results in Labor and Public Economics." *Journal of Economic Literature* 36: 1387–1425.

Fuller, D., and D. Geide-Stevenson. (2003). "Consensus Among Economists: Revisited." *Journal of Economic Education* 34: 369–387.

George, D. A. (2007). "Consolation for the Economists: The Future of Economic Orthodoxy." *Journal of Economic Surveys* 21(3): 417–425.

Gide, C., and C. Rist. (1909). *A History of Economic Doctrines.* London: G.G. Harrap.

Groves, R. M., F. J. Flowe, M. P. Couper, J. M. Lepkowski, E. Singer, and Tourangeau, R. (2004). *Survey Methodology.* New Jersey: Wiley and Sons.

Hayes, N. (2000) *Foundations of Psychology.* Andover: Thomson Learning.

Harcourt, G. C. (1972). *Some Cambridge Controversies in the Theory of Capital.* Cambridge: Cambridge University Press.

Hutchinson, T. W. (1953). *A Review of Economic Doctrines.* Oxford: Clarendon.

Kahneman, D., and A. Tversky. (1979). "Prospect Theory: An Analysis of Decision Under Risk." *Econometrica* 47(2): 263–292.

Kearl, J. R., C. L. Pope, G. C. Whiting, and L. T. Wimmer. (1979). "A Confusion of Economists." *American Economic Review, Papers and Proceedings* 69: 28–37.

Klamer, A., and D. Colander. (1990). *The Making of an Economist.* Boulder: Westview Press.

Klein, D. B., and C. Stern. (2006). "Economists Policy Views and Voting." *Public Choice* 126: 331–342.

Klein, D. B., and C. Stern. (2007). "Is There a Free-Market Economist in the House? The Policy Views of American Economic Association Members." *American Journal of Economics and Sociology* 66(2): 309–334.

Koppl, R. (2006). "Austrian Economics at the Cutting Edge." *Review of Austrian Economics* 19(4): 231–241.

Lawson, T. (2006). "The Nature of Heterodox Economics." *Cambridge Journal of Economics* 30(4): 483–505.

Lee, F. S. (2008). "Heterodox Economics." In *New Palgrave Dictionary of Economics,* 2nd ed. vol. 4. Eds. L. E. Blume and S. Durlauf, pp. 2–6. New York: Palgrave Macmillan.

——. (2009). *A History of Heterodox Economics: Challenging the Mainstream in the Twentieth Century.* London: Routledge

——. (2010a). "Pluralism in Heterodox Economics." In *Economic Pluralism.* Eds. R. F. Garnett, E. K. Olsen, and M. Starr, pp. 19–35. London: Routledge.

——. (2010b). "Heterodox Economics and its Critics." Paper presented at the EAEPE Conference 2010, Bordeaux, France, 27–31 October 2010.

——. (2011). "The Pluralism Debate in Heterodox Economics." *Review of Radical Political Economics,* forthcoming.

Lee, F. S., B. C. Cronin, S. McConnell, and E. Dean. (2010). "Research Quality Rankings of Heterodox Economic Journals in a Contested Discipline." *American Journal of Economics and Sociology* 65(5): 1409–1452.

Maki, U. (1997). "The One World and the Many Theories." In *Pluralism in Economics.* Eds. A. Salanti and E. Screpanti, pp. 37–47. Aldershot: Edward Elgar.

Mueller, D. C. (1995). "American and European Economists." *Kyklos* 48: 251–255.

Niehans, J. (1981). "Economics: History. Doctrine. Science. Art." *Kyklos* 34: 165–177.

Pesaran, H. (1987). *The Limits to Rational Expectations.* Bognor Regis: Basil Blackwell.

Prychitko, D. L. (1998). *Why Economists Disagree: An Introduction to the Alternative Schools of Thought.* New York: University of New York Press.

Randall, A. (1985). "Methodology, Ideology and the Economics of Policy: Why Resource Economists Disagree?" *American Journal of Agricultural Economics* 67: 1022–1029.

Roncaglia, R. (2005). *The Wealth of Ideas: A History of Economic Thought.* Cambridge: Cambridge University Press.

Urry, J. (Ed.) (1990). *Schools of Thought in Sociology Series.* Aldershot: Edward Elgar.

Whaples, R. (1996). "Is There Consensus Among American Labor Economists: Survey Results on Forty Propositions." *Journal of Labor Research* 17(4): 725–734.

——. (2006). "Do Economists Agree on Anything? Yes!" *Economists' Voice,* November.

Whaples, R., and J. C. Heckelman. (2005). "Public Choice Economics: Where Is There Consensus?" *American Economist* 49(1): 66–78.

Appendix

Table 6

The 40 Causes

Number	Cause
	International trade and European Union policy
1	Italian international trade specialization
2	higher international competition in goods and service markets
3	dumping and unfair international competition
4	set and quality of exported goods
5	low attraction of FDI
6	low firm propensity to internationalization
7	adoption of the Euro
8	European Commission economic policy
9	BCE monetary policy
10	primary commodity world price dynamics
11	difficult international political situation

Table 6 *Continued*

Number	Cause
	Firms' characteristics
12	small firms' size (more difficult to gain access to credit)
13	small firms' size (more difficult for internationalization activity)
14	small firms' size (more difficult for the adoption of new technologies)
15	small firms' size (more difficult for innovation activity)
16	ownership structure of Italian firms
17	role of the family in firm governance
18	low risk propensity of entrepreneurs
19	excessive protection of large domestic firms
	Structural characteristics
20	dynamic of investment in ICT
21	quantity and quality of infrastructures
22	quality of immaterial infrastructures (justice, authority, etc.)
23	low competition level, the existence of barriers to entry
24	bureaucratic impediments to private entrepreneurship
25	difficulties to gaining access to credit
26	persistence of the North-South economic divide
27	Mezzogiorno issue (crime)
28	Mezzogiorno issue (infrastructures)
	Labor market
29	productivity reduction caused by the labor market reform
30	low labor market flexibility
31	wage compression effect of "concertazione"
32	demographic dynamics
33	low human capital demand
34	low human capital supply
35	increasing number of immigrant workers
36	labor union behavior
	Government and public administration
37	public debt level and composition
38	type of policies adopted to reduce public debt
39	low efficiency of the public administration
40	low efficiency of the bureaucracy

Table 7

The 18 Policy Proposals

Number	Policy Proposal
1	proceed with more liberalizations
2	proceed with more privatizations
3	increase bureaucracy (public administration) efficiency
4	change trade specialization
5	improve quality of exported goods
6	induce internationalization activity by domestic firms
7	induce firms' size growth
8	create small and medium firms consortia
9	create and strengthen firm-territory link
10	increase public investment in strategic sectors
11	increase firms' investment in ICT
12	funding private research
13	funding public research
14	funding academic research
15	increase investments in physical infrastructures
16	make more flexible the labor market
17	reduce precarious jobs
18	reduce labor union power

Table 8

Fields of Specialization

	Nonmainstream	Mainstream	HetodooxJEL	MainstreamLarge	HeterodoxLarge	Heterodox	MainstreamExtra
Schools of Economic Thought and Methodology	8	2	15	1	14	15	1
Mathematical and Quantitative Methods	4	7	4	6	3	3	5
Microeconomics	10	19	11	16	9	7	18
Macroeconomics and Monetary Economics	24	25	13	30	23	23	31
International Economics	12	14	6	15	7	8	14
Financial Economics	3	5	2	5	1	1	4
Public Economics	12	10	11	13	7	8	12
Health, Education, and Welfare	2	0	4	0	2	2	0
Labor and Demographic Economics	7	14	4	12	4	4	11
Law and Economics	1	5	2	3	1	1	3
Industrial Organization	13	19	15	15	15	15	15
Business Admin. and Business Econ.; Marketing; Account.	0	0	2	0	1	1	0
Economic History	4	0	4	0	2	2	0
Economic Development, Tech. Change, and Growth	17	7	26	6	21	22	7
Economic Systems	1	0	0	0	1	1	0
Agricul. and Natural Resource Econ; Env. and Ecol. Econ.	3	3	2	2	2	2	2
Urban, Rural, and Regional Economics	5	2	19	2	5	4	3
Number of respondents in each group	220	59	54	86	98	92	91

Note: Percentage of respondents for each group that declares the specific JEL to be her field of research. Definitions of groups as in Table 2. Respondents could declare more than one field of research.

Table 9

Correlation Between Mean Opinions on Causes by Schools of Thought

	Eclec.	Inst./ Neo-Inst.	Keyn./ Neo-Keyn.	Keyn./ Post-Keyn.	Marxist Sraf./Neo-Marxist	Neocl./ Main.	Evolut.	No-School
Eclectic	1.00							
Institutionalist/Neo-Inst.	0.94	1.00						
Keynesian/Neo-Keynesian	0.96	0.88	1.00					
Keynesian/Post-Keynesian	0.94	0.87	0.95	1.00				
Marxist/Sraffian/Neo-Marxist	0.53	0.52	0.49	0.67	1.00			
Neoclassical/Mainstream	0.94	0.91	0.88	0.81	0.31	1.00		
Evolutionary	0.94	0.88	0.91	0.91	0.59	0.85	1.00	
No method	0.95	0.93	0.92	0.86	0.36	0.98	0.88	1.00

Note: Correlation coefficient between the mean response by school of thought computed on the 40 causes listed in Table 6. We considered only the schools of thought with more than five respondents.

Table 10

Correlation Between Mean Opinions on Policy Proposals by Schools of Thought

	Eclec.	Inst./ Neo-Inst.	Keyn./ Neo-Keyn.	Keyn./ Post-Keyn.	Marxist Sraf./Neo-Marxist	Neocl./ Main.	Evolut.	No-School
Eclectic	1.00							
Institutionalist/Neo-Inst.	0.96	1.00						
Keynesian/Neo-Keynesian	0.95	0.92	1.00					
Keynesian/Post-Keynesian	0.91	0.88	0.90	1.00				
Marxist/Sraffian/Neo-Marxist	0.83	0.81	0.75	0.94	1.00			
Neoclassical/Mainstream	0.53	0.51	0.57	0.25	0.07	1.00		
Evolutionary	0.95	0.89	0.90	0.92	0.87	0.36	1.00	
No-school	0.86	0.86	0.89	0.72	0.56	0.80	0.77	1.00

Note: Correlation coefficient between the mean response by school of thought computed on the 18 policy proposals listed in Table 7. We considered only the schools of thought with more than five respondents.

Index

for

STUDIES IN ECONOMIC REFORM AND SOCIAL JUSTICE:
SOCIAL COSTS OF MARKETS AND ECONOMIC THEORY